T3-BSD-336

THE SARGON LEGEND:
A STUDY OF THE AKKADIAN TEXT AND THE TALE OF THE HERO WHO WAS EXPOSED AT BIRTH

AMERICAN SCHOOLS OF ORIENTAL RESEARCH
DISSERTATION SERIES

edited by

David Noel Freedman

Number 4

THE SARGON LEGEND:
A STUDY OF THE AKKADIAN TEXT AND THE TALE OF THE HERO WHO WAS EXPOSED AT BIRTH

by
Brian Lewis

THE SARGON LEGEND:
A STUDY OF THE AKKADIAN TEXT AND THE TALE OF THE HERO WHO WAS EXPOSED AT BIRTH

by

Brian Lewis

Published by
American Schools of Oriental Research

Distributed by

American Schools of Oriental Research
126 Inman Street
Cambridge, MA 02139

THE SARGON LEGEND:
A STUDY OF THE AKKADIAN TEXT AND THE TALE OF THE HERO WHO WAS EXPOSED AT BIRTH

by
Brian Lewis

Cover design by Madeleine Churchill

Library of Congress Cataloging in Publication Data

Lewis, Brian, 1946-
The Sargon Legend.

(Dissertation series ; no. 4)
Includes the text of the legend in Akkadian and English.
1. Legend of Sargon. 2. Sargon I, King of Agade—Legends—History and criticism. 3. Abandoned children (in religion, folklore, etc.) 4. Assyro-Babylonian literature—History and criticism. I. Legend of Sargon. English and Akkadian. 1978. II. Title. III. Series.
PJ3771.L42L4 892′ .1 78-26335
ISBN O-89757-104-5

Printed in the United States of America

To My Parents

PREFACE

This manuscript represents a revised version of the dissertation I submitted to the Graduate School of Arts and Sciences of New York University in 1976. The most significant changes occur in Chapter III where the sections dealing with the dating and literary classification of the Sargon Legend have been rewritten to reflect my current thinking. The study of "the exposed-hero tale" in Chapters V and VI has been expanded by the addition of an Old Hittite version (tale 7) kindly brought to my attention by Prof. Marten Stol. Wherever possible the text has been updated to at least mention relevant publications that have appeared in the last two years. This manuscript has also benefited from critical readings by Prof. Stol and Prof. Raphael Kutscher.

I wish to thank the Trustees of the British Museum for granting me permission to include in this work the first published photographs of the Sargon Legend fragments. To Prof. E. Sollberger, Keeper of Western Asiatic Antiquities, and Mr. C. B. Walker of the British Museum thanks are due for allowing me to collate the Sargon Legend and related Sargon texts during the summers of 1975 and 1977. I want also to acknowledge the kindness of Profs. W. G. Lambert, A. Schaffer, and D. Kennedy who offered their expert opinions in the course of collation. Prof. Lambert was especially helpful in discussing with me literary and textual problems posed by the Sargon Legend text. In addition, I am grateful to Prof. B. Trell of the Classics Department of New York University for supplying me with her own translation of the passage from Suidas that appears in Chapter V.

Above all, I wish to express my gratitude to Prof. Stephen J. Lieberman, my teacher and dissertation advisor. It was my great privilege and honor to be his first doctoral student. For his patience, concern, and invaluable assistance, I am deeply appreciative. One could not hope to work under a finer scholar or a more thoughtful advisor.

September, 1978 B.L.

CONTENTS

Chapter | Page

TABLES

LIST OF ABBREVIATIONS

A	Lexical Series á A = *nâqu*
AAA	*Annals of Archaeology and Anthropology*
AASOR	*The Annual of the American Schools of Oriental Research*
ABAW	*Abhandlungen der bayerischen Akademie der Wissenschaften*
ABC	A. K. Grayson, *Assyrian and Babylonian Chronicles* (Locust Valley, 1975)
ABL	R. F. Harper, *Assyrian and Babylonian Letters* (London and Chicago, 1892-1914)
ABRT	J. Craig, *Assyrian and Babylonian Religious Texts* (Leipzig, 1895-97)
ACh	C. Virolleaud, *L'astrologie chaldéenne* (Paris, 1909)
L'adoption	E. Cassin, *L'adoption à Nuzi* (Paris, 1938)
AfO	*Archiv für Orientforschung*
AHw	W. von Soden, *Akkadisches Handwörterbuch* (Wiesbaden, 1965-)
AJSL	*American Journal of Semitic Languages and Literatures*
AKA	L. W. King, *The Annals of the Kings of Assyria* (London, 1902)
Ancient Mesopotamia	A. L. Oppenheim, *Ancient Mesopotamia*, Revised Edition Completed by E. Reiner (Chicago, 1977)
ANET	J. B. Pritchard, *Ancient Near Eastern Texts Relating to the Old Testament* (Princeton, 1950), 3rd Edition (Princeton, 1969)
AnOr	*Analecta Orientalia*
AnSt	*Anatolian Studies*
AO	Tablet Signature of the Louvre Museum (Paris)
AOAT(S)	*Alter Orient und altes Testament (Sonderreihe)*

AOB	*Altorientalische Bibliothek*
ARAB	D. D. Luckenbill, *Ancient Records of Assyria and Babylonia* (Chicago, 1926-27)
Archives	G. Cardascia, *Les archives des Murašû* (Paris, 1951)
ARM(T)	*Archives royales de Mari*
ArOr	*Archiv Orientální*
AS	*Assyriological Studies*
Atra-ḫasīs	W. G. Lambert, *Atra-ḫasīs* (Oxford, 1969)
Aussetzung des Kyros und Romulus	G. Binder, *Die Aussetzung des Königskindes Kyros und Romulus*, Beiträge zur klassischen Philologie, X (Meisenheim am Glan, 1964)
BA	*Beiträge zur Assyriologie*
BabLaws	G. Driver - J. Miles, *The Babylonian Laws* (Oxford, 1952)
BASOR	*Bulletin of the American Schools of Oriental Research*
BE	*The Babylonian Expedition of the University of Pennsylvania, Series A: Cuneiform Texts*
Bezold Catalogue, Supp.	L. W. King, *Catalogue of the Cuneiform Tablets in the Kouyunjik Collection, Supplement* (London, 1914)
BHLT	A. K. Grayson, *Babylonian Historical-Literary Texts* (Toronto, 1975)
BIN	*Babylonian Inscriptions in the Collection of J. B. Nies*
BiOr	*Bibliotheca Orientalis*
"Birth of Moses"	B. Childs, "The Birth of Moses," *JBL* 84 (1965), pp. 109-22.
Birth of the Hero	O. Rank, *The Myth of the Birth of the Hero* (New York, 1964)
BM	Tablet Signature of the British Museum (London)
Bo.	Tablet Signature of texts excavated at Boğazköy (Berlin, Istanbul)

Borger *Asarh.*	R. Borger, *Die Inschriften Asarhaddons, Königs von Assyrien,* AfO Beih. IX (Graz, 1956)
BRM	*Babylonian Records in the Library of J. Pierpont Morgan*
BSOAS	*Bulletin of the School of Oriental and African Studies*
BWL	W. G. Lambert, *Babylonian Wisdom Literature* (Oxford, 1960)
CAD	*The Assyrian Dictionary of the University of Chicago* (Chicago, 1956-)
CAH	*The Cambridge Ancient History*
Camb.	J. N. Strassmaier, *Inschriften von Cambyses, König von Babylon* (Leipzig, 1890)
Cat.	C. Bezold, *Catalogue of the Cuneiform Tablets in the Kouyunjik Collection of the British Museum* (London, 1889-99)
CBS	Tablet Signature of the University Museum of the University of Pennsylvania (Philadelphia)
CCEBK	L. W. King, *Chronicles Concerning Early Babylonian Kings* (London, 1907)
CH	Code of Hammurabi
Christusmythe	H. Zimmern, *Zum Streit um die "Christusmythe"* (Berlin, 1910)
"Contacts ethniques"	J. van Dijk, "Les contacts ethniques dans la Mésopotamie," *Syncretism,* Scripta Instituti Donneriani Aboensis, III (Uppsala, 1969), pp. 171-206.
CT	*Cuneiform Texts from Babylonian Tablets in the British Museum*
CTH	E. Laroche, *Catalogue des textes hittites, Etudes et Commentaires,* LXXV (Paris, 1971)
CTN	*Cuneiform Texts from Nimrud*
"Cuthaean Legend of Naram-Sin"	O. Gurney, "The Sultantepe Tablets IV. The Cuthaean Legend of Naram-Sin," *AnSṭ* 5 (1955), pp. 93-113.

Cyr.	J. N. Strassmaier, *Inschriften von Cyrus, König von Babylon* (Leipzig, 1890)
DA	A. Boissier, *Documents assyriens relatifs aux présages* (Paris, 1894-99)
EAK	R. Borger, *Einleitung in die assyrischen Königsinschriften* (Leiden, 1961)
Ebeling *Parfümrez*	E. Ebeling, *Parfümrezepte und kultische Texte aus Assur* (Rome, 1950)
ECTJ	A. Westenholz, *Early Cuneiform Texts in Jena* (Copenhagen, 1975)
EPAR	L. Delaporte, *Épigraphes araméens* (Paris, 1912)
Era	F. Gössmann, *Das Era-Epos* (Würzburg, 1955)
ERAS	M. J. Seux, *Épithètes royales akkadiennes et sumériennes* (Paris, 1967)
Exaltation of Inanna	W. Hallo and J. van Dijk, *The Exaltation of Inanna*, Yale Near Eastern Researches, III (New Haven, 1968)
Exodus	B. Childs, *The Book of Exodus* (Philadelphia, 1974)
FF	*Folklore Fellows (Communications)*
The Folktale	S. Thompson, *The Folktale* (New York, 1946)
"Fragment of Ancient Assyrian Mythology"	H. F. Talbot, "A Fragment of Ancient Assyrian Mythology," *TSBA* 1 (1872), pp. 271-80.
GAG	W. von Soden, *Grundriss der akkadischen Grammatik*, AnOr XXXIII/XLVII (Rome, 1969)
"Hebrew *tbh*"	C. Cohen, "Hebrew *tbh*: Proposed Etymologies," *JANES* 4 (1972), pp. 37-51.
"Historische Tradition"	H. G. Güterbock, "Die historische Tradition und ihre literarische Gestaltung bei Babyloniern und Hethitern bis 1200," *ZA* 42 (1934), pp. 1-91.
HSS	*Harvard Semitic Series*
HUCA	*Hebrew Union College Annual*

Hyginus, *Fabulae*	*The Myths of Hyginus*, trans. and ed. Mary Grant, Kansas Publications Humanistic Studies, LIV (Lawrence, 1960)
IAMN	*İstanbul Asarıatika Müzelerinesriyatı*
IM	Tablet Signature of the Iraq Museum (Baghdad)
"Inschriften der Könige von Agade"	H. Hirsch, "Die Inschriften der Könige von Agade," *AfO* 20 (1963), pp. 1-82.
ITN	E. Weidner, *Die Inschriften Tukulti-Ninurtas I*, AfO Beih. XII (Graz, 1959)
JANES	*Journal of the Ancient Near East Society of Columbia University*
JAOS	*Journal of the American Oriental Society*
JBL	*Journal of Biblical Literature*
JCS	*Journal of Cuneiform Studies*
JESHO	*Journal of the Economic and Social History of the Orient*
JNES	*Journal of Near Eastern Studies*
JRAS	*Journal of the Royal Asiatic Society*
K	Tablet Signature of the Kujunjik Collection of the British Museum (London)
KAH	*Keilschrifttexte aus Assur historischen Inhalts*
KAI	H. Donner - W. Röllig, *Kanaanäische und aramäische Inschriften* (Wiesbaden, 1968)
KAR	*Keilschrifttexte aus Assur religiösen Inhalts*
KAV	*Keilschrifttexte aus Assur verschiedenen Inhalts*
KB	*Keilinschriftliche Bibliothek*
KBo	*Keilschrifttexte aus Boghazköi*
Keilschrifttexte Sargons (Winckler, *Sar.*)	H. Winckler, *Die Keilschrifttexte Sargons* (Leipzig, 1889)

"Kish, Akkad and Agade"	H. Weiss, "Kish, Akkad and Agade," *JAOS* 95 (1975), pp. 434-53.
KTB	J. Lewy, *Die Kültepetexte der Sammlung Blanckertz* (Berlin, 1929)
KUB	*Keilschrifturkunden aus Boghazköi*
LA	F. Lenormant, *Lettres assyriologiques* (Paris, 1871-79)
LCL	*Loeb Classical Library*
Legends	L. Ginzberg, *The Legends of the Jews* (Philadelphia, 1910)
LIH	L. W. King, *The Letters and Inscriptions of Ḫammurabi* (London, 1898-1900)
Lyon, *Keilschrift-texte Sargon's*	D. Lyon, *Keilschrifttexte Sargon's* (Leipzig, 1883)
MAD	*Materials for the Assyrian Dictionary*
MAOG	*Mitteilungen der altorientalischen Gesellschaft*
Maqlû	G. Meier, *Die assyrische Beschwörungs-sammlung Maqlû*, AfO Beih. II (Berlin, 1937)
MDOG	*Mitteilungen der deutschen Orient-Gesellschaft*
MDP	*Mémoires de la Délégation en Perse*
MKNAW	*Mededelingen der Koninklijke Nederlandse Akademie van Wetenschappen*
MLC	Tablet Signature of the Morgan Library Collection
Mose und seine Zeit	H. Gressmann, *Mose und seine Zeit* (Göttingen, 1913)
Motif-Index	S. Thompson, *Motif-Index of Folk-Literature* (Bloomington, 1932-36)
"Motif of the Exposed Child"	D. Redford, "The Literary Motif of the Exposed Child," *Numen* 14 (1967), pp. 209-28.
MSL	*Materialien zum sumerischen Lexikon*
NAT	S. Parpola, *Neo-Assyrian Toponyms*, AOAT VI (Neukirchen-Vluyn, 1970)

Nbk.	J. N. Strassmaier, *Inschriften von Nabuchodonosor, König von Babylon* (Leipzig, 1889)
"New Light on Some Historical Omens"	E. Reiner, "New Light on Some Historical Omens," *Anatolian Studies Presented to Hans Gustav Güterbock on the Occasion of his 65th Birthday*, ed. K. Bittel (Istanbul, 1974), pp. 257-61.
"Nouveaux renseignements sur Šarrukin"	V. Scheil, "Nouveaux renseignements sur Šarrukin d'après un texte sumérien," *RA* 13 (1916), pp. 175-79.
OCD	*Oxford Classical Dictionary*
OECT	*Oxford Editions of Cuneiform Texts*
OIP	*Oriental Institute Publications*
OLZ	*Orientalistische Literaturzeitung*
Or	*Orientalia* N. S. Nova Series; S. P. Series Prior
PBS	*Publications of the Babylonian Section, University Museum, University of Pennsylvania*
PDT	M. Çiğ-H. Kizilyay-A. Salonen, *Die Puzriš-Dagan-Texte* (Helsinki, 1954)
PRAK	H. de Genouillac, *Premières recherches archéologiques à Kich* (Paris, 1924-25)
R	Rawlinson et al., *The Cuneiform Inscriptions of Western Asia*
RA	*Revue d'assyriologie*
RCAE	L. Waterman, *Royal Correspondence of the Assyrian Empire* (Ann Arbor, 1930-36)
"Reich Sargons von Akkad"	E. Weidner, "Das Reich Sargons von Akkad," *AfO* 16 (1952-53), pp. 1-24.
Les religions	R. Labat, *Les religions du Proche-Orient asiatique* (Paris, 1970)
RGTC	*Répertoire géographique des textes cunéiformes* (Wiesbaden, 1974-)
RISA	G. Barton, *The Royal Inscriptions of Sumer and Akkad* (New Haven, 1929)

RLA	*Reallexikon der Assyriologie*
Rm.	Rassam, Tablet Signature of the British Museum (London)
RQH	*Revue des questions historiques*
RTC	F. Thureau-Dangin, *Recueil de tablettes chaldéenes* (Paris, 1903)
"Seafaring Merchants of Ur"	A. L. Oppenheim, "The Seafaring Merchants of Ur," *JAOS* 74 (1954), pp. 6-17.
Sm.	Smith, Tablet Signature of the British Museum (London)
StOr	*Studia Orientalia*
Streck *Assurbanipal*	M. Streck, *Assurbanipal und die letzten assyrischen Könige*, VAB VII (Leipzig, 1916)
Study of Folklore	*The Study of Folklore*, ed. A. Dundes (Englewood Cliffs, 1965)
Sumerer und Akkader	F. R. Kraus, *Sumerer und Akkader, ein Problem der altmesopotamischen Geschichte*, MKNAW XXXIII/8 (Amsterdam, 1970)
The Sumerian King List	T. Jacobsen, *The Sumerian King List*, AS XI (Chicago, 1939)
"Tamar the Hierodule"	M. Astour, "Tamar the Hierodule," *JBL* 85 (1966), pp. 185-96.
TCL	*Textes cunéiformes du Louvre*
TCS	*Texts from Cuneiform Sources*
"A Technical Term for Exposure"	M. Cogan, "A Technical Term for Exposure," *JNES* 27 (1968), pp. 133-35.
TIM	*Texts in the Iraq Museum*
Titles	W. W. Hallo, *Early Mesopotamian Royal Titles*, American Oriental Society, XLIII (New Haven, 1957)
TMH	*Texte und Materialien der Frau Professor Hilprecht Collection*
TRD	H. de Genouillac, *La trouvaille de Drêhem* (Paris, 1911)

TSBA	*Transactions of the Society of Biblical Archaeology*
TSSI	J. Gibson, *Textbook of Syrian Semitic Inscriptions* (Oxford, 1971,1975)
TuL	E. Ebeling, *Tod und Leben nach den Vorstellungen der Babylonier* (Berlin and Leipzig, 1931)
UE	*Ur Excavations*
UET	*Ur Excavations, Texts*
"Untersuchungen zum Priestertum"	J. Renger, "Untersuchungen zum Priestertum in der altbabylonischen Zeit," *ZA* 58 (1967), pp. 110-88.
Untersuchungen zur akkadischen Epik	K. Hecker, *Untersuchungen zur akkadischen Epik,* AOATS VIII (Neukirchen-Vluyn, 1974)
UT	C. H. Gordon, *Ugaritic Textbook,* AnOr XXXVIII (Rome, 1965)
VAB	*Vorderasiatische Bibliothek*
VAT	Tablet Signature of the Staatliche Museen (Berlin)
VS	*Vorderasiatische Schriftdenkmäler der Königlichen Museen zu Berlin*
Winck. *Sarg.*	H. Winckler, *Die Keilschrifttexte Sargons* (Leipzig, 1889)
WO	*Die Welt des Orient*
YOS	*Yale Oriental Series. Babylonian Texts*
ZA	*Zeitschrift für Assyriologie*

CHAPTER I

INTRODUCTION

In the course of history, individuals appear whose lives and deeds affect the development of an entire civilization. Sargon of Akkad was such a man. Heroic figure, empire builder, and prototype for future rulers, Sargon secured for himself an enduring place in the historical traditions of Mesopotamia. Legends often spring up embellishing the accomplishments and perpetuating the memory of great men, and Sargon's importance is confirmed by the numerous inscriptions, omens, and literary texts that reveal his life and exploits.

Among the cuneiform tablets belonging to the collection of the British Museum are fragments of a composition which has come to be known as "the Sargon Legend" or "the Sargon Birth Legend."[1] The basis for the second title is the presence in the text of a birth story remarkably similar to the episode of the exposure of Moses in Exodus. This feature attracted the attention of the early Assyriologists and has contributed to the popularity of the text ever since.

In 1907, L. W. King published the most complete edition of the Sargon Legend to date including a cuneiform copy, transliteration, and translation of the first column and the badly mutilated second column. Nearly 70 years have passed since King's publication. This alone might justify a new attempt at improving the reading and solving the remaining obscurities. Recently, however, a copy of a previously unidentified fragment (K 7249) of the Legend was published by W. G. Lambert, raising hopes for a breakthrough in the interpretation of the second column. But perhaps more importantly, there has been, up to the present, no real attempt to explore the problems of origin and date of composition of the text or to evaluate its literary and historical significance. Also lacking has been a serious examination of the structure of the infant-exposure tale and of the position of the Sargon version vis-à-vis other stories of infant exposure. This study of the Sargon Legend aims to satisfy some of these needs.

Specifically, we shall:

1. Reedit the Sargon Legend texts K 3401 + Sm 2118, K 4470, and BM 47449 making use of the resources of the partially completed new dictionaries[2] and our improved knowledge of Akkadian grammar.
2. Offer the first transliteration, translation, and analysis of K 7249 as well as a partial reconstruction of column ii.[3]
3. Attempt to determine the connection between columns i and ii.
4. Treat textual and literary problems relating to the text. The relationships of the manuscripts will be studied, and we shall attempt the construction of a stemma.
5. Discuss the historical value of the Legend and its correspondence to other sources of Sargon tradition.
6. Discuss the genre of *narû*-literature or "pseudo-autobiography," including the identification of the Legend as a representative of the genre.
7. Analyze the tale of the hero exposed at birth through the use of the historic-geographic method developed by the Finnish school of folklore studies for the interpretation of folktales. Attention will be given to the relation between the Sargon version and the other occurrences, especially the biblical account of the abandonment of Moses.

Let us consider first the history of the study of the Sargon Legend texts.

Discovery of the Fragments

After being lost for over two millennia, the Sargon Legend was recovered as a result of the excavations carried out by Austen H. Layard and George Smith (on behalf of the British Museum) amid the ruins of Assurbanipal's library at Nineveh (modern Kujunjik). Three fragments of the Legend[4] from at least two different copies were discovered by Layard and his team during the early excavations at Kujunjik[5] (1848/50) and were sent back to the British Museum. More than two decades later, Smith uncovered a fourth fragment during his work at the site.[6] A fragment of a Neo-Babylonian practice tablet, preserving the first part of the Legend, also belongs to the collection of the British Museum.[7] The provenience of this text, which was catalogued in 1881, is Dilbat (Dailem).

Publication of the Text

In 1870, G. Smith published a partial cuneiform copy of K 3401 in *The Cuneiform Inscriptions of Western Asia*, Vol. III, pl. 4 no. 7,[8] identified as a "Tablet of Sargina I, King of Agane." Two years later Smith and H. F. Talbot offered the first treatments of the text in the inaugural volume of the *Transactions of the Society of Biblical Archaeology* 1 (1872). Interpreting the Legend as a copy of an original Sargon inscription, Smith prepared a translation of column i which showed that he was already in possession of the fragment Sm 2118.[9] His introduction to the text indicated an awareness of K 4470 and the existence of a second column.[10] In addition, he commented briefly on the "striking parallel" between the birth of Sargon and the account of the birth of Moses in Exodus. Smith's translation was adequate as a first effort, although many details remained confused or misunderstood.

Talbot's treatment of the Legend, which appeared as "A Fragment of Ancient Assyrian Mythology,"[11] was a more ambitious effort than Smith's. Talbot presented a translation, transcription, and cuneiform copy of twelve lines of column i along with a commentary of little or no value. Talbot's contribution lay in an awareness that the birth legend of Sargon belonged to a category of stories involving great figures in antiquity. His translation captured the gist of the text but was inferior to that of Smith. Like Smith he assumed that the text represented a Sargon inscription and speculated that it might have been copied from a Sargon statue at Agade. A personal rivalry may have existed between these two scholars, for Talbot seems to go to great length to point out that his paper was sent to the Society exactly three weeks before Smith's treatment was published and that any observations common to both were arrived at independently.

The year 1875 witnessed the appearance of five publications dealing in part with the Sargon Legend. Among these was the first treatment by a non-English scholar. Smith discussed the Legend in three new publications. A reprint of his first article with only minor revisions appeared in *Records of the*

Past, Vol. V (London, 1875), pp. 56-57. In a new book, *Assyrian Discoveries* (New York, 1875), pp. 224-25, Smith announced his discovery of "another fragment of the curious history of Sargon," followed by a short review of the contents of the Legend. In that same year, he presented *The Chaldean Account of Genesis* (New York, 1875), pp. 299-300, which featured an improved translation of the text. Here Smith expressed the opinion that knowledge of the Sargon birth story had most likely reached Egypt by the age of Moses and might have inspired the events related in Exodus II. He also advanced an etymology of the name Sargon that was essentially correct, namely, "true" or "legitimate king."[12]

Not to be completely outdone, Talbot published in *Records of the Past*, Vol. V, pp. 1-4, a rehash of his original treatment in *TSBA* 1, including a translation, commentary, and discussion of birth story parallels.

In his work *Babylone et la Chaldée* (Paris, 1875), pp. 98-100, J. Ménant offered a discussion and translation of the text, whose "nature toute particulière . . . a fixé depuis longtemps l'attention des assyriologues."[13] Ménant's translation, which took note of the treatments of Talbot, Smith, and Lenormant,[14] presented no real improvement in the reading of the text.

One year later, the first published treatment of the Sargon Legend in German appeared.[15] A. Gutschmid reproduced the translations of Smith and Talbot (lines 1-11) and discussed some of their findings. He correctly dismissed the identification of the Legend as a copy of an original inscription, suggesting that it be interpreted as the composition of a writer living many centuries later.

Another German scholar, F. Delitzsch, offered his own translation and transcription in *Wo lag das Paradies* (Leipzig, 1881)[16] a few years later. Delitzsch's translation did not include the end of column i but was superior to most of those which preceded.

Two references to the Legend appeared in works published in France during 1883. In "Deux textes très anciens de la Chaldée,"[17] J. Oppert provided an adequate translation of the entire remains of column i accompanied by a commentary and discussion. The second treatment is found in F. Lenormant's

Histoire ancienne de l'Orient (Paris, 1881-83), Vol. IV, pp. 76-77. Lenormant's effort was undistinguished and resembled Ménant's translation of a few years earlier. Whether he had based his treatment on Ménant, or the latter had used an earlier study of Lenormant, is unclear.[18]

In 1886, C. P. Tiele discussed the Legend in *Handbücher der alten Geschichte* I/4 (Gotha, 1886), pp. 112-15. As part of his treatment of Sargon of Akkad, he reviewed the contents of the text introducing the term "Sargons Geburtslegende" which became a popular designation of the whole composition. Also in that year, J. N. Strassmaier issued his *Alphabetisches Verzeichniss der assyrischen und akkadischen Wörter* (Leipzig, 1886). On page 1094 there appeared a partial cuneiform copy of K 3401 + Sm 2118.

Next, A. Sayce tried his hand at the text in *Lectures on the Origin and Growth of Religion*, The Hibbert Lectures (London, 1887), pp. 26-29. Sayce discussed the birth of Sargon and such other heroes as Cyrus, Romulus, and Perseus. He presented a translation that seems to have followed closely Smith's improved text in *The Chaldean Account of Genesis*.

The first bibliography of works treating the Sargon Legend appeared in 1891 in C. Bezold's *Catalogue of the Cuneiform Tablets in the Kouyunjik Collection* (London, 1889-99).[19] Accompanying the bibliography was a brief description of fragments K 3401 + Sm 2118 including their measurements.[20]

In the following year, H. Winckler supplied a good translation for E. Schrader's *Keilinschriftliche Bibliothek* III (Berlin, 1892), pp. 100-3. This publication is noteworthy because it represented the first effort to treat the mutilated portion of column ii. Despite its poor condition, Winckler gave a respectable transliteration of the traces preserved in the first 14 lines.

To T. G. Pinches belongs the credit for publishing in 1896 the first treatment of BM 47449, the Neo-Babylonian practice tablet that contains an extract from column i of the Legend. Pinches offered a cuneiform copy, transliteration, and translation of the Sargon passage followed by a list of variants with commentary.[21]

Shortly after the turn of the century, another English

scholar, L. W. King, published a new autograph copy of all known fragments of the Legend in *Cuneiform Texts from Babylonian Tablets in the British Museum*, Vol. XIII (London, 1901).[22] King's copy is reasonably accurate except for one glaring error.[23]

In 1904, A. Jeremias brought forth his important work *Das alte Testament im Licht des alten Orients* (Leipzig, 1904), which devoted a section to a discussion of the birth narrative of Moses and some of the most notable parallels in ancient literature. Special attention was given to the Sargon story by the author who offered a partial translation of the first column. Jeremias's translation followed Winckler's (*KB* III) except for a few details. The most interesting change was his interpretation of the difficult term *ēnetu* as "Vestalin," a word that approached the meaning more closely than any of the previous translations.[24]

The next treatment appeared three years later in O. Weber's *Die Literatur der Babylonier und Assyrier* (Leipzig, 1907), pp. 206-7. Weber provided a partial translation of column i followed by a brief discussion of the literary genre of the exposed infant.

The most important work done on the Sargon Legend in the first four decades since its initial publication was certainly L. W. King's treatment in *Chronicles Concerning Early Babylonian Kings* II (London, 1907), pp. 87-96. He produced a cuneiform copy, transliteration, and translation of both columns of the text. The translation was the best to date and included helpful notes on variant forms and proposed restorations. In addition, there was a selected bibliography of previous treatments.

One year later, the folklore scholar E. Cosquin published an article "Le lait de la mère et le coffre flottant,"[25] which contained a discussion of the Sargon Legend as an example of the floating box genre. Cosquin offered an excellent translation of the beginning of column i prepared by F. Thureau-Dangin. In this treatment, the distinguished French Assyriologist had perceptively interpreted *ēnetu* as "prêtresse de haut rang."

In 1909, A. Ungnad produced a new translation of both

columns for Gressmann's *Altorientalische Texte und Bilder zum alten Testament*, 1st ed. (Tübingen, 1909), p. 79. Ungnad also provided a list of the most recent treatments of the text. H. Zimmern followed the next year with a short translation in *Zum Streit um die "Christusmythe"* (Berlin, 1910), p. 26. In 1926, E. Ebeling issued his translation for the revised *Altorientalische Texte und Bilder* (Berlin and Leipzig, 1926), pp. 234-35.

Six years later, P. Jensen wrote an article "Aussetzungsgeschichte" for *Reallexikon der Assyriologie* I (Berlin and Leipzig, 1932), p. 322 in which the Sargon Legend figured prominently.

The most recent significant study of the Legend was published by H. G. Güterbock in his "Die historische Tradition und ihre literarische Gestaltung bei Babyloniern und Hethitern bis 1200."[26] Güterbock was the first to speak of the Sargon Legend as an example of *narû*-literature. He provided a paraphrased summary of column i, which was supplemented by valuable notes on difficult passages. There is a transliteration and translation of the second column that is clearly superior to any of the earlier efforts.

Since 1934 there has been little work done on the Legend with the exception of two new translations. The first was prepared by E. A. Speiser for *Ancient Near Eastern Texts Relating to the Old Testament*, edited by James B. Pritchard (Princeton, 1950), p. 119. A revised translation by A. K. Grayson appeared in *ANET*[3] in 1969. The latest effort is found in R. Labat's *Les religions du Proche-Orient asiatique* (Paris, 1970), p. 308. Both translations neglected the second column. In 1965, W. G. Lambert published a copy of K 7249,[27] which he identified as a fragment of column ii of the Sargon Legend.

The Legend has enjoyed some renewed interest in recent years as an example of the pseudo-autobiography. Four studies touching on this literary form have briefly mentioned the Sargon Legend.[28] Finally, recent archaeological reports of finds at Tell Mardikh concerning Sargon[29] and his contemporaries, if confirmed, may result not only in a new interest in Sargon, but in Sargon literature as well.

NOTES

CHAPTER I

[1]Neither title is completely satisfying because other "legends" are known concerning Sargon and a designation of the text by its opening motif ignores the possibility of its relative unimportance in the context of the entire composition. The birth story occupies only about a third of a column in a text that might have extended three or four columns. A title based on the incipit such as "the Legend of Sargon, Strong King" is clumsy. In any event, an attempt to change the title at this late date would surely result in confusion and resistance.

[2]Namely, the *Chicago Assyrian Dictionary (CAD)* and W. von Soden's *Akkadisches Handwörterbuch (AHw)*.

[3]In 1975, I had the opportunity to collate all the Sargon Legend fragments at the British Museum. Prior to a second collation in August 1977, the tablets were baked and soaked resulting in a slight improvement in the reading of some damaged signs.

[4]K 3401, K 4470, and K 7249.

[5]Not all tablets designated with a K catalogue number derive from Kujunjik. Some texts excavated at nearby Nimrud (Calah) also received K numbers. In addition, errors in classification are known to have occurred in the British Museum since fragments from Babylonian sites have been accessioned into the Kujunjik collection. Nevertheless, the likelihood is great that these fragments actually do come from the library of Assurbanipal.

[6]Designated Sm 2118, the fragment joins at the lower end of K 3401. Since Smith identifies the find spot as "the palace of Sennacherib at Kujunjik" (Smith, *Assyrian Discoveries* [New York, 1875], p. 224), this proves the provenience of K 3401 as well. Cf. n. 5.

[7]BM 47449 (81-11-8, 154).

[8]A Selection from the Miscellaneous Inscriptions of Assyria, prepared by Sir H. C. Rawlinson, assisted by George Smith (London, 1870).

[9]G. Smith, "Early History of Babylonia," *TSBA* 1 (1872), pp. 46-47. The translation concludes with the last preserved line of column i.

[10]Ibid., p. 46.

[11]*TSBA* 1 (1872), pp. 271-80.

[12]Cf. Talbot's earlier explication of the name as "king of justice," *TSBA* 1 (1872), p. 271. For a discussion of the

name Sargon, *šarru-kīn* "the king is the true one," see Chapter II, commentary to the text, col. i l.1.

[13]P. 99.

[14]The reference to a translation by Lenormant is puzzling. It should have appeared between 1870 and 1875, but I have not been able to find it. If it was published, it has been overlooked by the early bibliographies of Bezold and King (see below).

[15]A. Gutschmid, *Neue Beiträge zur Geschichte des alten Orients* (Leipzig, 1876), pp. 108-10.

[16]S.v. *Azupirānu*, pp. 208-9.

[17]In *Comptes rendus de l'Académie des Inscriptions et Belles Lettres quatrième série* 11 (1883), pp. 80-81.

[18]Cf. n. 14.

[19]Vol. II, p. 529.

[20]Similar descriptions of K 4470 and K 7249 appear on pages 635 and 840 respectively.

[21]In his "Assyriological Gleanings," *Proceedings of the Society of Biblical Archaeology* 18 (1896), p. 257.

[22]Pl. 42 and 43.

[23]See Chapter II, n. 12.

[24]On the problems surrounding the term *ēnetu*, see Chapter II, commentary to the text, col. i 2.1.

[25]In *Revue des questions historiques* N. S. 39 (1908), pp. 370-74.

[26]See *Zeitschrift für Assyriologie* 42 (1934), pp. 62-65.

[27]In *CT* XLVI (1965), pl. 45, no. 46.

[28]Lambert and Grayson, "Akkadian Prophecies," *JCS* 18 (1964), p. 8; Grayson, *Babylonian Historical-Literary Texts* (Toronto, 1975), p. 8, n. 11c, *Assyrian and Babylonian Chronicles*, TCS V (Locust Valley, 1975), p. 2, n. 14; and M. Astour, "Ezekiel's Prophecy of Gog and the Cuthean Legend of Naram-Sin," *JBL* 95 (1976), p. 572, n. 27.

[29]It now appears that an individual mentioned as a receiver of goods in the time of Ebrum is probably not Sargon of Akkad (cf. P. Matthiae, "Ebla in the Late Early Syrian Period: The Royal Palace and the State Archives," *Biblical Archeologist* 39 [1976], p. 102). The name, which is written *ša-ri-gi-nu*, was first interpreted as the Eblaite spelling of *šarru-kīn* (Sargon). But no title follows the name and the man's identity remains unclear.

CHAPTER II

THE SARGON LEGEND TEXTS

Textual Problems and Stemma

Four manuscripts of the Sargon Legend are known and may be used in the construction of its stemma. They are as follows:

A K 3401 + Sm 2118. Published by L. W. King, *CT* XIII, pl. 42. A translation, transliteration, and cuneiform copy were **published** by King in *CCEBK* II, 87-94. The obverse of A preserves parts of 30 lines of column i of the Legend on 27 separate lines. The reverse of the tablet is missing.

B K 4470. Published by L. W. King, *CT* XIII, pl. 43. The text is treated by King in *CCEBK* II, 87-94. B contains 22 lines of column i and 18 fragmentary lines of a second column on the obverse. The reverse is missing.

C BM 47449. Published by L. W. King, *CT* XIII, pl. 43.[1] The reverse of C preserves the first 6 lines of column i in a single column of a Neo-Babylonian practice tablet. Traces of three unrelated columns are also present on the same face. The Sargon Legend extract is treated by King in *CCEBK* II, 87-94.

D K 7249. Published by W. G. Lambert, *CT* XLVI, pl. 45 no. 46. This fragment, which appears to be from the reverse,[2] contains parts of 21 lines of text parallel to column ii of B. The other side is not preserved.

Texts A and B

Texts A and B are written in Neo-Assyrian script. Both preserve the beginning of column i, whereas B contains approximately the first third of 18 lines of a second column. Text A has slightly more of the first column (30 lines to 22 of B) and is in a better state of preservation. Both A and B grow more mutilated as they continue. Each lacks the lower right half as well as the bottom part of the tablet.

Over 22 lines of text overlap in A and B, so that a casual reading is sufficient to indicate that the two are almost identical. Components of the exposed-hero tale,[3] an integral part of column i, are present in A and B in exactly the same form. The record of Sargon's exploits after attaining kingship agrees in detail and order as far as both tablets are preserved. In fact, the vocabulary of the texts along with the order of the wording is virtually identical.

Those areas where A and B disagree are in cases of orthography, in two cases of vocalic or morphemic variants, and in one apparent change in vocabulary resulting from a scribal error. Unquestionably, A and B are closely related and derive from a common ancestor.

Variants in A and B

	A	B
1.	LUGAL.GI.NA LUGAL *dan-nu* LUGAL *a-ga-dè*^{ki} *a-na-ku*	LUGAL.G[I.NA LUG]AL⸢*dan*⸣*-nu* LUGAL *a-ga-*[*dè*^{ki} *a-na-ku*]
2.	*um-mi e-nê-tu*$_4$ *a-bi ul i-di*	*um-m*[*i*] *e-nê-tu*$_4$ *a-bi ul i-d*⸢*i*⸣
3.	ŠEŠ AD-*ja i-ra-mi šá-da-a*	ŠEŠ AD-*ja i-ra-mi šá-da-a*

Lines 1-3.--Despite the mutilated condition of the first line of B, an examination of the traces and a consideration of the spacing of words make a restoration identical to A certain. The content, vocabulary, and spelling agree and represent the way they must have appeared in the original. In A, lines 2 and 3 are written on a single line but are separated with a *Glossenkeil*.

	A	B
4.	*a-li* ^{uru}*a-zu-pi-ra-a-ni šá i-na a-ḫi* ^{íd}BURANUN *šak-nu*	*a-li* ^{uru}*a-zu-pi-ra-nu šá i-na a-ḫi* $^{í[d}$B]URANUN *šak-n*⸢*u*⸣

Line 4.--Text B preserves the syntactically correct form of the place name (*azupirānu*) with the nominative case ending *-u* (*ān*[*u*]).[4] The orthography in A, *a-zu-pi-ra-a-ni*, indicates the long vowel ā and ends in *-i*. This difference in case ending may be explained by loss of distinction in final vowels

common in Standard Babylonian.[5]

	A	B
5.	*i-ra-an-ni um-mu e-nê-tu*$_4$ *i-na pu-uz-ri ú-lid-an-ni*	*i-ra-an-ni um-mi e-nê-tu*$_4$ *i-na pu-*[*uz*]*-ri ú-lid-an-n*[*i*]
6.	*iš-kun-an-ni i-na qup-*⌈*pi*⌉ *šá šu-ri i-na* A.ESÍR KÁ-*ja ip-ḫi*	*iš-kun-an-ni i-na qup-pi šá šu-ú-*[*ri*] *i-na* A.ESÍR KÁ-*ja ip-ḫi*

Lines 5-6.--A and B differ slightly in line 5.

Text A reads *īranni ummu ēnetu* — the *ēnetu*-mother conceived me

Text B reads *īranni ummī ēnetu* — my mother, the *ēnetu*, conceived me

Although it is impossible to be certain which form is original, *ummī ēnetu* (B) is consistent with the autobiographical style in which the Legend is written. In addition, it is easier to explain how the morpheme *-ī* of the first person singular pronoun suffix could be lost than added. If we assume either (1) A or an ancestor of A was copied from a tablet in which "my mother, the *ēnetu*," was written with the logogram AMA without a phonetic complement, or (2) that a phonetic complement had existed but was damaged, then the loss of the morpheme could occur if the scribe decided to write the form syllabically. In any event, B seemingly represents the original form.[6]

In line 6 concerning the word *šūru* "reed," A and B differ, apparently, only in spelling. A reads *šu-ri* and B *šu-ú-*[*ri*] with vowel length indicated. That *ri* is to be restored to B rather than *šú*[7] follows from considerations of spacing.

It is very important to note that both A and B preserve the anomalous form KÁ-*ja*. Güterbock commented on the difficulty with this form, questioning whether the plural determinative had been lost KÁ<-MEŠ>-*ja* or whether a defect in grammar was involved.[8] The correct form in the singular would be *bābī* written KÁ-*i*.[9] This is the only example of an irregular form common to A and B; its significance for the stemma will be discussed below.

	A	B
7.	*id-dan-ni a-*⌈*na*⌉[Í]D *šá la e-le-e-*⌈*a*⌉	*id-dan-an-ni a-na* ÍD [*š*]*á la e-le-e-*⌈*a*⌉

Line 7.--This line appears to offer a major divergence in the text with two different verbs represented. A has *iddanni* from *nadû* "to throw down," "cast," "abandon," etc. The verb is a G preterit, third singular with a ventive pronoun suffix ending. Text B preserves *iddananni* a difficult form ostensibly from *nadānu* "to give" taken as a G preterit by King.[10]

A closer look at the verb form reveals that King was wrong; *iddananni* cannot be from *nadānu* as he has taken it. The 3rd person preterit of *nadānu* with the ventive suffix ending is *iddinanni*. Our form could be the 3rd person present (Assyrian), but this would be inconsistent with the pattern of verbs in the preterit in lines 5-12, all of which possess the same ventive suffix ending. No justification exists for assuming a present here. One is compelled to accept the reading of A, *iddanni*, as the original form. This is a good preterit and makes sense in context. Assuming A, B *iddananni* may easily be explained as a scribal error. Copying from a text with *iddanni*, the scribe of B or its ancestor may have inadvertently added a syllable, *an*, his eye resting on the line immediately above or below 7 as he inscribed the ending *anni*. Equally possible is that the error occurred when the scribe, dulled by the monotony of the ending, affixed the syllables *an-ni* to the verb stem.

An interpretation of *iddananni* as a scribal error based on an orthography *-dan*^{an} is also possible. Such spellings, involving CVC graphemes, are common in Old Akkadian and Sumerian and are attested, though infrequently, in later sources. For an example in a Neo-Assyrian royal inscription, see *TCL* III 37 ^{māt}*al-*^{la}*lab-ri-a* (cf. ^{māt}*al-lab-ri-a-a* ibid. 38).[11]

	A	B
8.	*iš-šá-an-ni* ÍD *a-na* U[GU] ⌜^{1}⌝*aq-qí* ^{lú}A.BAL *ú-bil-a*[*n-ni*]	[*iš-šá-an-ni* ÍD *a-na* U]GU [^{1}*aq-qí* ^{lú}A].BAL *ú-bi-la-an-*[*ni*]
9.	^{1}*aq-qí* ^{lú}A.BAL *i-na ṭí-i*[*b*] *d*[*a-l*]*i-*[*šú l*]*u ú-še-la-an-*[*ni*]	[^{1}]*aq-qí* ^{lú}A.BAL *i-na ṭí-ib d*[*a-li-šú l*]*u-u ú-še-la-an-n*[*i*]

10.	⸢1⸣*aq-qí* ^{lú}A.BAL *a-na ma-ru-ti-*⸢*šú*⸣ [*l*]*u ú-rab-ban-*[*ni-ma*]	[1]*aq-qí* ^{lú}A.BAL *a-na ma-ru-*[*ti-šú lu*] ⸢*ú*⸣*-rab-ba-ni-ma*[12]
12.	[*ina*] ^{lú}NU.KIRI$_6$ *-ti-já* ^{dingir}*iš-tar lu-u* ⸢*i*⸣*-ra-man-*⸢*ni*⸣*-*[*ma*]	[*i*]*-na* ^{lú}NU.KIRI$_6$ *-ti-já* ^{dingir}*i*[*š-tar lu-u i-r*]*a-man-ni-ma*

Lines 8-12.--Insofar as A and B are preserved, they are identical except for minor variations in orthography. The variants are: *ú-bil-an-ni* (A) against *ú-bi-la-an-ni* (B); *lu* (A) against *lu-u* (B); *ú-rab-ban-ni-ma* (A) against *ú-rab-ba-ni-ma* (B); and *ina* (A) against *i-na* (B).

	A	B
14.	[UN.M]EŠ SAG.GE$_6$.GA *lu-u a-be-el lu-u áš-*[*pur*]	[UN.M]EŠ *ṣal-mat* SAG.DU *lu-u a-b*[*e-el* . . .]
15.	[KUR]-⸢*e*⸣KALA.MEŠ *ina ak-kul-la-te šá* URUDU.ḪI.A *lu-u ár-*[*ḫi?-iṣ?*]	[KUR]-*i* KALA.MEŠ *ina ak-kul-la-t*[*e* . . .]
16.	[*lu*] *e-tel-li šá-di-i e-l*[*u-ti*]	[*lu e-tel*]*-li* KUR-*di-i* [ ]

Lines 14-16.--The variants in these lines are once again orthographic and hold little value for a developmental study of the text. Of interest in line 14 is the unusual form of the expression "black-headed (people)" found in A--SAG.GE$_6$.GA.[13] In contrast, B has the more common spelling *ṣal-mat* SAG.DU. In 15 and 16, A preserves the following orthographies for "mountain": KUR-*e* and *šá-di-i*, while B has KUR-*i* and KUR-*di-i*.

Genealogy of A and B

A reconstruction of a detailed stemma of the Sargon Legend text based on two or three partial copies is not possible.

We must be content with stating, through a comparison of variant forms, the obvious relationships that exist among the copies.

There are eleven places where variations in the text of the Legend are preserved in A and B. Three of these are of value in our study. The other eight are orthographic variants which shed no light on the genealogy of the text.

In one of the three significant variants, Text B preserves the correct form *azupirānu* against *azupirāni* in A. In the second, B again has what is probably the original form *ummī ēnetu* as opposed to *ummu ēnetu* in A. In the last one, A possesses the correct verb form *iddanni*, while B has *iddananni*.

Despite the overwhelming similarity of the texts in all other respects, obviously neither was copied directly from the other. To derive A from B, one would have to admit scribal errors in lines 4 and 5 and, at the same time, account for the correction of line 7 of B. This is quite unlikely. Just as unlikely is to take B from A; for, while one could understand the occurrence of the mistake *iddananni*, the improvement of A's errors in lines 4 and 5 would remain.

It seems reasonable to assume that A or its ancestor (A') had separated from B or its ancestor (B') before the corruption *iddananni* had appeared, or it too would have preserved it. B could not have descended from A and still maintained proper forms where corruptions had entered A. After some point we must assume a separate descent from a common ancestor (see fig. 1).

Let us now turn to the troublesome form in line 6, which is the only anomaly found in both texts. As indicated above, KÁ-*ja* is an error whether of omission of the plural sign MEŠ or in grammatical usage (the first person pronoun suffix -*ja* for -*ī*).[14] In either case, the nature of the error is not relevant to a discussion of the pedigree of the text. What is significant is that the form is found in both A and B. This leads to the conclusion that it had entered the transmission of the text at some point before the separation of A and B (see figure 2). Possibly the mistake occurred independently in the lines of A and B, but this seems much less likely. The simpler explanation in this case is to be preferred.

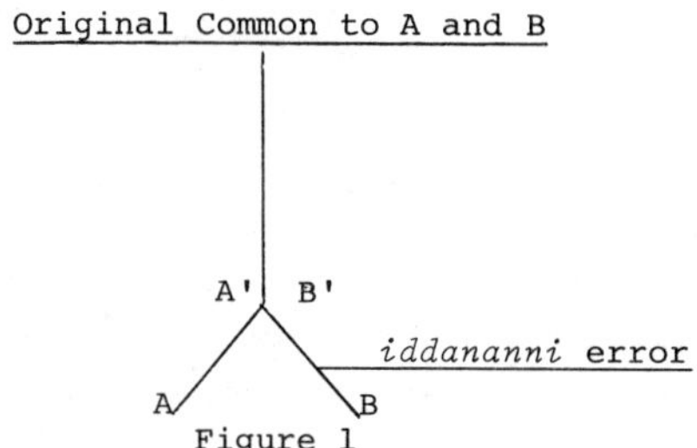

Figure 1

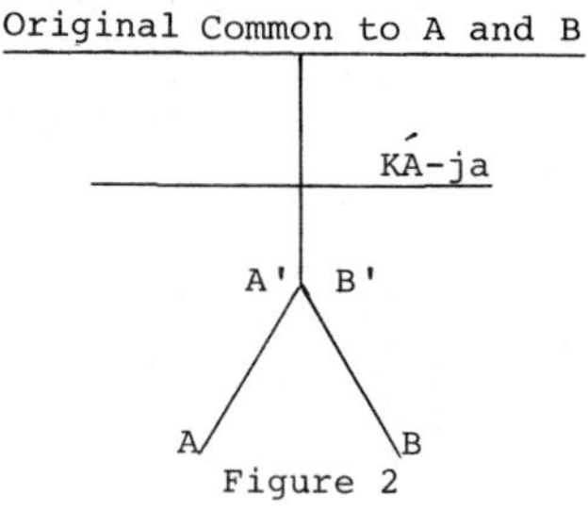

Figure 2

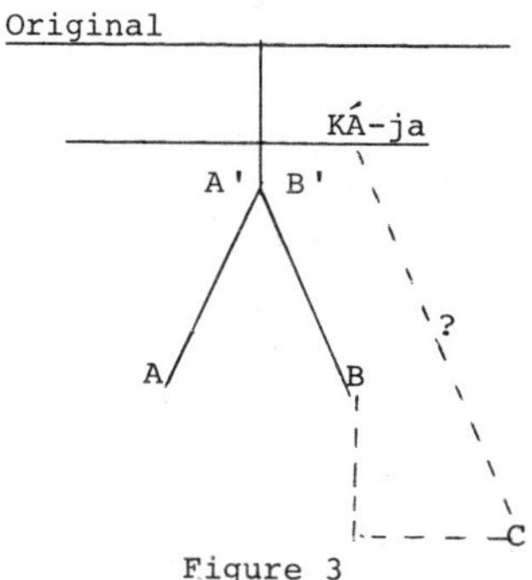

Figure 3

Text C

Text C is a practice tablet preserving four fragmentary columns each on obverse and reverse. One narrow column of the reverse contains lines 1-6 of the Legend (on 16 separate lines) written in Neo-Babylonian script. Unfortunately, the text is poorly preserved, three lines in the middle of the column are almost totally destroyed.

The text of the Legend, as found in C, is quite corrupt. A question arises immediately concerning its value in a developmental study of the Sargon Legend. For, on the surface, there are indications such as a lack of unambiguous first person elements which might, perhaps, be interpreted to cast doubt on C as a copy of an actual Sargon Legend text. That is to say, if parts are written about Sargon in the third person, possibly C represents the efforts of a student scribe to write down the gist of the tale rather than a true copy of an existing text before him. This argument must be rejected. A study of C shows that, with the exception of the missing word *anāku* in line 1, the presentation of the narrative is essentially complete in its order and detail. There are differences in orthography, grammar, syntax, and vocabulary; yet the structure of the tale and most of the words remain the same. With all its corruptions, C ultimately goes back to an ancestor common to A and B, and we shall see that it is possible to explain how many of the variants in C might have developed. Finally, the presence of the same form KÁ-*ja* found in the texts A and B argues compellingly that C was copied. If the scribe were writing from memory or dictation, one would expect him to write a form that represented the phrase he heard or understood, that is, either a singular or plural, not a mixed form. The repetition of KÁ-*ja* strongly suggests he was reproducing a spelling he had seen in writing, which had become part of the orthographic tradition of the text.

Variants in C

	C	A and B
1.	LUGAL.GIN LUGAL KALA	LUGAL.GI.NA LUGAL *dan-nu*
2.	LUGAL *a-ga-dè*^{ki}	LUGAL *a-ga-dè*^{ki} *a-na-ku*

Lines 1-2.--Note the spelling of Sargon's name in C, LUGAL.GIN, which is attested in the first millennium and is found often in Neo-Babylonian sources.[15] The orthography of the royal title that follows is extremely interesting; for, according to Seux's collection of the epithet,[16] the spelling LUGAL KALA does not occur at any period in Babylonia. It is found, however, in Middle and Neo-Assyrian inscriptions of Aššur-reš-iši I (1133-1116 B.C.) and Esarhaddon (680-669 B.C.).[17]

The most striking feature of C is the lack of the first person pronoun *anāku*. Was it left out by the scribe of C, or was it missing from his *Vorlage*? If the latter were the case, it might have occurred at some stage in the copying of a text damaged at the edge just as B is today.

	C	A and B
3.	AMA *e-nê-*tu_4	*um-mi e-nê-*tu_4 *a-bi ul i-di*
4.	AD *la i-ši*	

Lines 3-4.--The question here is how did the writer understand the logograms AMA and AD--as *ummu* and *abu* or as forms with the pronoun suffix understood? Elsewhere in C the pronominal suffix is indicated with a phonetic complement.[18] This might suggest that at some point in the transmission of the text the suffix was lost perhaps in copying from a damaged text.

In place of *ul i-di* in A and B, *la i-ši* is found in C. The form (*i-ši*) is a preterit of the defective verb *išû* "to have," "to own" which can be either first or third person. Consequently, it is no help in determining whether the subject was taken as *abu* or *abī*. One might speculate on the origin of this variant. A *di* sign[19] partially damaged could easily be restored by a copyist as *ši* producing a meaning as suitable as the original. The texts also differ in the choice of the negative particle. A and B preserve *ul*, used in the negation of declarative sentences and independent clauses, against *la* in C. The negative particle *la* is employed primarily in the negation of individual words and subordinate clauses, but *la* may replace *ul* in the negation of a main clause in Babylonian poetic texts.[20] The signs for *ul* and *la* are not easily confused in either their Assyrian or Babylonian forms, and one may assume that the variant in C is probably a secondary development.

	C	A and B
5.	*a-ḫu* AD-*ja*	ŠEŠ AD-*ja i-ra-mi šá-da-a*
6.	KUR-*d*[*a?*] [*i-ra*]-⸢*am*⸣-*mu*	

Lines 5-6.--These lines have been taken by Güterbock in the plural against A and B.[21] His position is apparently based on the verb *i-ra-am-mu* which seems to end in a plural morpheme -*ū* (G present 3rd plural). The difficulty with this interpretation lies in the construct subject of the sentence. The plural *status constructus* form of *aḫu* is *aḫḫī* not *aḫḫū*.[22] It is suggested here that C does not differ in number and that it may be properly taken in the singular. The vocalic ending -*u* may be explained in this fashion: final weak verbs ending in -*i* and -*u* were no longer carefully distinguished in Neo-Babylonian.[23] The form *aḫu* that is found in C does exist, according to *GAG*,[24] as a variant singular *status constructus* in Babylonian poetic texts. If this interpretation is correct, we are dealing with orthographic variations characteristic of the period in which C was copied and not with a basic alteration of the Legend. Note the change in word order involving *irammi šadâ* present in C. This is the only variant of this kind between the three copies.

	C	A and B
10.	AMA *e-né-tu*$_4$	*um-mu* (A) / *um-mi* (B) *e-né-tu*$_4$ *i-na pu-uz-ri ú-lid-an-ni*
11.	*ina pu-uz-zu*	
12.	*ú-lid-da-an-ni*	

Lines 10-12.--For line 10 refer to the discussion of C 3. In 11, Text C has the corrupt *puzzu* for *puzri*. This form might be explained as the result of confusion of the *rí* and *zu* signs , which are also similar in Neo-Babylonian script, though use of *rí* is rather rare in later periods. The error might well have been committed by the student scribe in copying from a text with *pu-uz-rí*, for *puzzu* has no known meaning. The orthography in C *ú-lid-da-an-ni* is anomalous and appears to be related to the problem of defective spellings involving words

written with CVC graphemes.[25]

	C	A and B
13.	*iš-ku-na-an-ni*	*iš-kun-an-ni i-na qup-pi*
		šá šu-ri (A) *šu-ú-[ri]* (B)
14.	*ina qu-up-pu*	
15.	*šá šu-ú-šú ina* A.ESÍR	

Lines 13-15.--Minor variations in spelling are present in 13 and 14. More importantly, C has *quppu* against the correct form *quppi* in A and B. This variant is easily explainable. A partially damaged *pi* sign might be mistaken for *pu* especially in a period when distinction in case endings had been lost, or it may simply be the result of loss of distinction of final vowels. In C 15 *šūšu* may represent the same kind of variant understandable as an error in transmission--a defective *ri* becoming *šú* → .[26] It is also possible that the confusion of two near synonyms *šūšu* "twig" and *šūru* "reed" might have resulted in the change.

Genealogy of C

Assuming C is a legitimate copy of a Sargon Legend text, as we believe it is, the question of its position in the family tree with A and B is a difficult one. The fact that it preserves the familiar KÁ-*ja* indicates it may have descended from an ancestor prior to the separation of A and B, or that it might be a descendant in the line of A or B. That it might be derived from an Assyrian copy is not impossible in view of its essential agreement with the other copies and also the presence of LUGAL KALA, an orthography attested only in Assyrian sources. Curiously (but probably coincidentally) a number of important variants in C occur exactly in areas damaged in B; for example, line 1--*anāku* which C omits is destroyed in B; line 2--*la i-ši* of C against *ul i-di* of B where the *di* sign is partially mutilated; and line 6 where C reads *šu-ú-šú* to *šu-ú-[ri]* in B, the last sign of which is lost. Although we have no way of knowing how and when the damage to B occurred, possibly C lies somewhere in its line. If C ran only one more line, the question might have been settled, for if the corrupt *iddananni* of B was preserved in C, we would be more confident of the connection. The possible relationship of all three copies of column i is given in figure 3.

Text D

Like A and B, D is written in the Standard Babylonian dialect in Neo-Assyrian script. This fragment, which preserves the same narrative found in column ii of B, overlaps in 13 lines allowing for the reconstruction of about two-thirds of the total line in some cases.

Variants in D

	B	D
8.	*ir-tap-pu-ud* ANŠE.E[DIN.NA]	*ir-tap-pu-ud sír-ra-mu*
9.	*il-lak šá-a-r*[*u*]	[*il*]*-lak* IM
12.	*šá pa-ri-i la-si-m*[*e*]	[*šá pa-r*]*e-e la-si-me* *a-a-i*[*t?*]

Lines 8-12.--Three variants[27] of an orthographic nature are apparent when comparing B and D. In line 8, D preserves the syllabic spelling of *serrēmu* "wild ass"--*sír-ra-mu* an orthography that is attested only in Neo-Assyrian.[28] Text B has the logogram ANŠE.EDIN.NA (=*serrēmu*). The other variants are *šá-a-r*[*u*] (B) against IM (D) and *pa-ri-i* (B) against *pa-re-e* (D). The poor state of preservation of column ii and the type of textual variants that do exist in B and D preclude any further refinement in our reconstruction of the development of the Sargon Legend text.

List of Manuscripts

Symbol	Museum Number	
A	K 3401+Sm 2118	reddish brown fragment from the obverse of a single column tablet measuring 9.5 cm. x 8.4 cm.; covers lines 1-32 of column i of the Legend.

Symbol	Museum Number	
B	K 4470	reddish brown fragment from the obverse of a two-column tablet measuring 7.7 cm. x 15 cm.; covers lines 1-22 of the first column and the beginnings of lines 1-18 of column ii.
C	BM 47449	dark brown fragment from the reverse of a practice tablet measuring 7.7 cm. x 8 cm.; covers lines 1-6 of column i.
D	K 7249	reddish brown fragment from the reverse (?) of a tablet measuring 5.9 cm. x 4.3 cm.; preserves 21 partial lines of column ii.

Critical Edition of the Text

As the basic text for column i of the Sargon Legend, A has been selected because its condition is superior to B and it offers almost eight more lines of text. The lines are numbered according to the sequence of the hypothetical text underlying A, so that, where two lines of text have been combined into one in A with a *Glossenkeil*, they have been separated and given individual numbers. This is done even when the text is destroyed and the combination can only be assumed from the context or spacing. Thus we follow King's numbering in *CCEBK* II, 87-94. Restorations are marked by brackets, uncertain readings or conjectural restorations by question mark and brackets.

The text of column ii has been reconstructed as a composite of the fragmentary sources B and D. Owing to the similar positions of the fragments relative to the whole text (they overlap in 13 lines), about two-thirds of some lines can now be restored. Here, the poor condition of the column has resulted in many conjectural readings.

Texts A, B, C, and D were collated by the writer first on photograph and later with the originals.

	Transliteration		Translation
	Column i		*Column i*
1.	LUGAL.GI.NA *(šarrukīn)* LUGAL *(šarru) dan-nu* LUGAL *(šar) a-ga-dè*^{ki} *a-na-ku*	1.	Sargon, strong king, king of Agade, am I.
2.	*um-mi e-nê-*tu_4 *a-bi ul i-di*	2.	My mother was a high priestess, my father I do not know.
3.	ŠEŠ *(aḫi)* AD-*ja (abīja) i-ra-mi šá-da-a*	3.	My paternal kin inhabit the mountain region.
4.	*a-li* ^{uru}*a-zu-pi-ra-a-ni šá i-na a-ḫi* ^{íd}BURANUN *(puratti) šak-nu*	4.	My city (of birth) is Azupirānu, which lies on the bank of the Euphrates.
5.	*i-ra-an-ni um-mu e-nê-*tu_4 *i-na pu-uz-ri ú-lid-an-ni*	5.	My mother*, a high priestess, conceived me, in secret she bore me.
6.	*iš-kun-an-ni i-na qup-*⸢*pi*⸣ *šá šu-ri i-na* A.ESÍR *(ittî)* KÁ-*ja (bābīja) ip-ḫi*	6.	She placed me in a reed basket, with bitumen she caulked my hatch.

1. LUGAL.GI.NA: C LUGAL.GIN; LUGAL *dan-nu*: C LUGAL KALA; *a-na-ku:* C omits
2. *um-mi*: C AMA; *a-bi ul i-di:* C AD *la i-ši*
3. ŠEŠ: C *a-ḫu; i-ra-mi:* C [*i-ra*]-⸢*am*⸣-*mu; šá-da-a:* C KUR-*da?* (The order is reversed in C: KUR-*da?*[*i-ra*]-⸢*am*⸣-*mu.*)
4. ^{uru}*a-zu-pi-ra-a-ni:* B ^{uru}*a-zu-pi-ra-nu*
5. *um-mu:* B *um-mi*, C AMA; *pu-uz-ri:* C *pu-uz-zu; ú-lid-an-ni:* C *ú-lid-da-an-ni*
6. *iš-kun-an-ni:* C *iš-ku-na-an-ni; i-na:* C *ina; qup-pi:* C *qu-up-pu; šu-ri:* B *šu-ú-*[*ri*], C *šu-ú-šú*

*Translation follows Text B.

7.	*id-dan-ni a-n⸢a⸣* [Í]D ([*nâ*]*ri*) *šá la e-le-e-⸢a⸣*	7.	She abandoned me to the river from which I could not escape.[29]
8.	*iš-šá-an-ni* ÍD (*nâru*) *a-na* U[GU (*mu*[*ḫḫi*]))] ⸢^{l}⸣*aq-qí* ^{lú}A.BAL (*dālî*) *ú-bil-a*[*n-ni*]	8.	The river carried me along; to Aqqi, the water drawer, it brought me.
9.	^{l}*aq-qí* ^{lú}A.BAL (*dālû*) *i-na ṭí-i*[*b*] *d*[*a-l*]*i-*[*šú l*]*u ú-še-la-an-*[*ni*]	9.	Aqqi, the water drawer, when immersing his bucket lifted me up.
10.	⸢^{l}⸣*aq-qí* ^{lú}A.BAL (*dālû*) *a-na ma-ru-ti-*⸢*šú*⸣[*l*]*u ú-rab-ban-*[*ni-ma*]	10.	Aqqi, the water drawer, raised me as his adopted son.
11.	⸢^{l}⸣*aq-qí* ^{lú}A.BAL (*dālû*) *a-na* ^{lú}NU.KIRI$_6$*-ti-šú* (*nukaribbūtīšu*) ⸢*lu*⸣*-u* [*i*]*š-kun-*[*an-ni*]	11.	Aqqi, the water drawer, set me to his garden work.
12.	[AŠ (*ina*)] ^{lú}NU.KIRI$_6$*-ti-já* (*nukaribbūtīja*) ^{dingir}*iš-tar lu-u* ⸢*i*⸣*-ra-man-*⸢*ni*⸣*-*[*ma*]	12.	During my garden work, Ištar loved me (so that)
13.	[5]5 MU.MEŠ (*šanāti*) LUGAL-*ú-ta* (*šarrūta*) *lu-u e-pu-u*[*š*]	13.	55 years I ruled as king.

---

7. *id-dan-ni:* B *id-dan-an-ni*

8. *ú-bil-an-ni:* B *ú-bi-la-an-*⸢*ni*⸣

9. *lu:* B [*l*]*u-u*

10. *ú-rab-ban-ni-ma:* B *ú-rab-ba-ni-ma* (from photo and collation; King's copy *ú-rab-ba-an-ni* is incorrect.)

12. AŠ: B *i-na*

14.	[UN.M]EŠ ([*niš*]*ê*) SAG.GE_6.GA (*ṣalmāt qaqqadi*) *lu-u a-be-el lu-u áš-*[*pur*]	14.	The black-headed people I took over (and) governed.
15.	[KUR]-⸢*e*⸣ ([*šad*]*ê*) KALA.MEŠ (*dannūti*) AŠ (*ina*) *ak-kul-la-te šá* URUDU.ḪI.A (*erê*) *lu-u ár-*[*ḫi?-iṣ?*]	15.	Difficult mountains I pas[sed through?] using copper picks.
16.	[*lu*] *e-tel-li šá-di-i e-l*[*u-ti*]	16.	The upper ranges I climbed again and again.
17.	[*lu*] *at-ta-tab-lak-ka-ta šá-di-i šap-l*[*u-ti*]	17.	The lower ranges I jumped over again and again.
18.	[*ma?*]-*ti ti-amat lu-ú al-ma-*⸢*a*⸣ [3]-⸢*šú*⸣ ([*šalāšīš*]*u*)	18.	The sea [land?] I besieged three times.
19.	⸢NI⸣.TUK^{ki} (⸢*ti*⸣*lmun*) *lu-u ik-š*[*u-ud qa-ti*]	19.	I conquered Tilmun . . .
20.	[*a-n*]*a* BÀD.DINGIR^{ki} (*dêr*) GAL-*i* (*rabî*) [*lu e-li*] ⸢*lu-u*⸣ *a*[*k?*]	20.	To greater Dêr I went up, I . . .
21.	[*ka?*]-*zal-lu ú-naq-qir-ma* [ ]	21.	[Ka]zallu? I destroyed . . .
22.	[*man*]-*nu* LUGAL (*šarru*) ⸢*šá*⸣ *i-la-a EGIR-ja* (*arkīja*)	22.	Whatever king may arise after me,
23.	⸢5⸣[5 MU.MEŠ (*šanāti*) LUGAL-*ú-ta* (*šarrūta*) *li-pu-uš*]	23.	[Let him rule as king 55 years??].

14. SAG.GE_6.GA: B *ṣal-mat* SAG.DU
15. KUR-*e*: B KUR-*i*
16. *šá-di-i*: B KUR-*di-i*

24.	[U]N.MEŠ *([ni]šê)* SAG.GE_6.GA *(ṣalmāt qaqqadi) li-b[e-el li-iš-pur]*	24.	L[et him take over (and) govern] the black-headed people.
25.	[KUR].MEŠ *([ša]dê)* KALA. MEŠ *(dannūti)* AŠ *(ina) ak-kul-l[a-te šá* URUDU.ḪI.A *(erê) li-ir-ḫi?-iṣ?]*	25.	[Let him pass through?] difficult mountains using co[pper picks].
26.	*[l]i-te-tel-li* KUR.MEŠ *(šadê)* AN.TA.MEŠ *(elûti)*	26.	Let him climb the upper ranges again and again.
27.	*[littatablakkata* KUR.MEŠ *(šadê)* KI.TA.MEŠ *(šaplūti)*]	27.	[Let him jump over the lower ranges again and again].
28.	*[m]a?-ti ti-amat lil-ma-a 3-šú (šalāšīšu)*	28.	Let him besiege the sea l[and?] three times.
29.	[NI.TUK^{ki} *(tilmun) li-ik-šu-ud qat-su*]	29.	[Let him conquer Tilmun . . .]
30.	*[a-na* B]ÀD.DINGIR^{ki} *([d]êr)* GAL-*i (rabî) li-li-ma*	30.	Let him go up to greater Dêr and . . .
31.	[*u]l-tu* URU-*já (ālīja) (a-ga-[dè*^{ki}]	31.	. . . from my city Agade
32.	[ ] *šu? ma? nâp? ri?*	32.	. . .

Column ii	*Column ii*
1. ⌈*a-na?*⌉	1. To? . . .
2. *ù* ŠU.L[Ú?] trace	2. and the *ḫūqu*-[bird? . . .
3. *ir-tap-pu-ud* ⌈U$_{10}$⌉ (*l*[*aḫru*]) or G[ANA$_6$] (*i*[*mmertu*]) [A]Š ([*in*]*a*) ⌈EDIN⌉ (⌈*ṣēri*⌉) *am-mī-ni la* [ ]	3. and the ewe ran about in the steppe, why not . . .
4. *ù* MAŠ.DÀ (*ṣabītu*) *iṣ*-⌈*ru*⌉/[*i*]*ṣ?-rat šá-a-ri lu-li-ma* [ ]	4. and the gazelle, the . . . of the wind, the stag . . .
5. *iṣ-ṣur-ru qa-du-ú šá iš-ta-s*[*u-ú*]	5. The Qaṭā-bird which was crying out
6. AŠ (*ina*) *ši-tas-si-šú mi-na-a il-qí*	6. In its continuous crying, what did it achieve?
7. *il-lik šá-a-r*[*u*]	7. The wind blew . . .
8. *ir-tap-pu-ud* ANŠE.E[DIN.NA] (*ser*[*rēmu*]) *a-a-i*[*t?*]	8. The wild ass ran about, what . . .
9. *il-lak šá-a-ru* AŠ (*ina*) A.RI[.A] (*na*[*mî*])	9. The wind blows from the steppe
10. *ir-tap-pu-ud* ANŠE.EDIN.NA (*serrēmu*) *i-bit* AŠ (*ina*) EDIN (*ṣēri*)	10. The wild ass ran about, he spent the night in the steppeland.
11. *i-šá-'u-ú* [ ]	11. The . . . runs . . .
12. *šá pa-ri-i la-si-me a-a-i*[*t?*]	12. of a swift onager what . . .

8. D: *sír-ra-mu*

9. D: IM

12. D: *pa-re-e*

13.	*ul i-šet* UR.BAR.RA *(barbaru) da-mi* [ ]	13.	The wolf did not escape the blood . . .
14.	UR.MAḪ *(nēšu) a-ki-lu da-mi* [ ]	14.	The devouring lion the blood . . .
15.	x-x-tu_4 *ta-bi-ik da-mi* [ ]	15.	. . . the spiller of blood . . .
16.	x-x-*šú la-pit da-mi* [ ]	16.	. . . the smearer of blood . . .
17.	*ir-tap-pu-ud* AŠ *(ina) di-in* ^{dingir}UTU *(šamaš) a-*⌈*na?*⌉]	17.	It ran about from the judgment of Šamaš to?
18.	[*il-lik*] *šá-a-ru* É *(bīt)* LÚ.[MEŠ?] *(a*[*mēlūti*]*)*	18.	The wind blew the house of men?
19.	[ ] *di-'a-ti* É *(bīt)* DINGIR.[MEŠ?]	19.	. . . tears? the temple of?
20.	[ ] *-lak na-mu-ta*	20.	. . . turns into wasteland
21.	DUMU.M[UNUS?]	21.	. . .
22.	traces	22.	. . .

15. B: not preserved

16. D: x-x-*šu*

Commentary to the Text

Column i

1.1 Sargon *(šarru-kīn)*, written logographically as LUGAL. GI.NA and LUGAL.GIN in the Legend, is best translated as "the king is the true one" taking the second element *kīn* as a G stative 3rd masculine singular of *kânu*. Other interpretations of the name such as "true king" *(šarru-kēnu)* and "the king he has established" *(šarru-ukīn)*[30] are not supported by the orthographic evidence. Waterman correctly argued against taking GIN as *kēnu*, an adjective, stating:

> if the latter were the ground meaning, then the form in our text [¹LUGAL-*ú*-*kîn* Letter 951 and passim] ought never to occur, but if *kênu* was original there ought to be some unquestioned early instances ending in *u*. So far as our evidence goes this is not the case.[31]

Waterman's spelling,[32] however, is not inconsistent with *šarru-kīn* since the *ú* of ¹LUGAL-*ú*-*kîn* can be understood as a phonetic complement of LUGAL. The interpretation *šarru-ukīn* is also not substantiated by the early orthographies.[33]

The Writing of the Name Sargon[34]

Third Millennium

The sources for the earliest orthography of Sargon's name include an original inscription found in Susa, the Maništušu Obelisk also from Susa, a number of Sumerian inscriptions that derive from Ur or the Ur III period, and a fragment of a calcite vase also from Ur. These indicate that the name of the founder of the Akkad dynasty was written *šar-ru*-GI[35] during the Old Akkadian period. An Ur III economic text from Drehem, which lists an offering to the statue of the deified Sargon in the Enlil temple at Nippur, preserves the orthography ᵈ*šar-ru-gin*ⁱⁿ.[36]

One may consider with caution the Old Babylonian copies of Sargon inscriptions made by the scribal school of Nippur "which attempt to reproduce faithfully the Sargonic dialect and system of writing."[37] In these copies of original inscriptions, Sargon appears in the Akkadian versions as *šar-ru*-GI and in the Sumerian counterparts as *šar-um*-GI.

The name Sargon is found as an element in a number of personal names in Old Akkadian and Ur III materials; for example: *šar-ru*-GI-*ì-lí; ur-*^{d}*šar-ru-gin; ur-*^{d}*šar-ru*-GIM;[38] *ur-šar-ru*-GIM; *šar-ru*-GIM; and *ur-šar-ru-um-*[GIM].

Second Millennium

In the Old Babylonian corpus we find the largest variety of spellings of the Sargon name. The orthographies attested in Mesopotamia proper are *šar-ru*-GI, *šar-um*-GI, *šar-um*-GI-*nê*, *šar-rum-ki-in*, *šar-ru-um-ki-in*, *šar-ru-ki-in*, *ša-ru-ki-in*, LUGAL-*ki-in*, and LUGAL.GI.NA.

The two most commonly attested forms are *šar-ru*-GI and *šar-ru-ki-in*. As we have already mentioned, the former represents the original spelling of the name which was employed by the scribes of Nippur in their copies of Old Akkadian Sargon inscriptions. This Old Akkadian orthography persisted during Old Babylonian times and appears in Akkadian inscriptions from Sumer (Nippur, Lagaš) and Akkad (Sippar), as well as in a Sumerian text from Kiš where it is preceded by the determinative for divinity. The spellings *šar-um*-GI and *šar-um*-GI-*nê* are found only in Sumerian sources from Nippur. The form *šar-um*-GI occurs in the Sumerian version of the Old Babylonian copies of Sargon inscriptions and in a copy of an economic text with a Sargon date name, while *šar-um*-GI-*nê* is attested twice in Sargon date names.

The most frequently attested spelling of the second millennium is also the most widespread geographically. The fully syllabic writing *šar-ru-ki-in* is found in Sumerian and Akkadian texts throughout the areas of Sumer and Akkad and in the regions of Mari and Assyria[39] in the north.

Note the remaining spellings which at present are known from one or two sources only: *šar-rum-ki-in*, *šar-ru-um-ki-in*, *ša-ru-ki-in*,[40] LUGAL-*ki-in*, and LUGAL.GI.NA.

First Millennium

LUGAL.GI.NA, employed in Text A and B of the Sargon Legend, is the most frequent spelling of the name in sources from the first millennium. The writings of this period are mainly logographic and consist of LUGAL.GIN (next in number after

LUGAL.GI.NA), LUGAL.GI, LUGAL-*ki-en*, LUGAL-*ú-kin*, MAN.GI.NA, MAN-*ki-in*, and *šar-ru-ki-in*.

That LUGAL.GI.NA was the normal way of writing Sargon's name in Assyria is seen in its almost exclusive usage in texts from Kujunjik (the library of Assurbanipal) and Assur. It occurs in a wide range of literature including omina, chronicles, literary, and scientific texts. One may assume that this orthography was common in the south as well from a Neo-Babylonian omen text from Uruk, a Neo-Babylonian version of the historical omens of Sargon and Naram-Sin (provenience unknown), and a royal inscription of Nabonidus.

The spelling LUGAL.GIN, attested only in the first millennium, appears to have enjoyed popular use in Neo-Babylonian literature. It occurs in Text C of the Sargon Legend from Dilbat, the World Map from Sippar, and a number of Neo-Babylonian chronicles, literary texts, and inscriptions whose proveniences are unknown. Evidence for an awareness of LUGAL. GIN in Assyria may be inferred from a commentary on the Astrological series *Enūma Anu-Enlil* discovered in the library of Assurbanipal. The line in question reads LUGAL *a-ga-dè*^{ki} : LUGAL.GIN:GI:*ta-ra-ṣa*. We may assume an additional orthography from this line, namely, LUGAL.GI, since the *Glossenkeil* seems to indicate a variant. For another possible case of LUGAL.GI in Neo-Assyrian period literature, see the Weidner Chronicle Ex. A Rs. 13, according to Weidner's emendations in *AfO* 13 (1939-40), p. 51.

Finally, for the first millennium we are aware of the compound spellings LUGAL-*ki-en* in an omen text from Assur, ^{1}LUGAL-*ú-kin* in a chronicle-like text concerning Nabonidus, MAN-*ki-in* in the series ḪAR-ra-*ḫubullu* (fragment from Assur), and MAN.GI.NA in an unpublished astrological omen.[41]

1.2 LUGAL *dannu*--the royal epithet here assumed by Sargon should be interpreted as "strong king."[42] Note that *CAD* translates the title in the Legend as "legitimate king" (Vol. D, p. 94 2). We see no justification for taking a secondary meaning of *dannu*, i.e. "legitimate" (basic sense: strong, hard, solid). As Hallo has shown, LUGAL KALA.GA replaced the earlier epithet NITA KALA.GA "strong male" after which it was patterned.[48] The epithet was employed as a standard title by important kings as a sign of their power and undoubtedly retained this essential meaning when used by usurpers. *CAD* does not explain why it translates *šarru dannu* as "legitimate king" when applied to Sargon, Kurigalzu, Arik-den-ili, Tukulti-Ninurta, Nabopolassar[44] and as "strong king" in the cases of Naram-Sin, Šu-Sin, Hammurabi, etc.[45]

The usage of the title by Sargon in the Legend is an anachronism, for it did not originate until the late Ur III period, too late to have appeared in original Sargon inscriptions. Its presence in first millennium copies of this literary text from Assyria, however, conforms to contemporary royal titulature since the title was commonly used by Assyrian kings from the late fourteenth century until the fall of the kingdom.

Historically, the title occurs in two forms: Sumerian--LUGAL KALA.GA and Akkadian--*šarru dannu* (with a variety of spellings attested).

Use in Babylonia

The title occurs as a royal epithet for the first time in Mesopotamia[46] during the reign of Amar-Sin of the Third Dynasty of Ur (2046-2038). Through a comparison of Amar-Sin's building inscriptions with his date formulae, Hallo has pinpointed the inception of its use to the eighth regnal year.[47] It is the Sumerian version of the title LUGAL KALA.GA that appears initially as a replacement for the older title NITA KALA.GA "strong male." The latter quickly fell into disuse when the new epithet was adopted by Amar-Sin's successors Šu-Sin and Ibbi-Sin. According to Hallo, the new title may have been introduced as a symbol of a higher status accorded kings arising from the tendency in the Ur III period to treat monarchs as divine. Gods were frequently called LUGAL but rarely NITA.[48]

The earliest occurrence of the Semitic version of the title dates from the reign of Šu-Sin. Here it is found in the syllabic spelling *šar-ru-um dan-núm*. Following the fall of the Third Dynasty of Ur, the title passed to the rulers of Isin, where it was first employed by Išbi-Irra and continued in use through Damiq-ilišu, the last of the line. The later kings of Ešnunna also made use of the title but only in its Akkadian form.[49]

Both the Akkadian and Sumerian versions were employed by

Hammurabi as his prerogative after achieving dominion over Ešnunna. In his inscriptions, the illustrious ruler of the First Babylonian Dynasty used the largest variety of spellings of the title of any king past or future. Samsuiluna and Ammi-ṣaduqa, successors of Hammurabi, also claimed the title "strong king" for themselves.

During the Kassite period, the Sumerian form of the title is found in Sumerian texts from Burnaburiaš through Kadašman-Enlil.[50] Spellings in Akkadian along with the Sumerian do occur, however, in the reign of Kurigalzu I. After the Kassite period, the title reappears after a hiatus of nearly a century in the inscriptions of certain Babylonian kings[51] shortly before the end of the second millennium.

In the Neo-Babylonian period, Šamaš-šum-ukin and Nabopolassar of the 10th and 11th dynasties respectively employed the epithet in their inscriptions.

Use in Assyria

The existence of the royal title "strong king" is attested in the inscriptions of the kings of Assyria from late Middle Assyrian times, appearing first with Arik-den-ili (1319-1308). After him the title was used regularly by all of the important rulers of Assyria until the fall of Nineveh in 612 B.C. Assumption of the title coincides with the beginning of the rise of Assyrian power following the end of Mitannian domination. The inception of Assyrian hegemony over the ancient Near East is generally placed during the reign of Aššur-uballiṭ I. While this monarch apparently did not use the epithet himself in his own inscriptions, it is interesting to note that Adad-nirari I, his grandson, did and even ascribed the title to his royal ancestor. This may well be an anachronism. In any event, the title was adopted in Assyria soon after improvement in the political situation.

Orthographies

Babylonia--A wide variety of spellings are found including syllabic spellings such as *šar-ru-um dan-nûm*, *šar-ru-um* . . . *da-an-nu-um*, *šar-ru da-an-nu and šar-ru dan-nu;* compound spellings--LUGAL *da-nûm*, LUGAL *dan-nu/ni*, LUGAL *da-an-num*, and MAN *dan-nu;* and logographic LUGAL KALA.GA.

Assyria--The following spellings were employed in writing the title in Akkadian: LUGAL *dan-nu*, MAN *dan-nu*, MAN KALA,[52] LUGAL KALA, and LUGAL KALA.GA. All of these occur in late Middle Assyrian and Neo-Assyrian sources. The most frequently attested forms are LUGAL *dan-nu* and MAN *dan-nu*.[53]

Conclusions

The epithet "strong king" came into use in the late Ur III period almost 240 years after the reign of Sargon of Akkad Neither in original inscriptions nor in Old Babylonian copies of original inscriptions was the title applied to Sargon or any member of the Akkad dynasty. Consequently, any ascription of the title to Sargon in later sources such as the Legend must be viewed as an anachronism resulting from the projection of a popular royal title back to a king who lived before its invention.

1.3 The second element of Sargon's titulary in the Legend is LUGAL *a-ga-dè*^{ki}. The spelling of Agade is that common one found in Sumerian and Akkadian texts from all periods of Mesopotamian history. That the title LUGAL *a-ga-dè*^{ki} originated in and was in frequent use during the Akkad period as part of the royal titulary of the dynasty is without doubt. Nevertheless, questions concerning the etymology, meaning, and historical relationships vis-à-vis the various usages of the term Agade remain unanswered.

During the late third millennium, the name was employed in two principal ways: to refer to the city that Sargon built[54] and made into his capital, and to represent the larger region of Northern Babylonia. As such it was considered as one of the two natural divisions of Mesopotamia proper. This is certainly the significance of the Sumerian royal epithet LUGAL KI.EN.GI KI URI (= *šar māt šumerîm u akkadîm*)[55] which is first attested during the reign of Ur-Nammu of the Third Dynasty of Ur.

The term Agade had a third use, namely,as a geographical designation for the northern part of the Mesopotamian plain.[56]

Origin of the Title

The epithet LUGAL *a-ga-dè*^{ki}[57] came into use with the rise to prominence of the Semitic dynasty of Akkad in the person of Sargon and his successors. Although no original inscription of Sargon is preserved with this title, nevertheless, it is found in the Old Babylonian copies of Sargon's original inscriptions from Nippur. There is no reason to deny its introduction during his rule. Among the Old Babylonian copies, the title occurs in the familiar orthography LUGAL *a-ga-dè*^{ki} in the Akkadian inscriptions b 7, b 8;[58] the Akkadian version of the bilingual inscriptions b 1, b 6; and in the Sumerian copy of b 6. The Sumerian version of bilingual b 1, however, preserves the interesting form a g - g i - d è $^{k i}$ which results from Sumerian vocalic harmony.

The epithet is not found among the original inscriptions or copies of Sargon's successor Rimuš, unless Goetze has correctly restored it in what he identifies as an Ur III copy of a Rimuš inscription.[59] No evidence exists for the use of the title by Maništušu himself.[60] Naram-Sin employed the title LUGAL *a-ga-dè*^{ki}[61] and even introduced the more pretentious DINGIR *a-ga-dè*^{ki}.[62] Šar-kali-šarri, the son of Naram-Sin, frequently used the epithet as part of his titulary.[63] Of the lesser rulers who presided over the downfall of the dynasty, Dudu, Elulu, and Šu-turul called themselves "king of Agade."[64]

Etymology

As noted, Agade served as a city name as well as the word signifying a region. The exact relationship between the two usages in terms of origin and derivation has yet to be clearly determined. The etymology of the name itself remains obscure. Whether it is Sumerian, Akkadian, or some other unidentified language is uncertain.[65] Poebel was probably correct in taking the two early spellings a g - g i - d è $^{k i}$ and *a-ga-dè*^{ki} as phonetic writings and suggesting that the original meaning of the name was unknown in Sargon's time.[66] This is compatible with the assumption that Sargon did not construct his city on virgin soil but chose a previously inhabited spot whose local name was retained, although its meaning had been forgotten. All of this must remain conjecture at least until the site of Agade is discovered.

Spelling

While the writing *a-ga-dè*[ki] was popular in all periods, a variety of spellings proliferated especially in the first millennium. For collections of the orthography of the name as city and region, see A. Boudou, *Or* SP 36-38 (1929), pp. 7, 9-10; E. Bilgiç, *AfO* 15 (1945-51), p. 32; S. Parpola, *AOAT* VI (1970), pp. 7-11; and Edzard, *RGTC* I, pp. 5-9.

Conclusions

The use of LUGAL *a-ga-dè*[ki] as part of Sargon's royal titulary is historically accurate. It is a title that Sargon originated and used in his own inscriptions. This was not the case with the preceding title LUGAL *dan-nu* which is used anachronistically in the Legend. Although the epithet "king of Agade" ceased to be used by kings of Mesopotamia after the end of the Akkad dynasty, knowledge of the title survived in the traditions surrounding the figures of Sargon and Naram-Sin.

2.1 An inadequate understanding of the term *ēnetu* had long posed serious difficulties not only in the interpretation of the motivation behind Sargon's exposure but also in the recognition of his true pedigree. That Sargon claims to be, at least partially, of noble descent is implicit in the status accorded his mother as an *ēnetu*.

In the early translations of the Sargon Legend, various definitions were offered for the term *ēnetu* such as "princess," "Herrin," "Vestalin," etc., to mention but a few.[67] These interpretations were proposed without much confidence and without any real attempt to understand the etymology of the word. More recently the word has been interpreted along two different lines: E. A. Speiser's translation of the Sargon Legend in *ANET*, p. 119 rendered *ēnetu* as "changeling,"[68] a participle derived from the verbal root *enû* "to change," "displace." The other interpretation proposed by Landsberger[69] sought to identify *ēnetu* with *ēntu* "high priestess," a feminine form of *ēnu*, a Sumerian loan word borrowed into Akkadian. A third position reflected by Güterbock's treatment of the Legend denied both proposals leaving the question open.[70] Landsberger's suggestion of *ēnetu* = *ēntu* has been accepted by *AHw*, *CAD*, C. Cohen, and B. Childs[71] on the basis of the lexical equation ba-ár BAR= *be-el-tú, en-e-tú* (A I/6: 286-87) and the publication of a text by W. G. Lambert which describes the *ēntu*-priestesses as belonging to a category of women prohibited from bearing children.[72]

Now that the identification of Sargon's mother as an *ēntu*-priestess has been settled, the reason for his exposure is clear (cf. below). A principal condition for holding the office was to avoid pregnancy if not actually to live chastely. Faced with the consequences of her transgression,[73] Sargon's mother had to dispose of him secretly.

Because the position of high priestess was customarily filled by members of the royal house,[74] Sargon's statement that his mother was an *ēnetu*, despite her indiscretion, served to establish his claim to high birth.

ēntu (ēnetu) as "High Priestess"

As we have already observed, the identification of *ēnetu* as a singular form of *ēntu* (pl. *ēnētu*) has been accepted by many authorities. *CAD* renders *ēntu* as "high priestess," a term attested from Old Akkadian on, written syllabically and NIN.DINGIR.[75] The Sumerian title NIN.DINGIR, "Lady (who is a) god" reflects the role and function of the "high priestess" in the cult. It is generally assumed that she played the part of a goddess in the "sacred marriage" or some similar cultic act.[76]

The "high priestess" normally lived within the confines of the temple in a special residence called the *gipāru*.[77] As chief priestess, her duties also included overseeing the lower orders of female temple personnel and managing the business affairs of the temple.[78]

The existence of another term for "high priestess" (EN) raises the question of the relationship of the *ēntu* (*ēnetu*) to the EN-priestess. Both *CAD* and *AHw* take *ēntu* as the female counterpart of the EN-priest.[79] On the other hand, in his study of the priesthood, Renger, while conceding many similarities, treats the two terms separately and draws a number of distinctions between them. The most important of these is the claim that the EN-priest or priestess was usually appointed to a great god of the opposite sex while the *ēntu*-priestess served a lesser deity of either sex.[80] Renger also argues that more than one *ēntu* might serve in a city and that the position of *ēntu* is always subordinate to the EN.[81]

Despite these alleged differences, the similarities between the two in terms of election, enthronement, service, and function, as observed by Renger himself, are so great that it is probable that we are dealing with the same office. The minor differences that exist as well as the variations in terminology may well be explained by differences in time and local custom.

Sexuality of the *ēnetu*

The primary restriction imposed upon the *ēntu* (*ēnetu*)-priestess, as we now see from Atra-ḫasīs, is the prohibition against bearing children. This raises a question concerning the sexuality of the *ēntu*. Was she expected to live in chastity as a requirement of her office, or was she permitted sexual contacts as long as conception did not occur? A variety of opinions has been expressed, yet the problem remains unsolved. *CAD* takes the position that both the *ēntu* and the *ugbabtu*-priestess ". . . were supposed to live in chastity, as is illustrated by numerous apodoses in the omen texts and by the cited passage from the Legend of Sargon of Akkad."[82] Driver and Miles imply the same in emphasizing that the *ēntu* alone of all the priestesses would be severely punished "if she frequented or kept an inn or, what is much the same thing, a brothel."[83] In addition, the *ēntu* was protected against any false slander concerning her moral conduct.[84] H. W. F. Saggs maintains that the *ēntu* was expected to live chastely and probably remained a virgin until reaching menopause.[85]

On the other side of the issue, Astour has argued most recently that the temple priestesses (including the *ēntu*) were actually sacred prostitutes who engaged in unnatural sex.[86] This assertion is based on the lexical equations in *malku-šarru: ugbabtum* = *assinnatum* and *ugbabtum* = *ēntum*.[87] The substantive *assinnatum* is understood as the feminine of *assinnu*, a term which he interprets as "male prostitute," "sodomite." As confirmation of the equation *assinnatum* = *ēntum* = sodomite, Astour points to the existence of an omen which describes a NIN.DINGIR (*ēntu*) as permitting anal intercourse in order to avoid conception.[88] The significance of the omen, however, is in doubt, for it is not clear from the protasis whether the apodosis is favorable or unfavorable; and in addition, one could argue that, by its very nature, the omen does not reflect the normal behavior of the priestess. Whether the *ēntu* would permit natural sex or any sex at all is unclear as is the identity of her partner in the omen.

According to the *CAD*, the *assinnu* (fem. *assinnatu*) is defined only as a member of the cultic personnel of Ištar. *CAD* goes on to assert that "there is no specific evidence that he was a eunuch or homosexual."[89] In *AHw* p. 75, von Soden offers the somewhat vague definition of *assinnu* as *Buhlknabe* "lover boy," "party boy(?)."

Astour's understanding of the sexuality of the *ēntu*, while impossible to dismiss, is as yet unproved. What can we say about the sexual conduct of the "high priestess?" If we assume, as the Sumerian title NIN.DINGIR implies, that the *ēntu* did take part in the "sacred marriage" or some such rite, we may condlude that, at the very least, she did not remain a virgin.[90] Whether any other sexual relations were permitted (as long as they did not lead to pregnancy) cannot be determined. The feeling here is that outside of her role as the goddess in the cult the *ēntu* was most likely expected to be chaste. It is possible, however, that lower members of the female priesthood may have been more active sexually.[91]

Enḫeduanna as High Priestess

The problems surrounding the figure of the high priestess can be seen to be more complex after considering the case of Enḫeduanna, EN-priestess of Ur. She has been identified from contemporary inscriptions found in Ur[92] as the daughter of Sargon of Akkad. She was apparently appointed by her father in an effort to solidify the political and religious hegemony of Agade over the Sumerian city-states.[93] The erstwhile princess held the office for at least twenty-five years serving into the reign of Naram-Sin, her nephew. According to van Dijk, Enḫeduanna, as EN-priestess of Ur, emerged as a kind of royal theologian promoting the syncretism of the Ištar-Inanna cults and elevating the figure of Ištar, the tutelary deity of Agade, to the top of the pantheon. Her theology is reflected in a cycle of beautifully written Sumerian temple hymns which have been accepted as her own work.[94]

The extent to which Enḫeduanna fits the generally accepted picture of an *ēntu*-priestess draws curious attention. That she was of royal birth and appointed to her post by the king agrees with the view held by Renger and others. But in her role in performing the cultic requirements of the office some problems are encountered. As EN-priestess to the moon god Nanna-Sin of Ur, Enḫeduanna might be expected to portray Ningal, the divine consort of Nanna-Sin, in the sacred marriage. No one, apparently, has tried to deal with the awkward question--who would act as her partner in the performance of the sacred marriage? That either her father or brother had exercised this privilege during their kingship seems unlikely. Are we to assume the existence of a figurehead ruler in Ur or perhaps a substitute king? Unfortunately, there is at this time no way of knowing.

Sargon and the *ēnetu*-mother

The identification of *ēnetu* as "high priestess" yields important information concerning the figure of Sargon implicit in the account of his birth. One is lead to believe that Sargon is of noble, if not royal, blood due to the status of his mother. The identity and social standing of his father, however, is still obscure.[95] If, according to the tradition preserved in the Legend, Sargon was thought to have been conceived during the ritual of the sacred marriage, then his father was a king and his pedigree beyond reproach. As Childs acknowledges, this argument would offer a consistent interpretation of the whole Legend and legitimate Sargon's claim to the throne.[97] In some occurrences of the exposed-hero tale the father is, in fact, a king or a god (see Chapter VI).

Nevertheless, we believe with Güterbock,[98] that certain facts present in the tale militate against this hypothesis in favor of Sargon's illegitimacy. The indications are these:

1. Sargon claims not to know the identity of his father.[99] If he were the product of a sacred marriage, he should know that his father was the king or, at least, a city ruler.
2. He does identify his paternal kin (literally his father's brother) as dwelling in the mountain region. Perhaps this may be taken as a hint that his father was a foreigner of nomadic stock.
3. Sargon was delivered in secret and disposed of quickly by his mother--obviously the actions of a woman unwilling or unable to publicly acknowledge her own child.
4. Sargon's mother is not identified by name. Is this because it was not known to this tradition[100] or just considered irrelevant? Perhaps the omission signifies a kind of censure on the part of the tradition, that giving birth in disgrace she is unworthy of specific mention.

In addition to these points, Childs argues in favor of Güterbock's interpretation that the function of the beginning of the text was not to legitimate Sargon's rule (by showing him to be the son of a king) but to serve as an introduction to the blessing oracles which follow; and, as such, the "*Märchenmotif*" of his birth "had no cultic or etiological role."[101]

The prohibition against bearing children which applied to the high priestess as well as the textual evidence discussed above, make it virtually certain that, in the eyes of this tradition, Sargon was considered illegitimate.

Yet, more importantly, at the same time, Sargon was considered of noble descent as a consequence of the status of his mother as high priestess.

2.2 *abī ul īdi*--literally "my father I knew not." Note the variant in C AD *la išī* "a father I (or he) had not," interpreted by Güterbock ("Historische Tradition," p. 62, n. 3) as an indication that Sargon was illegitimate. Cf. the expression in the lexical text *ana ittīšu* (*MSL* I Tablet III, col. iii, 28-31) where the foundling child is described as neither having (*i-šu-ú*) nor knowing (*i-du-ú*) his parents (cited below in the commentary, col. i, 10.2). Also cf. *ul īdi aba u umme amēli itti ištarātīja arbâ anāku* "I knew not a human father or mother, I grew up with my goddesses" in a prayer by Assurbanipal (*OECT* VI, pl. 11 K 1290:13); and the Gudea prayer to Gatumdu, cited above n. 96. Although it is probably not relevant to our text, note the existence of personal names of the type *a-ba-am-la-i-di*, *a-ba-la-i-di*, *a-ba-ul-i-di*, *a-bi-ul-i-di* and *aba-ul-īde* (AD.NU.ZU).[102] Such names were presumably given to foundlings or posthumous children.

3.1 The expression *aḫi abīja* has been taken literally as "my father's brother" or "my uncle" by all who have treated this text with the exception of Güterbock ("Historische Tradition," p. 62, n. 4). *CAD* accepts the traditional interpretation, rendering the line "My uncle dwells in the wilderness" (Vol. A, pt. 1, p. 200) as does von Soden (*AHw* p. 21, s.v. *aḫu(m)* I 1 a. *abim 'Onkel'* where this passage is listed). Güterbock was the first to realize that this reading does not make good sense in context. "Mit dem Satz dürfte auf keine bestimmte Person abgezielt sein, da die Figur eines Oheims für die Erzählung überflüssig ist"(n. 4). If Sargon does not know the identity of his father, he could not possibly refer to an individual as his paternal uncle. Since the figure of the father is essentially unimportant in the narrative and depicted in the vaguest way, the role of an uncle should not be worthy of mention.

Seeking an alternative understanding of the line, Güterbock offered the following translation of lines 3-4: "meinen Vater kenne ich nicht; er war einer von denen, die gern im Gebirge herumstreifen." Unfortunately, this interpretation presents even more difficulties, not the least being the interpretation of the verb *irammi* (see below, col. i 3.2).

We would suggest taking *aḫi abīja* as a general term signifying (paternal) "kinsman," or "clansman," thus reading the line "my (paternal) kin inhabit the mountain region." The purpose of line 3 then is to supply some additional information on Sargon's heritage, necessarily vague as a result of the dim reference to the father. This makes better sense than the previous translations and would indicate in broad terms that Sargon's paternal kin were unsettled tribesmen or at least non-indigenous.

In support of this interpretation, note that *CAD* does list as secondary meanings of *aḫu*: "brother, colleague, associate (as term for a specific social, political, legal, or emotional relationship)."[103] The plural of *aḫu* is attested in sources from Mari with the sense of "tribesmen,"[104] and in an inheritance text from Sippar it is clearly used as a general kinship term.[105]

Outside of Akkadian, *aḫu* is found with the meaning of "kinsman," and the phrase *'aḥ* + *'ab̲* occurs in Hebrew with this value (cf. below). For *'aḫ* as "kinsman" in Ugaritic, see Gordon's *UT* , 1965, p. 354, n. 128 s.v. *aḫu*; as "Genosse," in Canaanite see Donner-Röllig *KAI*, 1962-64, III, p. 2 s.v. 'ḥ. The expression *'aḥ* + *'ab̲* is attested three times in the Hebrew Bible meaning kinsman or relative(s), the best example being Genesis XXIX.12 where Jacob identifies himself to Rachel as *'ăḥî 'ăb̲îhā*, which cannot mean "her uncle" because their relationship is that of first cousins. It must be understood as "her kinsman." The other passages employing this meaning are Numbers XXVII.4 and Joshua XVII.4.

3.2 *irammi*--from *ramû* "to inhabit," a G present 3rd masculine singular. Güterbock's interpretation of the verb from *râmu* "to love" a G present with "overhanging" *-i* ("Historische Tradition," p. 62, n. 4) was based on the fact that *ramû* "to inhabit" was attested at that time only in the stative. This is no longer the case; see von Soden, *AHw* p. 953, 4, 5, 6.

Note the reverse order in C--*šadâ irammu*, for a discussion of this variant see Stemma: Variants in Text C.

4. Sargon's home town *Azupirānu* does not occur outside of this text. It was situated (if in fact it ever existed) on the bank of the Euphrates, an area which Bottéro would seek near the mouth of the river Khabur or Balikh.[106]

The place name has traditionally been derived from the *azupīru-azupirānu* plants whose precise identification is still in dispute. R. C. Thompson (*A Dictionary of Assyrian Botany* [London, 1949], p. 66 and passim) identifies the *azupirānu* as the "crocus saffron" used principally as a medicinal and coloring agent. *AHw* p. 93 follows this interpretation listing *azupīru, azupirānu, azupirānītu,* and *azukirānu* together as "Safran." On the other hand, *CAD* draws a distinction among them and rejects the identification as saffron (Vol. A, pt. 2, p. 531 2'). The plants are listed only as spices and medicinal plants. *CAD* does, however, refer to the geographical name in our text under *azupirānu* (Vol. A, pt. 2, p. 530 a).

5. *īranni*--from the root *erû* "to be pregnant" (intransitive), "to conceive" (transitive); this verb form is a G preterit (*īri*) 3rd feminine singular with the ventive and first person singular accusative pronominal suffix: *am* + *ni* > *anni*. The transitive meaning employed here is much less common than the intransitive; cf. *CAD* Vol. E, p. 326 s.v. *erû*, where only two other such uses are listed, both from Standard Babylonian sources.

6.1 *quppi*--King's copy *CT* XIII, pl. 42 indicates considerably more of the last sign of *qup-pi* than is now preserved on the tablet. Collation reveals [sign]. There is no doubt, however, that the sign is *pi* and not *pu* as in C. The basic meaning of the noun in Akkadian is, as von Soden notes (*AHw* p. 928 s.v. *quppu(m)* II) "box," "chest," "case," etc., and not "reed basket" which would render the phrase *quppi ša šūri* redundant. Cf. *quppu ša šūri* in A. Salonen, *Die Wasserfahrzeuge in Babylonien*, St Or VIII/4 (Helsinki, 1939), pp. 71-72.

6.2 The phrase KÁ-*ja*=*bābīja ipḫi* at the end of line 6 has been a source of interest and difficulty in the interpretation of the Sargon Legend. The problems involved are these:

1. Is the anomalous form KÁ-*ja* singular or plural?
2. What image is conveyed of Sargon's receptacle?
3. Are there literary allusions to the flood story underlying the birth narratives of Sargon and Moses?

That KÁ-*ja* represents a defective form was recognized by Güterbock ("Historische Tradition," p. 62, n. 5) and discussed above in the treatment of the stemma. It can be taken as a singular or plural resulting in considerable differences in meaning. *CAD* has apparently interpreted it both ways; see Vol. B, p. 24 under *bābu* which reads: *ina iṭṭî* KÁ-*ja ipḫi*--"she stopped up tightly with bitumen the chinks in my basket" (plural--referring to the spaces between the interwoven reeds??); and Vol. I/J, p. 311 d under *ittû, ina* A.ESÍR *bābīja ip̆hi*--"he! made the opening of my (basket) watertight with bitumen" (here the idea of a door or hatch is implied).

Among the meanings given for *bābu* in *CAD*, the most relevant appears to be no. 3 "opening of an object" which in special contexts translates as "hatch" of a vessel or receptacle. In agreement with C. Cohen (see below), we take KÁ-*ja* as the singular with the probable sense of "hatch," cf. Gilgameš XI 88, 93.[107] The description of Sargon's receptable clearly evokes images of vessels, while nautical terminology is employed (i.e., *bābu* = hatch). On page 24 b, *CAD* translates *bābu* as hatch of a ship (Gilg. XI 88, 93), listing the occurrence of the Legend passage among the referencesto the *bābu* of ships; cf. Cohen's "Hebrew *tbh*: Proposed Etymologies" in *JANES* 4 (1972), pp. 43-45 where the references are listed and treated. The verb *peḫû*, "to close," "shut" has the idiomatic sense "to caulk" when used of ships and hatches (*AHw* p. 853 4).

This leads to the question raised by Cohen in exploring the relationship of the use of *tbh* in both the birth narrative of Moses (Exodus II) and the biblical account of the flood: is there a definite literary allusion in Exodus II to Noah's ark (and for that matter, a connection between the image of Sargon's vessel and the Akkadian ark)? The problem requires further study, but the evidence seems to point to an affirmative answer.

As Cohen has recognized, the vessels in the Akkadian stories are described and prepared in similar fashion; both accounts employ the relatively rare sense of *bābu* as "hatch." From Gilgameš XI 88 and 93 we see that the final precaution taken to safeguard the inhabitant(s) prior to the vessel's use is the caulking of the hatch. An additional factor, which may have escaped attention, is that Utnapištim's vessel was also composed, at least in part, of reed (Gilg. XI, 20-24). The biblical tales, in addition to the obvious use of the same root **tbh* for the vessels, also agree on the preparation (caulking) of the receptacle and the substance used (pitch).

7.1 *iddanni*--a G preterit of the verb *nadû* with the ventive-accusative pronoun suffix analyzed above (see 5. *īranni*). The basic meaning of the root is "to throw," "to cast down." In this context, however, the secondary sense of "abandoning" is required. For examples of this usage, see *AHw* p. 706 under *nadû(m)* III, 15 *aufgeben*; also cf. Morton Cogan, "A Technical Term for Exposure," *JNES* 27 (1968), pp. 133-35, who refers to the usage of *nadû* in the Sargon Legend in his discussion of Hebrew השליך as a *terminus technicus* for abandonment.[108]

7.2 A difficult form to dissect, *e-le-e-a* has been treated in a variety of ways. Most previous attempts have been based on the root *elû*.

A form of *le'û* (preterit *ili*) with the sense "to overpower," or "to prevail over" would seem possible if the line had intended "the river which did not overpower me" or something similar. The difficulty is that one would expect the verb to have the accusative pronoun suffix--*anni* (with the ventive), unless the text read simply "the river which prevailed not."

Another possibility requires reading the end of the line *šá-la e-le-e-a* "I was able to bob" from *le'û* + *šalû* "to submerge," "plunge," "dip," etc.[109] Unfortunately, this nuance of *šalû* is apparently not attested elsewhere, unless we have an occurrence in a Neo-Babylonian text describing the river ordeal.[110] Here the verb *šalû* is found in the Š-stem, and the line in question reads x-x-*i-ti ú-šá-áš-la-áš-šum-ma šal-meš uṭ-ṭaḫ-ḫa-aš* ⌜*a*⌝-[*na kib-ri*] (Ea, king of the Apsu) . . . made him bob (?) or float (?) and safely brought him to the bank.[111]

King and Jensen[112] apparently interpreted the word as the preposition *eli* plus the suffix *ja* as the translation indicates in ". . . which (rose) not over me." The form is sound grammatically; however, the absence of a verb in the last half of the line makes the suggestion unlikely. Speiser's translation in *ANET*, p. 119 is identical to King's except that he places parentheses around the word "over." Are we to assume from this a G preterit of *elû* plus a dative suffix? Güterbock proposed taking *e-le-e-a* as a G infinitive in the genitive plus pronoun suffix, translating the line awkwardly "(sie warf mich in den Fluss) meines Nicht-Emporsteigens."[113] This interpretation seems equally untenable. Both dictionaries include the Sargon Legend occurrence under the verb *elû*. *AHw* cites this passage under the subheading *aus dem Wasser auftauchen* (*elû(m)* IV

p. 206 B 1b) without translating it. *CAD* offers the following translation: "She threw me into the river from which there should be no escape" (Vol. E, p. 121 8'); cf. another example of this sense of *elû* "to escape" cited by *CAD* from the Tukulti-Ninurta Epic--*ana pašuqti ḫalti ša la e-li-e ukimmi*[*r*] ("I heaped up [my people] in the narrow pit from which there is no escaping"[Vol. Ḫ, s.v. *ḫaštu* p. 143 b]).

The meaning required from context would seem to be that of escaping in the sense "to rise up and leave"; cf. Vol. E, p. 124 3 b. Therefore we suggest that line 7 be translated "she abandoned me to the river from which I could not escape,"[114] taking the verb as a G preterit 1st person singular with ventive ending. This solution fits the grammar and the context.

8. [1]*aq-qí*--according to this tradition, the name of Sargon's adoptive father. As Poebel had observed, *Aqqi* is an epithetic proper noun referring to his line of work as water drawer.[115] The name has been interpreted by Güterbock in similar fashion as a G preterit 1st person singular of *naqû*--*aqqi* = *ich goss*.[116] Poebel's attempt to read into the name of *Aqqi* a reflection of an etiological legend explaining the origin of the city name Agade is untenable.

9. The restoration *ina ṭīb dalīšu* proposed by Landsberger (apud Güterbock, "Historische Tradition," p. 63, n. 2) has been accepted by the dictionaries; cf. *CAD* and *AHw* under *dālu* "bucket." It makes good sense and fits the spacing.

Enough of the *li* is preserved to be confident of its restoration, but there is no trace of *šú* or any other sign immediately following *li* as King's copy seems to suggest.

The restored form **ṭīb* is derived from *ṭebû* (final weak) "to dip," "plunge," etc. and is presumably based on the nominal pattern *pars* (see *GAG* § 55b) *qat'* > *qāt*; for which cf. A. Goetze, "The Etymology of Akkadian *qātum* 'hand'" in *JCS* 2 (1948), pp. 269-70. This substantive is not attested elsewhere.

10.1 The principal problem with this line is whether to restore anything in the lacuna between *ana mārūtī*⌜*šu*⌝ and [*l*]*u urabbanni*. King's copy of the text (A) indicates a *šú* sign closely following *mārūti*. (It is not there, see below.) In addition, his translation in *CCEBK* II, 87-89 suggests the loss of part of the line by the use of brackets. Güterbock, following King, would restore something to Text A (probably *ilqanni*) while acknowledging that the corresponding line of B lacks the space for it. "In A zwischen *ana mārūtišu* und *urabbanni* noch ein wort zu erg. (vielleicht *ilqanni*), in B nicht."[117]

The proposal of *ilqanni* is based on the common expression *ana mārūti leqû* "to adopt" literally "to take in sonship." *AHw* accepts this restoration (s.v. *mārūtu(m)*, p. 617 3a), while *CAD* (s.v. *dālû*) hedges, returning to the use of brackets in the transcription yet translating the line with *leqû*.

Aqqi LÚ.A.BAL *ana mārūtišu* [. . .] *urabbanni*

Aqqi, the water drawer, adopted me and brought me up.[118]

The restoration is to be rejected on the basis of collation of A (space is not sufficient), comparison with B (unquestionably no room), and considerations of form and style. What King had taken as *šú* is really just a scratch in the clay. Collation reveals the position of the *šú* sign in the damaged portion of the line about 3-1/2 cm. from the end of *mārūti*. An unbroken part of the surface clay indicates the impressed lower edge of *šú*[119] . This reduces the remaining available space as does the certain restoration of a *lu* sign before *urabbani*; cf. the lines below for *lu-u* + verb.

If the line had another verb (*leqû*), one would expect *ilqanni* in harmony with the style of verb forms in this section of the text. One might also expect the asseverative particle *lu* which precedes the verbs from line 9 on; cf. line 14 in which two verbs occur back to back both preceded by *lu*. The limited space in this line might accommodate a TI sign = *leqû* but hardly TI plus phonetic complement(s) for the suffix.

Perhaps, more importantly, the sense of the line does not require another verb. As preserved it yields a complete thought--"Aqqi, the water drawer, raised me as his adopted son." Finally, compare the next line which also has but a single verb. It is similar in meaning and identical in structure. For the significance of the phrase "to raise in sonship" see CH § 185 and 10.2, below.

10.2 The word *mārūtu*, literally "sonship," refers to the practice common in Mesopotamia of adopting a son and heir, a practice in which the adoptee, in theory, severs all ties with his biological parents and enters the family of his adoptive parents. As a full-fledged member of his new family, all the privileges and responsibilities of "sonship" devolve upon him.

From such primary sources as the lexical series *ana ittīšu*, the Code of Hammurabi, and the *tuppi mārūti* from Nuzi,[120] it is apparent that adoption practices and procedures varied considerably depending on period and region. It is possible, however, to discern three basic types of adoption:

1. Adoptions contracted between the adoptive parents and the natural parents in which a written adoption contract (*tuppu*) is drawn up specifying the rights and obligations of the child with any special provisions that may also apply. The *tuppu* serves as proof of adoption guaranteeing the privileges granted to the adoptee.[121]
2. Adoptions arranged between parties where no written document is involved. One may assume here that the rights and duties of all sides are understood to be determined by law or local custom.[122]
3. Adoptions involving foundlings where the natural parents are unknown. Adoptions of this type would, of necessity, be instituted unilaterally by the finder or adopter with the obligations of parent and child determined by law or local custom.[123]

Based on laws §§ 185-86 of CH, which he believes apply to foundlings, Martin David assumes the existence of another category of adoption equivalent to a foster care relationship.[124] In both, the child is said to be adopted (*ana mārūtim ilqi*). Law § 185 adds the phrase *ina mêšu* which David reads "in his name" implying full adoption since the child is officially given the name of the adoptive parent. In this case the right of the natural parent to reclaim the child expires when he is grown. David maintains that the absence of this expression in § 186, which describes the search for the child's parents at the time of adoption, indicates that the adopter does not intend to raise the boy as a son but only as a foster child.

Driver and Miles disagree with David and do not admit the distinction of complete versus incomplete adoption.[125] They argue that the term *ana mārūtim* implies formal adoption and that the expression *ina mêšu* ("in his name") is to be understood as implicit in § 186 and the following laws.

The argument between David and Driver and Miles over complete versus incomplete adoption based on the inclusion of *ina mêšu* has become irrelevant, for the phrase is now interpreted "in (or from) his amniotic fluid," taking *mêšu* from *mû* "water" and not as an Akkadian word borrowed from Sumerian MU "name." See Borger apud *AHw* p. 665 a; E. Salonen *Glossar zu den altbabylonischen Urkunden aus Susa* in St Or XXXVI (Helsinki, 1967), s.v. *mû "Wasser"*-- *i-na me-e-šu ù da-mi-šu i-zi-ib-šu-ma* "ihn mit seinem Fruchtwasser und Blut verliess sie" *MDP* XXIII, 288 8 9; cf. *CAD* Vol. D, p. 77 3'. Therefore, one of the distinguishing factors between § 185 and § 186 affecting the right of the natural parent to reclaim the child would seem to be the age of the adoptee. If he were adopted immediately after birth and was figuratively or literally still wet, the adoption was considered permanent at his maturity.

Returning to law § 186, we believe Driver and Miles err in maintaining that the adoptee rather than the adopter is the one who searches for the natural parents.[126] The precise meaning of § 186 is obscure although the contrast with § 185 is clear; the right of the natural parent to reclaim the child does not expire when he is grown.

Why Did People Adopt?

Adoption was practiced in antiquity for a variety of reasons ranging from self-interest to simple compassion. It is generally assumed that the main purpose of the institution was to provide a legal and socially beneficial way for childless people[127] to adopt a son and heir in order to perpetuate the family line. No doubt religious considerations were involved, such as a desire on the part of a barren couple to insure that the appropriate rites would be performed after their deaths. Of more immediate concern were the services a son could provide during one's life. For poor people unable to afford servants or slaves, adoption would offer a way of obtaining cheap labor at home or at work. In addition, a son was expected to supply food, clothing, and support to his parents in their old age and a suitable burial at their death.

Childless individuals who had devoted their lives to building a business, practicing a trade, or acquiring material wealth would adopt a son not only to inherit from them but to continue their work. Adoption also provided a legal method of legitimizing extramarital offspring protecting their right of succession as well as their place in society.

Finally, one should not ignore humanitarian considerations as motives in adoption. These might come into play particularly in the case of foundlings who otherwise would suffer a cruel fate.

Rights and Duties of the Adoptee

Perhaps the party that benefited the most from the institution of "sonship" was the child who was accepted into a family and given the position of a natural son. Even if the relationship should be terminated at a later date by the adopter, the child is assured of part of his inheritance as compensation.[128]

Apprenticeship in the profession of the adoptive parent was one of the rights of the adoptee. In fact, failure to provide the child with this training was grounds for the natural parents to reclaim their child.[129]

It is fair to assume that, in many cases, adoption served as a means of upward social mobility for the children involved. For, as is often the case today, children available for adoption tend to come from broken homes and backgrounds of extreme poverty or illegitimacy.[130] To these children adoption meant the opportunity for a better life, for foundlings adoption could mean life itself.

In exchange for the benefits he received, a son was expected to respect and obey his parents, help them with their work, provide for them in their later years and perform the appropriate rites after their deaths. Adoption was a mutually beneficial relationship, a kind of social insurance in which both parties profited.

The Adoption of Sargon

The adoption of Sargon is an important component of the exposed-hero tale preserved in the extant portion of column i of the Legend. The characteristics of Sargon's adoption when compared to the relevant sections of *ana ittīšu* are clearly those of type 3--the adoption of a foundling. The foundling in *ana ittīšu* is described as *ša aba u ummu la išu . . . ša abašu ummašu la īdu* "one who had not a father and mother," "who knew not his father and mother." Obviously one of the distinguishing features of a foundling is not knowing who his parents are. Sargon, speaking of his own ancestry, admits in Text A *abī ul īdi* "I knew not my father" (note the variant in C--AD *la iši*--"a father I had not"). Sargon's mother is identified vaguely as an *ēnetu*-priestess.

Typically, foundlings were exposed in places of danger. According to *ana ittīšu*, the endangered infant might be found *ina būrti* "in a well," *ina pī kalbi* "at the mouth of the dog," or *ina pī āribi* "at the mouth of the raven." Sargon, on the other hand, was abandoned "to the river from which I could not escape" *ana nâri ša la ēlea*. The next stage in the process is the rescue by the future adoptive parent. The infant is "brought in from the street," *ina sūqi šūrub*, "snatched (from the mouth of the dog)," *ekimšu . . .*, or "released (from the mouth of the raven," *ušaddi*. . . . Aqqi, the water drawer, rescues Sargon by scooping him out of the river with his bucket *ina ṭīb dalīšu lu ušēlanni*. The rescue is an important aspect in the concept of foundling adoption, for in delivering the child from danger the adopter, in a sense, gives him life symbolizing the function of the natural parent and justifying his assumption of that role. Line 10 of the Legend is the official statement of the relationship between Sargon and Aqqi--*aqqi dālû ana mārūtīšu lu urabbani*. Sargon is raised in sonship by Aqqi with all the rights and duties implied in the adoptive relationship. The force of the verb *urabbanni* in the light of CH § 185 is to indicate that the bond between the two is permanent because Sargon has achieved his majority as Aqqi's son.

The implication of the next line . . . *ana nukaribbūtīšu lu iškuṇanni*[131] is consistent with the obligations incumbent upon an adoptive father. Even though Aqqi is not specifically called *nukaribbu* (gardener),[132] it is clear that his work involves horticulture so that we are dealing here with a reference to Sargon's apprenticeship in his father's profession.

In the Sumerian King List, Sargon's father or adoptive father (the word is partially destroyed) is called nu-giri$_{12}$ "gardener."[133]

We may conclude that the description of Sargon's origins as conveyed in the Legend agrees in form and detail with what is known about the institution of "sonship," particularly with respect to foundling adoption.

The Adoption Ceremony

Much information concerning the rules of adoption has been obtained from the study of the laws and contracts. Very little is known, however, of the ceremony or ritual that must have accompanied the undertaking of such an important commitment. One source on adoption, *ana ittīšu*, seems to offer a description of an adoption procedure following the taking up of a foundling. The finder of the infant goes before witnesses and performs some kind of act that apparently involves taking a seal impression of the measurement of the child's feet. The exact nature of that act and its purpose are unclear.

In her study of adoption at Nuzi, Cassin suggests the existence of an adoption ceremony, "très probablement pour donner publicité à l'affaire, une procédure fictive accompagnait l'acte d'adoption,"[134] and as an example, she cites *HSS* V 48, 16-29, 42ff. In this source, five men sent by the judges to the home of the adoptive parents call for the appearance of the adoptee in order to make his acquaintance. The boy is then introduced by the father as his son and sole descendant.

A. L. Oppenheim has most likely identified a Babylonian adoption ritual in a brief article discussing Stamm's interpretation of the Neo-Babylonian personal name *Ša-pī-kalbi*.[135] Disagreeing with Stamm who interprets *Ša-pī-kalbi* "(Who has been snatched) from the mouth of the dog" as the name given to a foundling who has actually suffered this experience, Oppenheim argues that it occurs too frequently to support such an interpretation. Based on a Neo-Babylonian legal text,[136] he maintains that the name *Ša-pī-kalbi* more likely refers to a particular type of adoption rather than the likelihood that the person so named narrowly escaped being devoured by dogs.

The text to which Oppenheim refers describes more accurately an adoption ritual than a type of adoption. It depicts a staged exposure and the subsequent adoption of a child by a man [1]Nur-Šamaš.[137] The lady with the child, whatever her relationship to him, abandons him by placing him on the street, i.e., "at the mouth of the dog." From here the child is taken up and rescued by the adopter. Oppenheim interprets the expressions *ana pī kalbi nasāku*, and *ištu pī kalbi našû* as legal terms denoting the symbolic acts of adoption.

It seems likely that this text actually refers to an adoption ceremony in which the participants acted out the roles that will determine the future of the child.[138] This ritual quite possibly may be formalizing a normal adoption, for in a genuine case of foundling adoption what would be the value of repeating the acts symbolically? The original act of discovery would be the one establishing and legitimizing the new relationship. It is not surprising that this adoption ritual was conceived of in terms of foundling adoption, for this may well be the oldest form of adoption. Before the considerations of legal inheritance arose, unwanted children must have been exposed to die. The situation of the foundling typifies what occurs in any adoption, so that a ceremony reflecting this concept is quite logical. Essentially, in any case of adoption, one party relinquishes claim to a child and the other party assumes it. The person abandoning the child in the ceremony (here the lady) surrenders all claims to him by exposing him to die. The person who first gave him life takes it away thereby terminating her rights as parent. The adopter rescues the child from danger which is tantamount to giving him life. In so doing he symbolically becomes the natural parent and the child belongs to him.

11. The abstract noun *nukaribbūtu* is based on a Sumerian loanword *nukaribbu*[139] (written [LÚ] NU.KIRI$_6$) which has been interpreted as "one who has to do with orchards."[140] In general, *nukaribbūtu* may be defined as "arboriculture," "orchard manage-

ment," or "gardener-work"; although, in most cases it pertains specifically to the cultivation of the date palm. The expression *ana nukaribbūti* found in contracts and legal contexts[141] is used in a slightly different sense. It refers to an institution common in Mesopotamia from Old Babylonian times on, based on a social and economic relationship between landowner and tenant farmer that was usually regulated by contract. In this relationship, the landowner contracts with the worker to till his land, care for the trees, and deliver the *imittu*-produce levied before the harvest.[142] In return the client receives a small percent of the *imittu* plus marginal use of the land to produce crops for his own needs.

Duties of the Client

The client farmer is expected first of all to till the soil. When empty land is involved, he must do the planting. In such cases longer contracts were called for, and the client did not deliver the crop until a few years had passed. The worker was also responsible for the maintenance and protection of the orchard. This included digging irrigation trenches, building protective walls around the grove, and caring for the younger palm sprouts. During the season his work involved pollinating the fruit and later laying out the dates for artificial ripening. Finally, at the end of the harvest came the delivery of the *imittu*, the yield of the orchard estimated beforehand by representatives of the owner.[143] The gardener was subject to penalties and indemnities if he failed to meet the *imittu*-quota or caused damage to the orchard through his negligence.

Benefits to Client and Owner

The institution of *nukaribbūtu* provided the poor garden worker with the opportunity to earn a meager living. For all his efforts he received a small percentage of the *imittu*-harvest. In addition, he was permitted limited use of the land (the space between the palm trees) to grow cereal crops to support himself. The gardener might also receive a *sissinnu*, apparently a bonus, consisting of a few kur of dates.[144]

Not unexpectedly, the chief beneficiary was the landowner, for this system supplied him with cheap labor to work his fields relieving him of the responsibility and the work. The bulk of the crop, which was assessed by his representatives, guaranteed his profit. The owner could lease barren land to someone as an investment, and with little expense (perhaps only the provision of seeds) he received a few years later not only his share of the harvest but a valuable, developed piece of land. The laws were designed to protect the owner, penalizing the worker for breaking the contract or damaging the property.

Who Became a *nukaribbu*?

Obviously, the first requirement for being an orchard gardener was some knowledge of arboriculture. According to Cardascia, the gardeners were poor folk, the servants or bondsmen of the landlord. "Ajoutons que les jardiniers sont toujours les 'esclaves' c.-a-d. les serviteurs d'un Murašû et que le bailleur est souvent leur maitre."[145]

Implications for the Sargon Legend

Sargon's adoptive father Aqqi is called [lú]A.BAL *(dālû)* "water drawer" or "gardener."[146] Drawing water from a well or other water source was a necessary part of the irrigation process. Aqqi's name as indicated in 8 above is an epithet indicative of his profession. Clearly, the tradition presents him as a lowly farmer engaged in backbreaking work. In line with Cardascia's description of members of his class, Aqqi may have been the servant of a nobleman or king. It is sometimes the case in other occurrences of the exposed-hero tale, that the adopter of the child is in the employ of a ruler who is related to the infant. Whether the Sargon Legend represents a simplified version of an older, more detailed exposure narrative will be considered in Chapter VI.

Now let us ponder the meaning of Sargon's statement in line 11 that *Aqqi . . . ana nukaribbūtīšu lu iškunanni*--"(he) set me to his garden work."[147] This interpretation is to be preferred to the traditional rendering by King, Speiser (*ANET*), etc., which is somewhat ambiguous--"he appointed me as his gardener." Sargon does not contract with a landowner (Aqqi) to work his orchard; rather he is allowed, as a youth, to learn his father's profession by helping him in his work. One may surmise that Sargon continued his garden work by himself, and that during his career as gardener, he developed his special relationship with Ištar, for, as we shall see, she had a weakness for arboriculturists. This weakness will be discussed below (12).

12. ^{d}*ištar . . . iramanni*--the verb *râmu* is used in expressing the concept of love in all its dimensions, including specifically sexual love.[148] According to this line which is sadly lacking in details, Sargon apparently attracted the attention of Ištar while pursuing his career as gardener and became the object of her desire. Not unexpectedly, the goddess of love--Sumerian Inanna, Akkadian Ištar[149]--enjoyed quite a few romantic interests often with unpleasant consequences for those who caught her fancy. Inanna (Ištar) seems to have been particularly susceptible to gardeners.

1. *Inanna and Dumuzi*--Many versions of this myth are found. In essence, Dumuzi courts Inanna, they become lovers and later marry. In the Sumerian version "Inanna's Descent to the Nether World,"[150] Inanna, angered by Dumuzi's apparent indifference to her ordeal in the underworld, condemns him to dwell there forever as her ransom.
2. *Ištar and Išullanu*--The existence of this myth is known from Gilgameš VI, 64-78. Ištar fell in love with Išullanu, her father's gardener (*nukaribbu*), who had been conscientiously providing her with dates and food. Because he spurned her explicit sexual invitations, Ištar turned him into a *dallalu*-creature.[151]
3. *Ištar and Gilgameš*--Watching Gilgameš, king of Uruk, clean and dress himself, Ištar was so smitten by his good looks that she offered herself to him sexually as lover and wife. Aware of the fate of those whom the goddess had so favored, Gilgameš refused her, recounting the history of her shameless conduct towards them.[152]
4. *Inanna and Šukallituda*--According to this Sumerian myth,[153] Šukallituda, a gardener and discoverer of the technique of

"shade tree" arboriculture, apparently got the best of Inanna. Spying her from his garden in a state of exhaustion brought on by her travels, Šukallituda took the opportunity to cohabit with her. The next day the humiliated goddess arose to seek her revenge. She visited three plagues against the land without achieving her purpose. Ultimately, the two are somehow reconciled since Šukallituda emerges with Inanna's blessing.

5. *Inanna and Enkimdu*--A Sumerian myth "Inanna Prefers the Farmer"[154] relates the contest over the goddess between Dumuzi, the shepherd god, and Enkimdu, the farmer god. While Dumuzi apparently triumphs in the end, it was the farmer who had been the real object of Inanna's affection.
6. *Ištar and the roller-bird, the lion, the horse, the shepherd*--Tablet VI 48-63 of the Gilgameš Epic briefly describes Ištar's affairs with all of the above and the grief they suffer in the end.

Sargon and Ištar

In view of the literary traditions concerning Ištar's love affairs, it is difficult to avoid the impression that the author of the Sargon Legend was drawing on such allusions and that Sargon, like his mythic predecessors, had become the object of Ištar's desire. This is not to deny the likelihood that historically the goddess had been associated with Sargon's career. That Ištar had achieved a new position of importance during the Akkad Dynasty has been recognized and the subject of recent studies.[155]

Both Hallo and van Dijk have sought to explain the career of Sargon through a personal relationship between him and the goddess (or her representative). Whether this crucial influence came from his mother who was a high priestess (of Inanna perhaps), or a priestess whom he had married, or even his daughter Enḫeduanna remains speculation.[156]

Sargon's rise to prominence and specifically his 55 years of kingship seem to follow as a direct consequence of line 12, that ". . . Ištar loved me *so that*" (if we assume this force for the enclitic -*ma*). Note that as an inducement to love the goddess, promises of kingship are offered to Gilgameš who though already a king would attain even greater dominion. "Before thee shall bow down kings, rulers, (and) princes. The yield of mountain and plain they shall bring thee in tribute."[157]

13. Here was preserved in the beginning of the line the length of Sargon's reign. Both A and B, unfortunately, are broken at the edge, so that only a small portion of one figure remains . King and Güterbock among others had postulated a double digit figure ending in four (x+4).[158] *CAD* has, quite erroneously, assumed a figure of only four years: 4 *šanāte šarrūta lu e-pu-uš*-- "for four years I was king . . ." (Vol. E, p. 219, s.v. *šarrūtu*). This is impossible for a number of reasons. From the context it is obvious that "Sargon" is speaking at the end of his long, glorious reign. He enumerates his greatest accomplishments, challenging future monarchs to emulate him (lines 22ff). Clearly, the narrative is not set early in his career, nor is it possible to argue that his rule lasted only four years. From a collation of A and B it is certain that requirements of space alone reject *CAD*'s interpretation. For if the line had begun with the number four, one would have to assume that of all lines preserved in A and B, only this line began indented. Furthermore, enough of the figure is preserved to rule out an elongated sign stretching the length of two regular signs.

Now the cuneiform signs for the numbers four and five are quite similar, and both possess phonetic values as well--*šá* and *já* respectively. Happily, both these values are employed in the text providing the basis for comparison. After collating the signs for size, shape, and style, the traces in both texts appear to be those of the number five. Therefore, we would restore the complete figure for Sargon's reign as 55 years in agreement with one tradition preserved in the Sumerian King List.[159]

According to Jacobsen, six sources L_1, P_2, P_3, S, Su, and Su_{3+4} preserved the figure of 55 years; one source WB differed in reading 56. Of the six copies with the number 55, three are from Nippur, two are from Susa, and one is of unknown provenience. All these copies date from the Old Babylonian period; WB is roughly contemporaneous and may derive from Larsa.

We may now recognize in line 13 of the Sargon Legend a reflection of a very old tradition concerning Sargon's length of rule, a tradition that is attested in Babylonia in sources as early as the 19th century B.C.

14. The restoration of the end of this line . . . *lu abēl lu aš[pur]* was first proposed by H. Winckler (*KB* III, p. 102 13). Winckler's reading has gone unchallenged and has been adopted in recent translations of the Legend.[160] *CAD* accepts the reading in its article on the verb *bêlu* (Vol. B, p. 200 c'). Further support of the proposed restoration comes from a knowledge of the idiom compounded of *bêlu* and *šapāru* with the meaning "to take over (and) govern." This idiom is attested in the annals and royal inscriptions of Assyrian kings dating from the first quarter of the ninth century B.C.[161] Collation of Text A reveals remains of three horizontals after the end of the preceding *áš* sign. These traces, not present in King's copy, are compatible with the beginning of a *pur* sign .[162]

The basic meaning of the root **špr* in Akkadian as well as the other cognate languages in which it occurs is "to send (a message)" and secondarily "to write." The verb is attested with these values in Old Akkadian and Old Babylonian, while forms of *šapāru* occur frequently with or without the substantive *ṭēmu* ("order," "command," "decree," etc.) in Middle Babylonian letters and Assyrian royal correspondence.[163]

A further development in meaning appears in certain noun formations of the root in Old Akkadian, Old Babylonian, and Middle Assyrian period sources. This third value of **špr* reflects the concept of "commanding" and is expressed by the words *šipru* (a command), *šāpiru* (a commander), *šāpirūtu* (rule), and perhaps *šabrû* (a temple administrator).[164]

If we were to speculate on the semantic development of this sense of *šapāru*, we would posit a military or administrative milieu as its *Sitz im Leben*. From the original idea of sending a message, it is easy to perceive the evolution of the nuance "commanding" in such a situation. The substantive *šipru* a message, issued by someone in a position of authority, whether human or divine,[165] would, in effect, constitute a command. One who sends messages (*šāpiru*) to subordinates is a commander, a governor, or, in the religious sphere, a temple official *(šabrû)*.

In summary we note:

1. The root **špr* with the sense of commanding or ruling developed from the basic meaning "to send (a message)" possibly from political or military situations.
2. Noun forms of the root with this value are attested as early as Old Akkadian.
3. The idiom *bêlu* plus *šapāru* "to take over (and) govern" seems to be a Neo-Assyrianism.
4. This value of **špr* is a development unique to Akkadian and, as far as we can determine, unknown in the other Semitic languages.

The idiom *bêlu* + *šapāru* "to take over (and) govern"

1.	*ana bêli šuknuše u šapāri*	*AKA* p. 268 1 42 *CTN* II 267 25	Aššurnaṣirpal II 883-859 B.C.
2.	*ibēluma ultašpiru*	Winck. *Sar.* p. 170 5	Sargon II 721-705 B.C.
3.	*ibēl u išpur*	Winck. *Sar.* p. 38 236ff.	Sargon II 721-705 B.C.
4.	*labēl lašpur*	Borger *Asarh.* 67:7'	Esarhaddon 680-669 B.C.

15. The last word of the line has been restored by King and others as *ub*[*bit*] from *abātu* "to destroy." *CAD* is in agreement translating the line KUR-*e dannūte ina ag-gul-la-te ša erî lu-u ub*-[*bit*]--"he cut down the difficult mountains using copper pickaxes" (Vol. A, pt. 1, p. 44 2 e);[166] cf. the usage of *abātu* in KUR.MEŠ *ubbitma būlšunu ušamqit*--"he destroyed the mountain regions and felled their beasts" (Gössman Era IV 147 [*CAD* ibid., p. 43 C]); and *Marduk nasiḫ murṣu muabbit* KUR.MEŠ "who removes sickness, destroys the mountains" (Craig *ABRT* I 59 K 8961:8 [*CAD* ibid.]). The meaning of the verb with *šadû* in both cases is "to ruin a region," "to lay waste."

Because the context here seems to require a different sense from that of destroying mountains, we suggest as an alternative possibility the restoration of *ár*-[*ḫi-iṣ*] from *raḫāṣu* "to pass through" (see *AHw* p. 943 3 a *Land durchlaufen;* esp. *Gebirge riḫiṣ* [*RA* 46 [1952], 94 67]). According to *CAD*, the pickaxe *akkullu* is a tool used for cutting through stony terrain in building a road, canal, pit, etc. (Vol. A, pt. 1, p. 276 b). Thus the line might mean "difficult mountains I passed through using copper picks (to cut roads)." In the lines which immediately follow, Sargon claims to have ascended and crossed over various mountain ranges. The achievement seems to lie in securing passage through the mountain barriers, not in destroying them.

16. Clearly something is to be restored to the beginning of this line and the next. The traditional restoration of the asseverative particle is appropriate, although the spacing would require the simple spelling *lu* instead of *lu-u*.

17. *at-ta-tab-lak-ka-ta*--from *nabalkutu* "to pass over," "cross," "go beyond," an Ntn perfect 1st person singular with ventive ending. Cf. *GAG* §39, p. *50; *AHw* p. 696, s.v. *nabalkutu(m)* II: Ntn; and for a general study of the quadri-literal verb, see Alexander Heidel, *The System of the Quadriliteral Verb*, AS XIII (Chicago, 1940), esp. 112ff. Note p. 126 where this form is identified erroneously as an Ntn preterit. There is, apparently, one other case of an Ntn perfect of *nabalkutu*, an anomalous form *it-ta-ta-bal-ki-tu* preserved in the annals of Adad-nirari II (*KAH* II, 84 31); concerning this form see *GAG* § 110d and von Soden, "Verbalformen mit doppelten t-Infix im Akkadischen," *Or* N.S. 19 (1950), p. 395.[167]

18.1 In this line, we find one of the major problems of the first column. Because the beginning of the first word is destroyed (in the corresponding line 29 as well), the reading in uncertain. There have been two basic approaches to the interpretation of the line during the last seventy years. King proposed the reading *ma-ti ti-amat lu-u al-ma-a* III *šanîtu* "the Country of the Sea three times did I besiege,"[168] apparently a reference to campaigns against the Sea Land, a political entity within the confines of Babylonia at the head of the Persian Gulf.[169] *CAD* accepts the restoration *ma-ti* but interprets the line differently, rendering [*mā*]*ti tiāmat* as "the shores of the ocean" (three times I circled).[170] The translations of Speiser (*ANET*) and Labat (*Les religions*) belong in this camp.

An alternative interpretation was proposed by Güterbock, who suggested reading [*siḫir*]*ti tiāmat* with the sense of "dreimaliges Umfahren des Meeres (?)."[171] Most recently, Grayson has followed this path reading [*si-ḫi-ir*]-*ti ti-amat* . . . "the entire sea I went around (lit. 'surrounded')."[172]

Collation of the text indicates room for one small sign only (before -*ti*) in both lines 18 and 29. The form *māti*, written KUR-*ti* or *ma-ti* is possible; *siḫirti*, even written with the logogram NIGIN(-*ti*) is not. Line 29 reveals a trace of the end of the sign in question , a vertical with the slightest traces of three horizontals suggesting *ma-ti*.

Assuming *māti tiāmat*, the precise meaning of the line is still unsettled. The form *māti* in *māti tiāmat* is somewhat irregular.[173] One might have expected *māt* or *mātāt* in a construct phrase. In any event, we cannot be sure whether we are dealing with a specific geo-political unit--the Sea Land--or a general reference to lands bordering on or beyond the sea.

18.2 *ti-amat*--note the relatively unusual spelling of *Ti'āmat* with the GEME sign (=*amat*). This orthography represents the uncontracted substantive in the absolute state.[174] Such forms in the absolute are not uncommonly derived from regular nouns used as personal names.[175] *Tiāmat* from *ti'āmtum* (later *tâmtu*) was the personification of the sea, a central figure in the Babylonian Creation Epic. One encounters this particular spelling regularly in the *Enūma Eliš* and occasionally in literary and historical texts from the first millennium.[176]

19. The identification of Tilmun[177] is still a matter of debate nearly a century after H. C. Rawlinson's proposal of Bahrain Island.[178] While scholarly consensus has settled on Bahrain and parts of the Arabian littoral as the location of ancient Tilmun, dissident opinions range from the eastern Persian Gulf area south of Elam to the western coast of the Indian subcontinent.

The arguments for and against each localization appear throughout the literature on Tilmun, and it is neither possible nor desirable to repeat them here. Instead, we offer a bibliography of the most important treatments of the subject including the most recent literature to date.[179]

20.1 The beginning of this line is damaged; however, the presence of a vertical suggests the first word is [*a-n*]*a*.

20.2 Restore [*lu-u e-li*] after *Dêr rabî* following the corresponding line (30), which preserves . . . BÀD.DINGIR[ki] GAL-*i li-li-ma* "let him go up to Greater Dêr." Both of these restorations (*lu e-li* and *a-na*, see 20.1) are already found in King *CCEBK* II, p. 92. In the second half of this line after *lu-u*, one might expect a preterit verb in the first person singular. There are traces [illegible] which might possibly be *ag/ak/aq*, perhaps from *agmur* "I annihilated," *akšud* "I conquered" or "I reached," *aqqur* "I devastated," or even *akšuš* "I mastered."

Although the second half of the line is destroyed, it seems likely that the tradition recalls the capture of Dêr.[180] Aside from brief mention of the land of Dêr as part of the empire of Sargon in the Geographical Treatise,[181] there is no other reference to Dêr in Sargon sources. The city is known to have existed in the late third millennium, for Rimuš claims to have destroyed it.[182] According to Oppenheim, Dêr was politically important for only a short time during the Old Babylonian period.[183] Later it is mentioned in the inscriptions of Neo-Assyrian kings. It is conceivable that Sargon had an encounter with the city perhaps during an Elamite campaign.[184]

21. J. Nougayrol's proposed reading [*ka*]-*zal-lu ú-naq-qir-ma* offered in *RA* 45 (1951), p. 179, n. 2 has been adopted in the third edition of *ANET* 1969, p. 119. It rests on a Sargon tradition[185] and fits the context well. Unhappily, the space from the estimated edge of the tablet does not seem to allow a sign as large as *ka*, leaving us with the difficult alternative x-*ni lu ú-naq-qir-ma*.

23. For line 23 a restoration ⌜5⌝[5 MU.MEŠ LUGAL-*ú-ta li-pu-uš*] should be considered for a variety of reasons. Follow-

ing the *Glossenkeil* there are traces of a sign not incompatible with the number 50 , and in line 13 we have 55 years. Further support is furnished by the apparent parallel structure of the narrative in this part of column i. Line 22 functions as a transition between the enumeration of Sargon's deeds (lines 13-20) and the subsequent section in which future kings are exhorted to repeat these same feats. Thus the first identifiable line of this repetition repeats the deed of line 14, line 25 repeats line 15, 26 follows 16 and so on. They continue in sequence until line 28, assuming that the counterparts of 17 and 19 existed and were located after *Glossenkeilen* in the missing portion of the text, i.e., to the right of lines 26 and 27. It is unclear whether the pattern breaks down after line 28 or even if the difficult line 21 is part of the pattern. In any event, it is not unreasonable to suppose that line 23 was in fact the counterpart to line 13, the opening statement of Sargon's accomplishments.

26. Restore [*l*]*i-te-tel-li*; traces of a *li* sign are present. The form is a Gtn perfect precative of *elû*, rare but attested, see *GAG* §81 e.[186] Unquestionably, another line followed after a *Glossenkeil* in the second half of the line. From the pattern of the text, that line may be reconstructed as [*littatablak-kat(a) šadê šaplūti*] (cf. lines 16-17). The verb form *littatablakkat(a)* would be an Ntn perfect precative (with ventive ending).

32. At the bottom edge of text A, portions of four or five badly mutilated signs are visible. No treatment of the Legend has ever attempted to identify these signs. With reservation we suggest reading *šu? ma? nâp? ri?*.

Column ii

1. Although the upper edge of Text B is missing along column ii, what traces do remain are definitely from the first line of the column. Here the lower portions of the first two signs are visible. King's copy is a bit inexact; in particular, the horizontal is placed too low. The traces appear as follows:  The first sign seems likely to be the remains of *a*, the next probably *na* or, less likely, DU.

2. The line apparently begins with the conjunction *ù* (cf. line 4) and is followed by ŠU, then traces of what may be LÚ. A bit more of the sign is visible than the copy indicates but not enough to be certain of its identification. An animal name would seem appropriate (cf. below, esp. line 4); ŠU.LÚ^{mušen}= *ḫazû*, *ḫūqu* "a kind of bird" is possible (see *AHw* p. 339 under *ḫāzû*; *CAD* Vol. Ḫ, p. 166, 244). The alternatives *šurānu*, *šūru*, *šurdu* seem unlikely from the traces.

3.1 Reconstructed from B 3 and D 2. The verb *irtappud* is derived from *rapādu*, a Gtn preterit 3rd feminine singular "it ran about" (cf. *AHw* p. 954, Gtn 1 b).

3.2 The sign following the verb is DARA$_4$ which has the values GANA$_6$ *(immertu)* "ewe" (see *AHw* p. 378 lex. for the equation ga-nam/na-(am) ganam$_{6,5,4}$=*im-mer/me-er-tu/tum YOS* I, 53, 180// *CT* XXXV, 5 15 [Ea]) and U$_{10}$ *(laḫru)* "ewe" (see *AHw* p. 528; and *CAD* Vol. L, p. 42 lex). Güterbock's proposed restoration "*ai*[*alu* (od. *tur*[*aḫu*])" in "Historische Tradition," p. 64 3 is to be rejected. According to *CAD*, *ajalu* "stag" is written with DÀRA.MAŠ=(DARA$_3$.MAŠ) not DARA$_4$ (Vol. A, pt. 1, p. 225 lex.). For *turaḫu* "ibex," cf. *CAD* (ibid.) which gives the equation DÀRA=*turaḫu*.

3.3 It is likely that D 2 and B 3 belong to the same line of text, based on the certain correspondence of D 4 and B 5. Working backwards, D 3 should connect with B 4, which *CAD* does in fact claim (see Vol. L, p. 241 1 sub *lulīmu*).[187] If we assume that different recensions are not involved, the sequence of lines in B and D would place them together. D reads x ⌜EDIN⌝

⸢*am*⸣-*mi̅-ni la̤* [. . .]. Preceding EDIN, Lambert's copy suggests a trace of a sign, possibly the stem of a vertical. Collation of the text, however, reveals the end of a horizontal, which might be restored as AŠ *(ina)*. This proposal allows the reconstruction and meaningful interpretation of B 3 and D 2--*irtappud laḫru ina ṣēri ammīni la* [. . .], "the ewe ran about in the steppe, why not. . . ."

4. *CAD* takes B 4 and D 3 as the same line offering as a transliteration under *lulīmu* (Vol. L, p. 241 1): MAŠ.DÀ *iṣ-rat šá-a-ri lu-li-ma CT* XLVI, 46 3 and dupl. *CT* XIII, 43 K 4470 ii 4. These two lines may in fact be related, notwithstanding the fact that B reveals traces of a sign after GIŠ which is much more likely to be *ru* than *rat* . D on the other hand is broken in the middle of the sign preceding *rat*, so that it cannot be identified with certainty. Consequently, we are not sure that the problem is merely one of reconciling two variant forms of the same word *iṣ-ru* (B) and *iṣ-rat* (D). Further complicating the connection proposed by *CAD* is the matter of interpretation. A translation of the line is conspicuously absent from *CAD*, and one wonders how it understood the phrase *iṣrat šāri*. Does *CAD* derive the form from *iṣratu* "plan," "design," "border" (Vol. I/J, p. 206) and, if so, what does the phrase really mean? Other possibilities that come to mind, *giš-rat/ru-ti (gašru) šāri* "the power or strength of the wind" or *esru/rat šāri* "the captive of the wind" are equally unconvincing. A collation of D rules out *AHw*'s restoration [*u*]*rrad šá-a-ri* (see p. 1192 sub *šāru(m)* I).

5.1 B 5 and D 4 obviously duplicate each other with four signs overlapping between them. From this correspondence we are able to align and reconstruct the narrative of column ii insofar as the two sources permit. B 5 preserves *iṣ-ṣur-ru qa̤-du-*⸢*ú*⸣. Following the *du* sign which is in poor condition, there are remains of two horizontals and the tops of two or three verticals --definitely a *ú* sign. The parallel line in D is broken at the beginning--[*iṣ-ṣur-r*]*u qa-du-ú šá iš-ta-s*[*u-ú?*]. Together they provide about two-thirds of the length of the line. On the identification of the Qaṭā-bird *(iṣṣūru qadû)* as *Pterocles alchata* "Large Pin-tailed Sandgrouse," see A. Salonen, *Vögel und Vogelfang im alten Mesopotamien* (Helsinki, 1973), pp. 241-43; and cf. B. Landsberger, *WO* 3 (1966), pp. 264-65; *CAD* Vol. I/J, pp. 208-9 sub *iṣṣūr qādê* "owl"; and *AHw* p. 892 sub *qadû(m)* I "Käuzchen."

5.2 Restore *iš-ta-su-ú*, from *šasû* "to cry," "call out," a Gtn preterit *(ištassi)* 3rd masculine singular subjunctive. Note that line 6 begins with a Gtn infinitive of *šasû: ina šitassīšu*.

6. For *leqû* with the apparent meaning "to achieve" or "to accomplish," see Grayson, *ABC* p. 281 sub Chronicle 2 27 who translates the passage in our text. Cf. ibid. p. 89 Chronicle 2 27, commentary to 27; p. 96 Chronicle 3 69; and Landsberger, *WO* 3 p. 264 C.

7. *il-lik šá-a-*⌈*ru*⌉--"the wind blew," cf. line 9.

8.1 Restore in B ANŠE.E[DIN.NA] *(ser[rēmu])* "wild ass," traces of EDIN are visible on the clay. King was first to correctly identify the animal as "wild ass," transcribing the name *pur*[*imu*] (*CCEBK* II, p. 95 8,10). Nougayrol has subsequently shown the correct reading to be *serrēmu*, the BU sign having the value *sír*; see "*Sirrimu* (non **purimu*) 'âne sauvage'" in *JCS* 2 (1948), pp. 203-8. Copy D confirms the restoration preserving the syllabic spelling *sír-ra-mu*.

8.2 The last sign at least partially preserved may be *id/t/ṭ* (see D 7). Lambert's copy shows the beginnings of three horizontals ; whereas, the traces appear to indicate . If this identification is correct, then the second half of the line begins *a-a-it*, perhaps from *ajītu* feminine singular interrogative-indefinite pronoun (masculine *ajû*). This particular orthography is attested: *a-a-i-te* (var. *a-a-it*) *epšēti šanâti mātitan* "what strange deeds (are happening) everywhere" *BWL* Ludlul II, 10; see *CAD* A, pt. 1, p. 235 5'. Perhaps the second half of the column, which is largely missing, contained a series of interrogative expressions, cf. *ammīni la* line 2;

a-a-it? line 12.

9.1 *il-lak šá-a-ru*/IM--"the wind blows"; cf. line 7 where we find *alāku* in the preterit.

9.2 Restore A.RI[.A?] = *(na[mî])* "prairie," "steppe," from *namû* (Old Babylonian *nawû*) written syllabically and A.RI.A; cf. *AHw* p. 771 sub *nawûm* I. The proposal makes sense and fits the background of the narrative. As a less probable alternative, one might consider a form of the root *erû*, whose meaning until recently was obscure. See *CAD* Vol. A, pt. 2, p. 317 under *arû* D, which cites the occurrence *lillik šāru qaqqara li-e-er-ri*--"let the wind blow let it . . . the ground" *BRM* IV, 1 15 (OB Atraḫasīs). Lambert has recently provided an interpretation and discussion of the root *erû* "to be parched," D "to parch" in *Atra-ḫasīs*, p. 72 Tablet II, col. i 15; notes to Tablet II, p. 156, i 14-17.

10. *i-bit*--perhaps from *bâtu* "to spend the night," "to delay," occasionally used of animals, cf. *ARM* I 50 19.

11. There is a *Glossenkeil* between EDIN (line 10) and *i-šá-['u-ú]* on D, which Lambert's copy overlooked. Thus D and B agree that 10 and 11 are separate lines. The verb form seems to be a G present 3rd plural(?) of *ša'û* "to run" and not *šâ'u* "to fly," see *AHw* p. 1205 sub *ša'û(m)* II 1.

12. Perhaps the same word as line 8: *a-a-it?*

13.1 The difficulty here lies in identifying the verb. The early translators including King proposed *i-lak* from *alāku*, a G present. While this is not impossible (the spelling does occur), the usual orthography is *il-lak*. The meaning is passable in context. Güterbock, however, read the signs *i-šet* and translated the line "nicht hält stand der Wolf" ("Historische Tradition," p. 64 13). In view of the activity and the nature of the animals in the narrative, we prefer *išēt* from *šêtu* (basic meaning "to leave over or behind") with the sense of "to get away, " "to escape (from)," cf. *AHw* p. 1221 sub *šêtu(m)* II 6.

13.2 Before the line breaks off in D, the syllables *da-mi*-x? are preserved here and in lines 14-16. Considering the predatory animals involved in this section (*nêšu* and *barbaru*) along with the expression *tābik dami* (in line 15), it is a good bet that the word is *damu* "blood" perhaps followed by a pronominal suffix.[188]

14. *nêšu ākilu*--"the devouring lion"; cf. *CAD* Vol. A, pt. 1, p. 266, which translates *ākilu* adj. as man-eating, apparently based on this occurrence--*nēšu a-ki-lu damī* . . . "the man-eating lion [consumes(?)] blood," and Borger *Asarh.* 109 iv 7 *ina qātē nēši a-ki-l*⌈*i*⌉ [*limallû*]*kunu* "may (the deities) hand you over to a man-eating lion." We prefer the more literal and neutral translation "devouring lion." No proof exists that the lion in column ii of the Legend is consuming humans and not other animals. Borger translates the passage in *Asarh.* ". . . eines gefrässigen Löwen. . . ." Note the common usage of devouring animals in treaty curses of which Borger *Asarh.* is an example. Cf. D. Hiller's "Treaty Curses and the Old Testament Prophets," *Biblica et Orientalia* 16 (1964), pp. 54-56.

15.1 This line is found on D only. From line 5 the sequence and correspondence of lines between B and D have been established with certainty, and it is a bit disturbing to find them ostensibly broken. Actually, it is quite likely that line 15 was preserved on B, occupying the right half of the line shared by B 14. It should be noted that D 12 (=B 14) consists of widely spaced signs indicating a line of fairly short length. In B, however, the same signs are compressed, just as we would expect if the scribe had required the right side of the tablet for a second line of text following a *Glossenkeil*.

15.2 x-x-tu_4--there appears to be enough room for two signs. One might look for an animal name followed by *tābik dami* in apposition but nothing suitable comes to mind. The form *ta-bi-ik* (from *tabāku* "to spill") could be either a G participle masculine singular construct *(tābik)* or a stative 3rd masculine singular *(tabik)*. The preference is for *tābik dami* "the spiller of blood" especially since the expression is attested elsewhere. Cf. *CAD* Vol. D under *damu*, p. 75 top; and *AHw* p. 1296 s.v. *tabāku(m)*f. Landsberger would restore the first words of this line and the next as *ḫabbātu* and *šaggāšu* respectively (*WO* 3, p. 246 C Reihe: *ṣabītu* . . . [*ḫabbā*]*tu*, [*šaggā*]*šu*). While one cannot reject these suggestions outright, the traces at the beginning of line 16 do not seem to support a reading *šaggāšu*.

16. We encounter here difficulties comparable to those in the preceding line. B preserves x-x-*šú la-pit* against x-x-*šu la-pit da-mi-?* in D. The grammar and structure may parallel line 15--*tābik dami*//*lāpit dami*.

17. A vestige of the sign following *a* is visible and might be *na* or less likely *du*  .

18.1 Restore *il-lik* or *il-lak* [*š*]*á-a-ru* on analogy with lines 7 and 9.

18.2 After É LÚ, the top of a vertical is present. Is it MEŠ?

19. *di-'a-ti*--the reading is conjectural. If correct, it may be the plural of *dīmtu* "tears," "weeping," cf. *CAD* Vol. D, p. 147 *dī'ātu* NA.

20. *namūta*--an abstract noun from *namû*. Note the idiom *namūta alāku* "to become wasteland," "to fall to ruins," and in the Š-stem "to make a wasteland," cf. *CAD* Vol. A, pt. 1, p. 316 under *alāku namūtu*. Possibly, we have here an occurrence of the idiom in the present G or Š (of *alāku*). Note, however, that the normal order seems to be *namūta alāku*.

NOTES

CHAPTER II

[1]King's copy of the cuneiform includes only the column dealing with the Sargon Legend.

[2]Prof. Lambert has suggested to me the possibility that D might be from the reverse of the missing portion of A. The script is in fact quite similar, and one might expect D, based on the overlap of lines with col. ii of B, to belong close to the lower left edge of A. A treatment of D, previously unedited, appears below as part of the critical edition of the text.

[3]See Chapters V and VI.

[4]For a discussion of the ending *ānu*, see *GAG* § 56r; and cf. A. Goetze, "The Akkadian Masculine Plural in *ānū/ī* and its Semitic Background," *Language* 22 (1946), pp. 127-30; and G. Buccellati, "The Case Against the Alleged Akkadian Plural Morpheme *-ānū*," *Afroasiatic Linguistics* Vol. 3/2 (1976), pp. 28-30.

[5]Cf. E. Reiner, *A Linguistic Analysis of Akkadian* (The Hague, 1966), p. 61.

[6]Cf. line 2 where A and B agree on *ummī ēnetu*. Here, the phrase is probably to be read as "my mother was an *ēnetu*." It is also possible to argue that *ummu* (A5) is the basic form and that *ummī* (B5) resulted from contamination by line 2.

[7]Cf. Text C which reads *šu-ú-šú*.

[8]Güterbock, "Historische Tradition," p. 62, n. 5.

[9]This particular spelling is not attested among the occurrences listed under *bābu* in *CAD*. The spellings KÁ plus *-šu*, *-ša*, and *-ka* in the singular are common.

[10]King, *CCEBK* II, p. 89, n. 3.

[11]I am grateful to Marten Stol for calling my attention to a number of examples of this phenomenon in Middle Assyrian, Neo-Assyrian, and Late Babylonian texts. Cf. *na-an-*^{na}*nab-šú* (*EAK* I 101 27); *lil-*^{li}*lik-ma* (*RCAE* 749 r. 11); *dun*^{un}*-nu-nim-ma* (*PBS* XV 80 i 20); and ^{d}EN-*ri-man*^{an}*-ni* (*Camb.* 150:12, cf. ^{d}EN-*ri-man-ni* [*Cyr.* 260:9]).

[12]King's copy of K 4470 (B) in *CT* XIII, pl. 43 is mistaken. Line 10 ends, according to King's copy, **ú-rab-ba-an-ni*. My collation of B and the photo show that the tablet in fact reads *ú-rab-ba-ni-ma*.

[13]For a brief discussion of the term with references, see *CAD* Vol. Ṣ, p. 76 3'.

[14]See the commentary to the text, col. i 6.2.

[15]See the discussion of the orthography of Sargon's name in the commentary to the text, col. i 1.1.

[16]See M. J. Seux, *Épithètes royales akkadiennes et sumériennes* (Paris, 1967), pp. 293-97.

[17]A slightly different form of the title with KALA--MAN KALA is attested in the inscriptions of four other Assyrian kings: Tiglath-Pileser I (1115-1077); Šamši-Adad IV (1054-1051); Sargon II (721-705); and Assurbanipal (668-627).

[18]See AD-*ja* in line 5 and KÁ-*ja* in line 16.

[19]This process is just as likely to have occurred in a Babylonian antecedent → .

[20]On the use of the negative particle, see *GAG* § 122; and cf. K. Riemschneider, *Lehrbuch des Akkadischen* (Leipzig, 1969), 20.16.

[21]Güterbock, "Historische Tradition," p. 62, n. 4.

[22]See *AHw* p. 21 sub *aḫu(m)*I.

[23]For the most recent treatment of the question with references to previous literature, see David B. Weisberg, *Guild Structure and Political Allegiance in Early Achaemenid Mesopotamia*, Yale Near Eastern Researches, I (New Haven, 1967), pp. 106-11.

[24]*GAG* §64c; cf. *abum St. constr. abu*, paradigm 4 pp. 6*-7* and n. 1; also *AHw* p. 21, s.v. *aḫu(m)*I.

[25]See p. 14 and n. 11. Also cf. the spelling in ^{d}Ningal. . . *a-lid-da-at* (*VAB* VII/2 p. 288 6).

[26]As King suggests in *CCEBK* II, p. 81, n. 1.

[27]A more serious discrepancy involving line 4 of B and line 3 of D will be discussed in the commentary. See col. ii 4.

[28]See *AHw* p. 1038, sub. *serrēmu*.

[29]Literally: rise from.

[30]So Leroy Waterman, *Royal Correspondence of the Assyrian Empire*, Vol. III (Ann Arbor, 1930-36), p. 266, n. 951, who follows King and others.

[31]Ibid.

[32]See also *RCAE* Letters 542 and 1016 (LUGAL-*ú-kin*).

[33]For example, the early Old Babylonian spellings *šar-rum-ki-in* and *šar-ru-um-ki-in*, and perhaps the third millennium personal name *ur-*^{d}*šar-ru*-GIM = *ur-*^{d}*šar-ru-ken*$_{x}$, see n. 38 below

concerning *ur*-^{d}*šar-ru*-GIM, also referred to in the Appendix.

34 See the Appendix for a listing of the orthographies and sources along with spellings for Sargon I and II.

35 The actual form of the name was *šarrum-kīn*, "the king is the true one." This compound spelling (with GI) reflects a common feature of Sumerian orthography--representing the initial syllables in writing and omitting the end. For a discussion of the subject, see M. Civil, "The Sumerian Writing System: Some Problems" in *Or* N.S. 42 (1973), pp. 30-31.

36 See *PDT* 605 6 and the commentary to lines 5-6 on p. 227.

37 I.J. Gelb, *Old Akkadian Writing and Grammar*, 2nd ed. (Chicago, 1961), pp. 30-31.

38 David Owen accepts names like this as evidence of a value *ken*$_x$ for GIM; see *JNES* 33 (1974), p. 419, s.v. p. 28.

39 The occurrence of Sargon's name in an inscription of Šamši-Adad I excavated in Nineveh is the earliest reference to the King of Agade that derives from Assyria. See the Appendix 7f.

40 This spelling is found in an unedited Sargon text copied by van Dijk in *Sumer* 13 (1957), p. 99, pl. 16 I 9' and now republished in *TIM* IX as no. 48, pl. 36 I 9'.

41 See Chapter IV *V*. 19 and n. 40.

42 See W.W. Hallo's treatment of the title in *Early Mesopotamian Royal Titles*, American Oriental Society, XLIII (New Haven, 1957), pp. 89-99. For another opinion see Guy Bunnens, "À propos de l'épithète royale šarru dannu," *Annuaire de l'Institut de Philologie et d'Histoire Orientales et Slaves* 20 (1968-72), pp. 145-54.

43 Hallo, *Titles*, p. 89.

44 *CAD* Vol. D, pp. 94-95.

45 Ibid., p. 95 3b.

46 Note its previous attribution to the divine Gilgameš (LUGAL KALA) in *RA* 10 (1913), p. 101; also cf. K. Tallquist, *Akkadische Götterepitheta*, Studia Orientalia, VII (Helsinki, 1938), p. 233. For the possibility of an earlier occurrence outside of Mesopotamia, see Hallo's discussion of Annu-banini of Lulubum, *Titles*, pp. 97-98.

47 *Titles*, pp. 89-91.

48 Ibid., p. 99.

49 In a seal inscription dedicated to him by an underling, Šu-ilia, an early ruler of an independent Ešnunna, is called LUGAL *da-núm*. There is no evidence, however, that he used the title for himself (ibid., p. 95).

[50]Whether these sources refer to Burnaburiaš I or II, and Kadašman-Enlil I or II is uncertain; see M. J. Seux, *Êpithètes royales akkadiennes et sumériennes* (Paris, 1967), p. 423.

[51]Namely, Adad-šuma-uṣur; Itti-Marduk-balaṭu; and Nebuchadnezzar I.

[52]Note that these three spellings: LUGAL *dan-nu*, MAN *dan-nu*, and MAN KALA are found in sources of Sargon II.

[53]The orthographies used in Babylonia and Assyria may be found in Seux, *ERAS*, pp. 294-96.

[54]As Kraus has recently suggested, Sargon may very well have built his capital on a previously inhabited or partially developed site; see F. R. Kraus, *Sumerer und Akkader, ein Problem der altmesopotamischen Geschichte*, MKNAW N.R. XXXIII/8 (Amsterdam, 1970), p. 24. For the latest attempt to identify the location of Agade, see H. Weiss who argues for Išan al-Mizyad in "Kish, Akkad and Agade," *JAOS* 95 (1975), pp. 434-53.

[55]The earliest evidence of the title in Akkadian occurs in a building inscription of Lipit-Ištar (1934-1924), see C. J. Gadd, *The Early Dynasties of Sumer and Akkad* (London, 1921), pl. 3 i 14-17 and p. 33. It is probably safe to assume that the Akkadian goes back to the late third millennium. For a discussion of the term see Hallo, *Titles*, pp. 77-89; also cf. Kraus, *Sumerer und Akkader*, pp. 28-30, 36.

[56]E. Unger, "Akkad" in *RLA* I (1932), p. 62 2.

[57]Most likely meaning of the title is "king of (the city) Agade." This form is analogous to LUGAL Kiš^{ki}.

[58]These designations follow H. Hirsch, "Die Inschriften der Könige von Agade," *AfO* 20 (1963), pp. 34-51.

[59]See A. Goetze, "Akkad Dynasty Inscriptions from Nippur" in *JAOS* 88 (1968), p. 54, r. 9, 10.

[60]Note an inscription of Šamši-Adad I which reads *Ma-an-iš-ti-šu* DUMU *šar-ru-ki-in* LUGAL *a-ga-dè*^{ki} (*EAK* I, p. 9 9-10). The title probably belongs to Sargon.

[61]Hirsch, "Inschriften der Könige von Agade," s.v. Naram-Sin b 4, vs. kol. i 2.3, 8.9 and passim.

[62]V. Scheil, *MDP* VI, pl. 1-2, p. 6.

[63]H. Hilprecht, *BE* I, no. 1.

[64]For Dudu, see *PBS* V, 39 pl. 98; Elulu, *AfO* 10 (1935-36), p. 281; and Šu-turul, *Iranica Antiqua* 2 (1962), p. 156.

[65]For the latest discussion of the question, see Kraus, *Sumerer und Akkader*, p. 24.

[66]*PBS* IV/1, p. 231.

[67]For *ēnetu* as "princess," see G. Smith, *The Chaldean Account of Genesis* (New York, 1876), p. 299; as "Herrin," F. Delitzsch, *Wo lag das Paradies* (Leipzig, 1881), p. 209; and as "Vestalin," A. Jeremias, *Das alte Testament im Lichte des alten Orients* (Leipzig, 1904), p. 400.

[68]Note that A. K. Grayson has replaced "changeling" with "high priestess" in *ANET*[3] 1969, p. 119.

[69]See "Zu den Frauenklassen des Kodex Hammurabi" in *ZA* 30 (1915-16), p. 71. Note that in 1908 Thureau-Dangin had suggested the interpretation of *ēnetu* as "prétresse de haut rang," see Chapter I, p. 6.

[70]In his "Historische Tradition," p. 62, n. 2; cf. Driver and Miles, *The Babylonian Laws* (Oxford, 1952), II, p. 199, n. 2.

[71]For the identification of *ēnetu* with *ēntu*, see *AHw* p. 220 s.v. *entu*; *CAD* Vol. E, p. 172 s.v. *ēntu*; Chayim Cohen, "Hebrew *tbh*: Proposed Etymologies" in *JANES* 4 (1972), pp. 46-51; and Brevard Childs, *The Book of Exodus*, Old Testament Library (Philadelphia, 1974), pp. 8-10.

[72]W. G. Lambert, *Atra-ḫasīs* (Oxford, 1969), p. 102 vii, 1-8; p. 165, note on vii, 6-7 and 8-9.

[73]According to Astour, the priestess, if discovered, would face death by burning. For the argument see M. Astour, "Tamar the Hierodule" in *JBL* 85 (1966), pp. 193-94.

[74]See J. Renger, "Untersuchungen zum Priestertum in der altbabylonischen Zeit" in *ZA* 58 (1967), p. 126 20 and also n. 97.

[75]*CAD* Vol. E, p. 172.

[76]J. Renger, "Untersuchungen zum Priestertum, p. 144 50. For a discussion of the *Heilige Hochzeit*, see Renger's article in *RLA* IV (1975), pp. 251-59.

[77]See the article on the *gipāru* by R. Harris in *RLA* III (1968), pp. 377-79.

[78]Renger, "Untersuchungen zum Priestertum," p. 140 45.

[79]*CAD* Vol. E, p. 179 3' s.v. *ēnu*, where EN-priestess is written NIN or NIN.DINGIR, and note the discussion which follows; cf. *AHw* p. 220 c' s.v. *enu(m)*; Driver and Miles, *BabLaws* I, p. 361; and M. Astour, "Tamar the Hierodule," p. 188.

[80]Renger, "Untersuchungen zum Priestertum," p. 143 49.

[81]Ibid., p. 143 48.

[82]*CAD* Vol. E, p. 173; for earlier material dealing with this problem see J. Nougayrol, "NIN.DINGIR(.RA) = *ugbabtum* (non **ukkurtum*)" in *JNES* 9 (1950), pp. 51-52, and "Textes hépatosco-

piques d'époque ancienne conservés au Musée du Louvre (III)" in *RA* 44 (1950), pp. 27-29, 39.

[83]*BabLaws* I, p. 363, based on CH § 110.

[84]Ibid.

[85]H. W. F. Saggs, *The Greatness that was Babylon* (New York, 1968), p. 333.

[86]For earlier advocates of this position, see B. Meissner, *Babylonien und Assyrien* (Heidelberg, 1920, 1925), II, pp. 68-69, 437; and I. Diakonoff, *Epos O Gilgameš* (Moscow, 1961), p. 150; cf. *CAD* Vol. E, p. 204 s.v. *assinnūtu*.

[87]*Malku-šarru* I, 131-35, see the edition by A. Draffkorn Kilmer in *JAOS* 83 (1963), pp. 421-46.

[88]See *CAD* Vol. E, p. 325 s.v. *erû*; *ēntu aššum la erîša qinnassa ušnâk* (*CT* XXXI, 44 obv. (!) i 10, dupl. *BRM* IV, 12 32 and Boissier *DA* 220 10).

[89]*CAD* Vol. A, pt. 2, p. 341. Note the apparent contradiction with the earlier position taken in Vol. E, p. 204 s.v. *epēšu assinnūtu* where the idiom is translated "to practice sodomy." According to Bottêro and Petschow (see "Homosexualität" in *RLA* IV [1972-75], esp. pp. 463-68), the *assinnu* was in fact a homosexual.

[90]Assuming that the sex act was actually performed and not simulated. For the archaeological evidence bearing on this question, see J. S. Cooper, "Heilige Hochzeit" B in *RLA* IV (1975), pp. 259-69.

[91]There is some evidence that there existed higher and lower members of the *ēntu*-order, for references and discussion see Driver and Miles, *BabLaws* I, p. 363.

[92]These inscriptions are now listed by H. Hirsch in his "Inschriften der Könige von Agade," p. 9, sub 2; also see I. J. Gelb *MAD* II, 1961, p. 194.

[93]Cf. the recent article by J. van Dijk, "Les contacts ethniques dans la Mésopotamie" in *Syncretism*, Scripta Instituti Donneriani Aboensis, III (Uppsala, 1969), pp. 193-94.

[94]Attributed to Enheduanna by the colophon. For a recent edition of the hymns, see Å. Sjöberg, *The Collection of the Sumerian Temple Hymns*, TCS III (Locust Valley, 1969); cf. also Hallo and van Dijk, *The Exaltation of Inanna* (New Haven, 1968).

[95]Unless the father should prove to be the king, he is most likely irrelevant in establishing Sargon's nobility.

[96]According to A. Falkenstein, Gudea may also have been the result of a sacred union between his mother, high priestess of the goddess Gatumdu, and the ruler. In a prayer to Gatumdu, Gudea says "I have not a mother, you are my mother. I have not a

father, you are my father." (Cyl. A iii 6-10). For Falkenstein's argument, see *Die Inschriften Gudeas von Lagaš*, AnOr XXX (Rome, 1966), pp. 1-3.

[97]Childs, *Exodus*, p. 9.

[98]See "Historische Tradition," p. 62, n. 3; and Childs, *Exodus*, p. 9.

[99]In another tradition preserved in a Sumerian text, the Sargon-Lugalzagesi Legend, Sargon's father is identified as *La'ibum*; see *TCL* XVI, pl. 142, no. 73 11; and cf. Chapter IV *III* 6.

[100]In *TCL* XVI, no. 73 11, Sargon's mother might have been named. Unfortunately, the text is broken in the crucial place a d - d a - n i *la-i-bu-um* a m a - [n i? . . .].

[101]Childs, *Exodus*, p. 10.

[102]See J. J. Stamm, *Die Akkadische Namengebung* (Leipzig, 1939), p. 321.

[103]*CAD* Vol. A, pt. 1, p. 195 2.

[104]See *ARM* I, 6 9; IV, 1 18; V, 73 r. 12'; and passim.

[105]The text mentions four people as the *aḫḫū* of a *nadītu*. Only one is a brother, the others are nephews (see R. Harris, "On Kinship and Inheritance in Old Babylonian Sippar," *Iraq* 38 [1976], p. 131).

[106]Bottéro et al., *The Near East: The Early Civilizations*, Delacorte World History (New York, 1967), p. 103.

[107]Note *erub ana libbi elippima peḫi bābka* "Enter the ship and seal your 'hatch'" (88); and *ērub ana libbi elippi apteḫi bābī* "I entered the ship and sealed my 'hatch'" (93).

[108]Note the variant *iddananni* found in B. An analysis of this corrupt form is offered above in our discussion of the stemma, Genealogy of Texts A and B.

[109]See *AHw* p. 1152 s.v. *šalû(m)* I. Cf. Zimmern's treatment in *Christusmythe*, p. 26 ". . . sie wollte, das (ich) darin untersanke." For Zimmern's contribution to the study of the Legend, see Chapter I, p. 7.

[110]W. G. Lambert, "Nebuchadnezzar King of Justice," *Iraq* 27 (1965), p. 6 5.

[111]Cf. Lambert's translation ". . . he made him jump in and safely brought him [to the bank]." Ibid., p. 9.

[112]See Güterbock's summary of the previous treatments of this form in "Historische Tradition," p. 63, n. 5.

[113]Ibid.

[114]Cf. Labat's translation in *Les religions du Proche-Orient asiatique* (Paris, 1970), p. 308 which seems to anticipate my interpretation. "Elle me jeta dans le fleuve, sans que j'en puisse sortir."

[115]*PBS* IV/1, p. 231.

[116]Güterbock, "Historische Tradition," p. 63, n. 1.

[117]Ibid., p. 63, n. 3.

[118]Vol. D under *dālû*, p. 57 f.

[119]This location of *šú* is very important because, if correct, it makes the restoration of *ilqanni* in the available remaining space impossible.

[120]See Landsberger's edition of *ana ittīšu* in *Materialien zum sumerischen Lexikon* I, Tf. III, col. iii, pp. 43-46; for a recent treatment of CH §§ 185-93, see Driver and Miles, *BabLaws* II, pp. 74-75; and for the Nuzzi material see E. Cassin, *L'adoption à Nuzi* (Paris, 1938). As a partial bibliography including sources, see M. David, "Adoption" in *RLA* I (1932), pp. 37-39; A. Falkenstein, "Die neusumerischen Gerichtsurkunden," *ABAW* N. F. Heft 39 (1956), pp. 110-11, 336-40 ; G. Boyer, *ARMT* VIII (1958), pp. 178-82; R. Haase, *Einführung in das Studium keilschriftlicher Rechtsquellen* (Wiesbaden, 1965), pp. 71-72; V. Korošec, *Orientalisches Recht*, in Handbuch der Orientalistik, ed. B. Spuler, Abt I Erg. Bd 3 (Leiden, 1964), pp. 112-13; R. Harris, *Ancient Sippar, A Demographic Study of an Old-Babylonian City* (Istanbul, 1975), pp. 137, 347, 355-57; and M. Ellis, "An Old Babylonian Adoption Contract from Tell Harmal," *JCS* 27 (1975), pp. 130-151. On adoption in the Neo-Babylonian period, see M. San Nicolo, "Neu-babylonische Urkunden aus Ur" in *Or N.S.* 19 (1950), pp. 221-22; "Babylonische Rechtsurkunden des 8. und 7. Jahrhundert v. Chr.," *ABAW* N. F. Heft 34 (1951), pp. 1-3; San Nicolo and Petschow, "Babylonische Rechtsurkunden aus dem 6. Jahrhundert v. Chr.," *ABAW* N. F. Heft 51 (1960), pp. 6-9; and Driver and Miles, *BabLaws* I, pp. 383-406.

[121]For an example of such a contract, see Cassin, *L'adoption*, p. 285ff.

[122]CH §§ 185-93, which deal with adoptions by free men, craftsmen, and officials but do not explicitly refer to a contract, may reflect this type of adoption.

[123]On this type of adoption, see *ana ittīšu MSL* I Tf. III, col. iii, p. 44 27ff.

[124]M. David, *Die Adoption im altbabylonischen Recht*, Leipziger rechtswissenschaftliche Studien, XXIII (Leipzig, 1927), pp. 24-28.

[125]Driver and Miles, *BabLaws* I, pp. 389-91.

[126]Cf. *CAD* Vol. Ḫ, s.v. *ḫâṭu* p. 161 3 for a translation of the law. *CAD* interprets *awīlum* as the subject of *iḫiāṭ* "search." Driver's contention that *awīlum* as subject of *iḫiāṭ*

is hardly possible grammatically is not clear to me.

[127] Those who already had sons were still permitted to adopt; cf. Driver and Miles, *BabLaws* I, p. 384.

[128] Driver and Miles, *BabLaws* I, p. 385; cf. CH § 191.

[129] CH §§ 188-89.

[130] Cf. A. L. Oppenheim, "'Siege Documents' from Nippur," *Iraq* 17 (1955), pp. 69-89, which describes children sold to avoid starvation. The purchaser is addressed, "Take my small child and keep (her) alive *(bulluṭu)*! She shall be your small child (slave-girl). Give me x shekels of silver so that I may (have something to) eat *(akālu)*!" p. 71.

[131] Cf. the commentary on column i, 11 below.

[132] Note *CAD* defines *dālû* as "water drawer," "gardener," Vol. D, p. 57; cf. 36 ERIM LÚ.A.BAL *ša* 6 *ūmī* 6 (text 4) ERIM. MEŠ *maḫāḫu* . . . "36 gardeners, (i.e.) six men on six days for preparing the soil, . . ." (*TCL* I, 174 6ff), ibid., p. 57.

[133] T. Jacobsen, *The Sumerian King List*, AS XI (Chicago, 1939), pp. 110-11 32 and n. 238.

[134] Cassin, *L'adoption*, p. 39.

[135] "Assyriological Gleanings" 1 in *BASOR* 91 (1943), pp. 36-37.

[136] Strassmaier *Nbk.* 439.

[137] The text, *Nbk.* 439, in Oppenheim's transliteration and translation, reads as follows:
an-nu-tu ^{amēl}*mu-kin-ni-e ša ina pa-ni-šú-nu* ⌜SAL⌝*-ra-a* ^{amēl}[ ]-tum? (-)*x-šú a-na* [*pi-i*] *kal-bi ta-as-su-qú* ^{m}Nur-^{d}Šamaš [*i*]*š-tu pi-i kal-bi iš-šu-ú-'-ma* [^{amēl}*mukinni*] "these are the witnesses in the presence of whom Lady X-ra has thrown her! to the mouth of the dog(s) and Nur-Šamaš has taken (him) away from the mouth of the dog(s) and has x-ed him witness."

[138] So also E. Cassin, "Symboles de cession immobilière" in *L'année sociologique* 3e (1952), pp. 118-19.

[139] See *AHw* p. 802.

[140] See D. O. Edzard, "Sumerische Komposita mit dem 'Nominal-prafix' nu-" in *ZA* 55 (1963), p. 92 B 1.

[141] For the most recent treatment including summary of previous material, see G. Cardascia, *Les archives des Murašû* (Paris, 1951).

[142] Note that the term *imittu* is attested only in late sources (Neo-Babylonian), although the practice is unquestionably older. Cf. *CAD* Vol. I/J, p. 123, s.v. *imittu* B.

[143] Ibid., p. 125 s.v. *imittu* B; cf. B. Landsberger, *The Date Palm and its By-products According to the Cuneiform Sources*,

AfO Beiheft XVII (Graz, 1967) esp. p. 10.

[144]See *AHw* p. 1051 *sissinnu(m)* (3). Note that this term is also attested in Late Babylonian sources only.

[145]Cardascia, *Archives*, p. 137.

[146]Cf. n. 132.

[147]Cf. Labat's translation: "Aqqi, le puiseur d'eau me mit à son métier de jardinier" in *Les religions*, p. 308.

[148]See *AHw* p. 951 1 c-d for cases of the sexual connotations of *râmu* involving a deity; and p. 952 4 7 for relations between humans.

[149]The two goddesses are syncretized by the Old Babylonian period, partially perhaps as a result of the policy of Sargon of Akkad, see J. van Dijk, "Contacts ethniques," pp. 188-91; and cf. above 2.1 Enḫeduanna as High Priestess.

[150]See *ANET*3 1969, pp. 52-57, n. 6.

[151]Generally taken to be a mole; cf. *CAD* Vol. D, p. 52 ("a small animal, perhaps a frog").

[152]Gilgameš VI, 44-79,

[153]See S. N. Kramer, "A Blood Motif in Sumerian Mythology" in *ArOr* 17 (1949), pp. 399-405; and cf. C. J. Gadd, "Some Contributions to the Gilgamesh Epic," *Iraq* 28 (1966), 2 pp. 117-18.

[154]See under the title of "Dumuzi and Enkimdu, The Dispute between the Shepherd-God and the Farmer-God" in *ANET*3 1969, pp. 41-42.

[155]See W. Hallo and J. van Dijk, *Exaltation of Inanna*, pp. 1-11; and J. van Dijk, "Contacts ethniques," pp. 188-206.

[156]Cf. van Dijk, "Contacts ethniques," pp. 189-90 and Hallo and van Dijk, *Exaltation of Inanna*, pp. 6-7.

[157]Alexander Heidel, *The Gilgamesh Epic and Old Testament Parallels* (Chicago, 1963), p.50 (VI), 16-17.

[158]Note Labat reads x+6 years. The traces preclude this figure (*Les religions*, p. 308).

[159]T. Jacobsen, *The Sumerian King List*, pp. 23-28.

[160]Most notably Speiser's translation in *ANET*, p. 119 and Labat's in *Les religions*, p. 308.

[161]A list of occurrences of the idiom appears below.

[162]Based on my first collation in 1975. When the tablet was baked in August 1977, all trace of the *pur* sign was lost. See Chapter I n. 3.

[163]For examples in Old Akkadian, see I. J. Gelb, *MAD* III, p. 281, s.v. *š*pr* (*šapāru*); in Old Babylonian, *awatum ša tašpuram* "the command that you sent" (King, *LIH* I, pl. 12f, and 3 p. 65 [K8]); in Middle Babylonian, *belī ṭēma lišpura* "let my lord send a command" (Lutz, *PBS* I/2 no. 49 22, 62, 33-34); in Neo-Assyrian, *ṭēmu la išparunissu* "a command he has not sent him" (Waterman, *RCAE* 158 20-21).

[164]The word *šipru* is a *pirs* noun form whose basic meaning is "message," (see Gelb *MAD* III, p. 281); *šāpiru*, a G participle (ibid.); *šāpirūtu*, an abstract noun form based on the G participle (*ARM* XV, p. 264); and *šabrû*, a back loan from the Sumerian word written PA.AL (*MAD III*, p. 281; and *AHw* p. 1120, s.v. *šabrû(m)*. See also *AHw* p. 1171 sub *šapāru* 7.

[165]Note *in šipri* ᵈInanna *PBS* V 36, r. 1-3.

[166]Although Güterbock accepted *abātu*, he apparently sensed the real meaning called for by the text, "*Wortl. 'zerstörte' nämlich um sie gangbar zu machen*" ("Historische Tradition," p. 63 n. 5).

[167]For the identification of an idiom *šadê nabalkutu* "to jump over mountains" used in dating the text along with a list of occurrences, see Chapter III n. 57.

[168]King, *CCEBK* II, p. 92 18.

[169]Cf. A. L. Oppenheim, *Ancient Mesopotamia*, Revised Edition Completed by E. Reiner (Chicago, 1977), p. 414, s.v. Sealand.

[170]*CAD* Vol. L 3', pp. 70-71.

[171]Güterbock, "Historische Tradition," p. 63 and n. 8.

[172]Grayson, *ABC*, p. 234.

[173]Cf. Chapter III n. 50.

[174]Unless GEME is read as *amtu* or *amti*; cf. W. von Soden, *Das akkadische Syllabar*, AnOr XLII (Rome, 1967), p. 60 303.

[175]See T. Jacobsen, "The Battle between Marduk and Tiamat" in *JAOS* 88 (1968), p. 105.

[176]For example, *Enūma Eliš* IV 93 and passim. This orthography occurs in sources of Sargon II and Assurbanipal; for Sargon II see *RCAE* 381 7, a letter from Ashurrisua to Sargon; and the Silver Inscription, Lyon, *Keilschrifttexte Sargon's*, p. 23 25; for Assurbanipal see Streck, *Assurbanipal* III under *tâmtu* and *tiāmat*. Note the spelling in a literary text from Assur, see Ebeling *Parfümrez*, pl. 26 13.

[177]The locations of Makan and Meluḫḫa, lands associated with Tilmun, are also uncertain.

[178]*JRAS* N.S. 12 (1880), pp. 207-27.

[179]Arguing for an identification with Bahrain, Durand and Rawlinson, "Extracts from Report on the Islands and Antiquities of Bahrain. With Notes by Major-General Sir H. C. Rawlinson." *JRAS* N.S. 12 (1880), pp. 189-227; F. Hommel, *Ethnologie und Geographie des alten Orients*, Handbuch der Altertumswissenschaft (Munich, 1904-1926), 123, pp. 538-43; M. Streck, *Assurbanipal* (Leipzig, 1916) III, Glossar, s.v. Dilmun (includes bibliography); B. Landsberger, "Über die Völker Vorderasiens im dritten Jahrtausend," *ZA* 35 (1923-24), p. 217, n. 2, "Exkurs I," *WO* 3 (1966), p. 261; C. Burrows and A. Deimel, "Tilmun, Bahrain, Paradise," "Bemerkungen zu Burrows" in *Or* 30 SP (1928), pp. 3-24, 25-34; W. F. Albright, "The Mouth of the Rivers," *AJSL* (1919), pp. 182-85, "A Babylonian Geographical Treatise on Sargon of Akkad's Empire," *JAOS* 45 (1925), pp. 237-38; P. B. Cornwall, *Dilmun: The History of Bahrein Island Before Cyprus*, an unpublished Ph.D. thesis Harvard (1944), "On the Location of Dilmun" in *BASOR* 103 (1946), pp. 3-11 (which contests Kramer's article in the same journal [1944] and presents a review of the evidence for Bahrain); also see "Two Letters from Dilmun," *JCS* 6 (1952), pp. 137-42; E. Weidner, "Ausgrabungen in Bahrein," *AfO* 15 (1945-51), pp. 169-70, "Das Reich Sargons von Akkad," *AfO* 16 (1952-53), pp. 1-24, "Ausgrabungen am persischen Gulf," *AfO* 22 (1968-69), pp. 118-20; A. L. Oppenheim, "The Sea Faring Merchants of Ur," *JAOS* 74 (1959), pp. 6-17; W. F. Leemans, "The Trade Relations of Babylonia" in *JESHO* 3 (1960), pp. 27-30, "Old Babylonian Letters and Economic History," *JESHO* 11 (1968), 215-26, *Foreign Trade in the Old Babylonian Period* (Leiden, 1960); K. Jaritz, "Tilmun-Makan-Meluḫḫa" in *JNES* 27 (1968), pp. 209-14; G. Bibby, *Looking for Dilmun* (New York, 1969) based on archaeological excavations conducted on Bahrain, Failaka, and other sites on the Arabian coast; I. J. Gelb, "Makkan and Meluḫḫa in Early Mesopotamian Sources," *RA* 64 (1970), pp. 1-8; R. Borger, "Buchbesprechungen" (Parpola *NAT*) in *ZA* 62 (1972), pp. 136-37; G. Komoróczy, "Tilmun als 'Speicher des Landes' im Epos 'Enki und Ninhursag,'" *Iraq* 39 (1977), pp. 67-70; and cf. S. Parpola, *Neo-Assyrian Toponyms*, AOAT VI (Neukirchen-Vluyn, 1970), p. 103 for listing of occurrences.

Arguing for a localization in Iran, P. Jensen, "Kiš," *ZA* 15 (1900), pp. 225-26; A. Poebel, "A New Creation and Deluge Text" *PBS* IV/1 (1914), p. 62; S. Langdon, "Sumerian Epic of Paradise," *PBS* X/1 (1915), pp. 8-10; S. N. Kramer, "Dilmun the Land of the Living," *BASOR* 96 (1944), pp. 18-28, "Dilmun Quest for Paradise," *Antiquity* 37 (1963), pp. 111-15 (which is a follow-up of his previous study in *BASOR* 96 placing Dilmun in Iran. Kramer would now extend its eastern boundary to include that part of India where Harappan civilization flourished).

For a convenient summary of previous opinions, see J. Hansman, "A Periplus of Magan and Meluḫḫa," *BSOAS* 36 (1973), pp. 553-54; and for an attempt to locate Dilmun along with Makan and Meluḫḫa in western India, see R. Thapar, "A Possible Identification of Meluḫḫa, Dilmun, and Makan," *JESHO* 18 (1975), pp. 1-42; cf. D. Chakraberti, "Gujarat Harappan Connection with West Asia: A Reconsideration of the Evidence" in *JESHO* 18 (1975), pp. 337-42, a criticism of Thapar's use of the archaeological evidence.

[180]A city located beyond the Tigris toward Elam.

[181]See Chapter IV, *VI* 3.

[182]See E. Unger, *RLA* II (1938), p. 199, s.v. Dêr; cf. G. Barton, *RISA*, p. 122 166.

[183]Oppenheim, *Ancient Mesopotamia*, p. 403.

[184]See Chapter IV for the Old Babylonian copies of Sargon's inscriptions that mention such a campaign, especially inscriptions C 2 and 5.

[185]See King *CCEBK* II, p. 5 9 (Sargon Chronicle); p. 33 31 (Sargon Omens--Neo-Assyrian version); and p. 41 2 (Sargon Omens--Neo-Babylonian version).

[186]One might also consider interpreting the verb as a Gtn preterit precative based on a spelling *li-* [te]*tel-li*. Cf. *AHw* p. 208, s.v. *Gtn* 1b which indicates such a spelling but lists it as a Gtn perfect. Also cf. n. 11 above.

[187]There is a problem with this connection that *CAD* overlooks, but it need not be considered impossible. Cf. 4.

[188]In line 15 after *da-mi* there is a faint trace of what may be a *šú*.

CHAPTER III

THE SARGON LEGEND: LITERARY PROBLEMS

Narû-Literature

The Sargon Legend has been relegated to a subcategory of historical-literary texts called by scholars at various times "*narû*-literature," "poetic autobiography," or, most recently, "pseudo-autobiography." Each designation attempts to capture a distinctive feature of the genre. The term *narû*-literature[1] was originally suggested because of the obvious resemblance of these compositions to the form of *narû*-inscriptions. A *narû* is a stela on which a royal inscription is engraved. These inscriptions begin with a self-introduction that may include a list of royal epithets and then follow with a first person narrative relating noteworthy events in the king's reign. They conclude with an epilogue consisting of a blessing oracle or curse formula intended for anyone who might disturb the *narû*.

Recognizing that *narû*-literary texts were, in effect, apocryphal inscriptions that were most likely never inscribed on stelae, some scholars began to feel that the term "*narû*-literature" was unsatisfactory. A. K. Grayson and W. G. Lambert proposed a new designation to avoid confusion between this genre and authentic inscriptions written on stelae; the name they suggested was "poetic autobiography."[2] Grayson has now emended this to "pseudo-autobiography."[3]

The literary works usually assigned to the genre of pseudo-autobiography are few in number and for the most part poorly preserved. Nevertheless, these texts appear to share certain distinguishing characteristics:

1. The texts concern the figure of a great king and record either significant events or unusual experiences during his rule.
2. They are pseudepigraphical and purport to be genuine royal inscriptions.
3. They are written in the first person in the style of an autobiography.

4. Following the pattern of the royal inscription, they are constructed with a prologue, narrative, and epilogue.
5. The prologue begins with a self-presentation and may include information concerning the king's origin or the cause of the predicament he faces in the narrative section.
6. The narrative is devoted to a specific episode in the life of the king.
7. The epilogue contains a message for future kings expressed in the form of a blessing oracle or curse formula.
8. The texts are didactic in nature; there is a moral to be learned from the personal experiences of the king that can be acquired by reading his "stela."
9. They are written in a poetic or semipoetic narrative style.

The Pseudo-Autobiographies

The texts that belong to the genre of pseudo-autobiography have been most recently listed along with bibliographical information by Grayson.[4] By far the most important of these, at least from the standpoint of completeness, is the so-called Cuthean Legend of Naram-Sin. O. Gurney has been able to reconstruct parts of all 175 lines of the text using Neo-Assyrian fragments from Sultantepe and Kujunjik.[5] Actually, it is from this composition that most of the generalizations concerning the structure and characteristics of the genre are based, for the other examples, excluding the Sargon Legend,[6] are in such poor condition that they preserve only a few of the features listed above.

In the Legend of Naram-Sin, the characteristic structure is clearly visible. The prologue (lines 1-30) begins with a self-introduction by Naram-Sin who calls himself the son of Sargon.[7] Because the beginning of the text is so badly mutilated, it is not possible to determine what other information concerning Naram-Sin's origins or early career may have been included. At the end of this division is an enigmatic observation that the Sumerian hero Enmerkar incurred punishment for himself and his family, living and dead, through his failure to leave behind a *narû*-inscription of his reign.[8]

The main body of the text extends from line 31 to line 146 and focuses on the consequences of an invasion of

Naram-Sin's empire by warriors who, in some way, give the appearance of birds. Naram-Sin inquires of the gods as to what course to take; but, when the oracles are negative, he chooses to ignore them. Disaster ensues as three of his armies are annihilated by the enemy, and the land is laid waste. Confused, despondent, and filled with self-doubt, Naram-Sin questions his value as king. Finally, Ea intercedes for the tragic figure, and Naram-Sin emerges a victorious but chastened ruler.

The epilogue (lines 147-75) contains the familiar blessing oracles addressed to future kings. They are advised to read Naram-Sin's "stela" and bless him, learn from his experiences, and leave their own *narû* so that one day their posterity will bless them.

The Cuthean Legend was intended to convey a number of teachings. Perhaps, as Grayson has observed, the main theme is "that a king must heed the diviners or suffer dire consequences."[9] Still additional advice is given to the future king in the recommendation "to adopt a policy of passive resistance"[10] and in the belief that a pious ruler had to record his reign in a *narû*-inscription for the benefit of succeeding generations.

This discussion of the Naram-Sin Legend has been based on Neo-Assyrian copies of the text. That the composition is at least related to earlier sources is affirmed by the existence of a Hittite version and a late Old Babylonian copy dated by Finkelstein to the reign of Ammiṣaduqa.[11]

Another example of the pseudo-autobiography is the legend of a king of the Second Dynasty of Isin, who has tentatively been identified by Brinkman as Nebuchadnezzar I.[12] A single fragment of this text has survived from a Neo-Assyrian copy. The text was published by G. Smith (III *R* 38, no. 2) and edited most recently by H. Tadmor.[13] The fragment that is preserved comes from the narrative portion of the text; the prologue and the epilogue are lost. The style is autobiographical, and there are similarities to the situation faced by Naram-Sin in the Cuthean Legend. The narrative on the obverse reveals Babylon at the mercy of an Elamite enemy that has destroyed the cult centers and swept away the people of Sumer and Akkad. The reverse pictures a figure (no doubt the king) overwhelmed by fear, reduced to "speaking (to himself) in panic, trouble, and despair."[14] The hero sets out to meet the Elamites in battle but is forced to flee when his troops are stricken with a plague sent by Nergal. The king prays that Enlil's anger be assuaged and, while the text is destroyed at this point, it seems likely that the god relented enabling the king to defeat the enemy and free Babylonia from foreign domination.[15]

A comparison of the plot with that of the Naram-Sin Legend reveals the following correspondences:

1. Destruction of the land by a foreign invader.
2. Initial attempts to defeat the enemy fail because of divine displeasure.
3. The hero enters a period of despair, mourning, and self-doubt followed by the intercession of a deity.
4. The king triumphs over the enemy and rescues his people.

If this text does in fact belong to the class of pseudo-autobiography, it is important in dating the genre, for it would prove that *narû*-literature was still being composed as late as the end of the second millennium and possibly the early first millennium. Should Brinkman's proposed identification of Nebuchadnezzar I be correct, then the composition could not be earlier than the last quarter of the twelfth century (1124-1103). Tadmor is more cautious in admitting that any of the first four kings of the dynasty might be the ruler in question.[16] Even in this case one is left with a *terminus post quem* of the second half of the twelfth century.[17]

A third text that has been assigned to this genre on the basis of its incipit is an Old Babylonian Sargon composition. Regrettably, only the beginning of the text is preserved: "I (am) Sargon, beloved of Ištar, who roams the entire world."[18]

Also included in this category is the pseudo-autobiography of an unidentified king of the Kassite period. Fragments of the text (K 2599, K 3069, and K 10724) were published by Lambert in *CT* XLVI, nos. 49 and 50. The text has not been edited.

Listed by Grayson as possible pseudo-autobiographies are a Naram-Sin text[19] and the so-called "Sin of Sargon" text.[20] Should the latter be conclusively proved to be a *narû* composition, then we would have a case of a pseudo-autobiography written as late as the reign of Esarhaddon.[21]

The Sargon Legend and the Pseudo-autobiography

The Sargon Legend was identified by Güterbock as representative of *narû*-literature.[22] No one, to our knowledge, has ever challenged this classification. Let us examine the text in light of the characteristics of the genre outlined above.

1. The Legend, as far as it is preserved, is devoted to the figure of a king--Sargon, the founder of the Akkad dynasty.
2. The text is obviously pseudepigraphical and was written much later than the Old Akkadian period.[23]
3. The text, written in the first person, evinces a retrospective viewpoint.
4. Three divisions are discernible corresponding to a prologue, narrative, and epilogue.[24]
5. Sargon introduces himself in the beginning of the text and supplies information about his origins.
6. A section describes Sargon's accomplishments as king.
7. An address to future kings corresponds to the blessing-curse formula of the royal inscription.
8. The moral lesson, assuming one existed, is uncertain. It may simply be that to achieve greatness a king must emulate Sargon's accomplishments.
9. The Legend is written in semipoetic language. Parallelism is utilized but no regular meter.

According to the criteria that we have established, the Sargon Legend would appear to qualify as a pseudo-autobiography Nevertheless, there are grounds for questioning the traditional classification of the text. The portion of the first column that corresponds to the "narrative" exhibits some irregularities. It is extremely short--only nine lines--and can hardly be considered a true narrative in comparison with the other pseudo-autobiographies. Unlike the Legend of Naram-Sin and the Isin II text which contain lengthy narrative tales involving the king and an invading enemy, the Sargon Legend "narrative" is composed of independent statements of Sargon's chief exploits. In this respect the Sargon Legend more closely resembles the narrative section of a royal inscription than the historical tale featured in other examples of pseudo-autobiographies.

As we have indicated, the Birth Legend displays all the characteristics of a *narû*-literary text within its first 30 lines. Note, however, that the epilogue with its advice to future kings begins on line 22. The blessing-curse oracles logically conclude literary works such as royal inscriptions, "law codes,"[25] and the only complete pseudo-autobiography that has survived, the Cuthean Legend of Naram-Sin. Yet, if we assume a minimum of a single column text, it seems likely that the Legend[26] continued past the point where it is broken (line 32) for perhaps another 25 lines or so.[27] There are indications that the text extended from two to four columns, for Text B (K 4470) preserves part of a second column on its obverse (the first column duplicates K 3401). The width of K 4470 makes it unlikely that more than two columns were written on each face. Therefore, the possibility of a third and fourth column on the reverse belonging to the Sargon Legend must be considered. That column ii of Text B does in fact belong to the same work as column i, and that the Sargon Legend was therefore at least two columns long is supported by W. G. Lambert's observation (communicated to me orally) that Text D, which duplicates col. ii, was probably from the same scribal hand as Text A and may have come from the reverse of A (K 3401).

If the Legend is a pseudo-autobiography and our identification of prologue, narrative, and epilogue is essentially correct, then we are hard put to account for the contents of the major portion of the text that has not survived. Surely the epilogue did not extend 1 1/2 to 3 1/2 columns. In view of the estimated length of the composition, the question arises whether the Legend, in its entirety, is a text of the same species as the Cuthean Legend of Naram-Sin. Although the first 30 lines of the Sargon Legend may resemble the style of a pseudo-autobiography, the entire work may have been a composite text whose opening section took the form of a miniature *narû*.

The closest parallel to such a literary phenomenon may be the epilogue to the laws of Hammurabi. The "law codes," as Finkelstein has noted,[28] are really royal inscriptions of the apologia genre and are cast in the familiar three-part structure of the *narû*-inscription. In the case of the Hammurabi "Code," the epilogue seems to represent the *narû* form in microcosm, that is, it contains the basic features of a complete inscription. There is a self-introduction by the king, a list of exploits, advice to future kings, and the concluding blessing-curse oracles. Similarly, we cannot completely exclude the possibility that the first 30 lines of the Legend belong to a prologue that also resembled a *narû* in microcosm. If this is the case, the Legend may, in fact, be a pseudo-autobiography. The only complete model that we possess, however, does not reflect this pattern in either its prologue or epilogue.

In sum, difficulties exist with the traditional classification of the Legend as a pseudo-autobiography that have been previously overlooked. Until more of the missing portions of the text are recovered, it will not be possible to determine whether the Sargon Legend is a genuine pseudo-autobiography or something else. One may not rule out the possibility that the text, at least in its Neo-Assyrian form, was actually a pastiche, one section of which took the form of a pseudo-autobiography. This raises the question of an older Sargon *narû* on which lines 1-30 may have been based, as well as the nature of the sources underlying the text.

The Sargon Legend: Source Analysis

What is preserved of column i of the Sargon Legend is cast in a definite literary form, whose components have already been identified. There is a prologue (lines 1-12), a narrative (lines 13-21), and an epilogue (lines 22-30?). The same structure was observed in the Cuthean Legend.

An examination of the prologue reveals two distinct sections that most likely derive from independent sources of tradition. The first (1-4) is an introduction in the form of a statement of origins; the second (5-12) contains folk traditions about Sargon embedded in an infant-exposure tale. This section may be further broken down into three apparently unrelated units. The first of these (5-7) represents the basic exposure motif including the adoption of the infant; the second (8-11) involves Sargon's career as gardener; and the third (12) seems to reflect the theme of Ištar's desire for the gardener.

The main body of the text of the first column, which

corresponds to the narrative (13-21), consists of simple statements of Sargon's most noteworthy accomplishments. Each exploit is related in the briefest possible manner in an independent episode. There is no apparent chronological order.

The third major division, the epilogue (22-30?), resembles the form of a blessing oracle. After addressing whatever kings may arise after him (22), Sargon challenges them to repeat the same feats that had established his greatness (23-30).[29] The tablet is broken at this point; only traces of lines 31-32 are preserved, but they do not appear to repeat anything found earlier in the text. Whether the column continued with another part of the epilogue or moved on to a new narrative cannot be determined.

It may seem arbitrary to impose these particular divisions upon the contents of column i, but we hope to show that at least some of these units can be traced to independent traditions occurring in separate sources.

The introduction of the prologue gives a statement of Sargon's origins:

My mother was a high priestess,
My father I do not know
My paternal kin inhabit the mountain region
My city (of birth) is Azupirānu . . .[30]

This information is disclosed in a definite pattern that seems to be a formula.[31] We have already noted the existence of a similar formula in an early second millennium text written in Sumerian, the Sargon-Lugalzagesi Legend. The corresponding lines read:

At that time, Sargon whose city was . . .
Whose father was Laibum, whose mother was . . .[32]

In his discussion of this text, Güterbock suggests the existence of an earlier Sumerian composition upon which this passage is based. The hypothetical source, in his view, contained information about Sargon's origins and may have been a parallel to the Akkadian "Birth Legend."[33] That some ancient source existed with information about Sargon in language similar to both the Sargon Legend and the Scheil text seems likely. But an ancient Sumerian version of our text appears improbable for two reasons. Such a work would have to be extremely early--late Ur III or very early second millennium--to serve as source material for the Sargon-Lugalzagesi Legend, and pseudo-autobiographies are not attested before the late Old Babylonian period. Secondly, there is no proof that *narû*-literature was ever written in Sumerian. It is better, therefore, to posit a Sumerian composition of a literary type unrelated to the Sargon Legend that circulated around the turn of the second millennium. The relationship between the hypothetical text and the Birth Legend is conjectural. One might expect, however, an indirect descent through an Akkadian version of the aforementioned text or an Old Babylonian epic, perhaps even a Sargon *narû*, that had incorporated the relevant section.[34]

Lines 5-12 of the prologue involve folk traditions that grew up around the figure of Sargon. While it is risky to try to separate the exposed-hero tale from the association of Sargon with the gardening profession of his adoptive father, it is possible that two originally independent traditions have been merged. In the Sumerian King List, there is a statement that connects Sargon to date farming, "his . . . was a date grower."[35] Who this person was--his father, adoptive father, or someone else--is not clear.[36] What is significant is that the association with gardening is very old and must have arisen shortly after Sargon's death if not during his lifetime. The structure of the note resembles the formula found in the Scheil text, and one might look for its source in a Sumerian text of Sargon's origins such as the one Güterbock has postulated. Whether the original source also included an exposure tale is impossible to tell; the King List note is too short to give any indication. It would seem that the tradition of Sargon as gardener preceded the much more complex exposed-hero tale, and the latter was combined with it at a later date.[37]

We may have a vestige of another folktale in line 12, which concludes the prologue. This would have dealt with Sargon's relationship to Ištar. The goddess is known to have shown a sexual preference for gardeners.[38] She made overtures to Išullanu and Enkimdu and was ravished by Šukallituda, also a gardener. It is not impossible that a folktale existed, based on the pattern of these myths, connecting Sargon and Ištar during his career as gardener. Such a tale may have served to explain Sargon's rise from obscurity and the special attention he lavished on the Ištar cult as the consequence of a liaison that took place back in the days when he was a lowly gardener. This type of story may have circulated orally and never have been written down. Like the story of Išullanu referred to in Gilgameš VI, 64-78, it may have been lost except for the allusion in our Sargon text.

It has been observed that the narrative portion of column i is devoted to the celebration of Sargon's most important achievements. At least the Legend singles them out as such, since they are to stand as the criteria with which future kings are to measure their greatness. The feats of which Sargon boasts are recited in sparse detail. With the possible exception of lines 16-18, the exploits appear to be individual units of tradition strung together like beads on a string in no particular order. Where are we to look for the source of this material? On the surface these statements bear some resemblance to the historical omens of Sargon in their terseness but not in their content. The type of material involved would appear at home in a royal inscription or a chronicle. Yet, there is no correspondence between the extant copies of Sargon's inscriptions from Nippur and these traditions. Of course Tilmun is mentioned in Sargon's inscriptions, but there is no claim to have conquered it. Dêr is not spoken of at all nor is there any reference to cutting through mountains, governing mankind, or ruling for 55 years. A Sargon chronicle remains a possibility, although one consisting of traditions like these is unknown. Two chronicles containing Sargon material that have survived, the Chronicle of Early Kings and the Weidner Chronicle,[39] reveal no points of contact.[40] Whatever the nature of the source, the concise formulation of each statement would seem to indicate that the author of the Sargon Legend excerpted and reduced his material.

Column ii of the Legend is so poorly preserved that its plot cannot yet be determined. It describes real animals rather than mythological ones moving about in their natural habitat, the steppe. Assuming that column ii is part of the Sargon Legend, one can only guess at its theme; perhaps it is the prelude to an adventure story or a hunting motif. The solution to this problem must await the discovery of additional copies or fragments of the text. Whatever its nature, column ii does seem to represent a source unrelated to anything found in lines 1-30 of column i.

The Problem of Dating the Sargon Legend Text

In view of the popularity that the Sargon Legend has enjoyed, witnessed by the numerous translations that have appeared since 1872,[41] it is surprising that no one has seriously tackled the problem of establishing the date of composition of the text. One explanation for this may be that the text is preserved only in late copies and that there seems to be little, if any, internal evidence with which to assign a date.

Nevertheless, a consensus among scholars has developed that would ascribe a relatively early date of composition to the Legend, sometime within the first half of the second millennium or roughly, the Old Babylonian period. Few scholars, however, have bothered to offer arguments in support of this "assumption."

The problem of determining the date of composition is further complicated by the question of the literary classification of the text. If the Legend is indeed a pseudo-autobiography,[42] then one is faced with an extremely long period during which it might have been written, for compositions that have been identified as pseudo-autobiographies are attested as early as the Old Babylonian period and as late as the beginning of the Neo-Assyrian period.

It may in fact be impossible to establish with certainty the origins of the Sargon Legend based on the available evidence. The text is in fragmentary condition and a section with a colophon has not survived. The text also lacks any obvious grammatical, lexicographical, or philological feature that would allow a precise dating. Aside from its possible mention in two inventories of literary works from Kujunjik,[43] there are no known references to the Sargon Legend in cuneiform literature.

The copies whose fragments we possess are relatively late. Three fragments belonging to the Kujunjik collection are written in Neo-Assyrian script, and a fourth fragment written in Neo-Babylonian is probably even later. The question is: are these late copies of a text that had originated in a much earlier period, or are they the remnants of a late composition that may have been only loosely based on earlier sources?

In theory, the Legend might have been composed at any time following the reign of Sargon of Akkad down to the period of the Neo-Assyrian king Assurbanipal in whose archives manuscripts A, B, and D were presumably found. Now we have seen that the use of the royal epithet *šarru dannu* "strong king" (in line 1) is an anachronism in a text attributed to Sargon of Akkad, for the first occurrence is to be found in the eighth regnal year of Amar-Sin (2039) of the Third Dynasty of Ur and thus follows by 240 years the end of Sargon's rule.[44] Therefore, the ascription of the title to Sargon in this work proves that the Legend (at least in the form that we have it) was written after 2039 and establishes the *terminus post quem* for our text. The presence of copies in the library of Assurbanipal (668-627) provides a *terminus ante quem* of the mid-seventh century.[45]

For an Early Date

With the upper and lower limits now set, let us examine the arguments favoring an early date of composition.

1. The Old Babylonian period was one of great literary activity in Sumerian and Akkadian, and Sargon literature was both popular and abundant. As examples we may mention the Sargon-Lugalzagesi Legend first treated by Scheil, the Sargon epic edited by Nougayrol, the fragment of a Sargon *narû* edited by Clay, the Sargon epic published by van Dijk, and probably the *šar tamḫāri* epic as well.[46] A forerunner of the Sargon Legend would not be out of place in such company.
2. Many traditions preserved in the Sargon Legend are demonstrably old and are found in sources from the early second millennium. The traditions that Sargon ruled for 55 years and was associated with someone in the gardening profession are both preserved in the Sumerian King List. The special relationship that he enjoyed with the goddess Ištar is alluded to in the incipit of the Sargon text published by Clay. In addition, the details of Sargon's adoption follow closely the classical description of foundling adoption outlined in the lexical series *ana ittīšu*.[47] Of course the presence of old traditions in a late copy of a

literary text (i.e., the Legend) does not prove that the work is as old as the material it contains.

3. Texts preserving information on Sargon's origins may have been common during the early second millennium. The Sumerian text about Sargon and Lugalzagesi contains a section similar to the statement of Sargon's origins in the Legend. Güterbock speculates that an even older Sumerian composition circulated, which was devoted to the origins of the king of Agade and may have been parallel to the Legend. It was presumably upon this source that the Sargon-Lugalzagesi passage was based.
4. Jacobsen argues for the presence of epic-historical literature as early as the third millennium as the source material from which the historical notes of the King List derive. In particular, he points to the "narrative of the 'Birth Legend'" as the source of the reference to Sargon's connection to date growing.[48]
5. Perhaps the strongest support for an early date is the fact that literary texts written in the style of a pseudo-autobiography are attested in the first half of the second millennium, namely, the fragment of a Sargon composition published by Clay and the Old Babylonian version of the Legend of Naram-Sin.[49]

For a Late Date

The arguments supporting a late date of composition may be listed as follows:

1. In the Sargon Legend text (as far as it is preserved), there is nothing of a lexical, grammatical, or orthographical nature that need be early. There are no recognizable archaisms.[50] This is, of course, but an argument based on negative evidence and should be considered accordingly.
2. Literary compositions displaying the characteristics of *narû*-literature were also produced at a late date even perhaps as late as the beginning of the first millennium. The Isin II text, the *narû* of an unidentified king of the Kassite period, and possibly the "Sin of Sargon" text demonstrate not only that the genre was still in vogue but that heroes of the recent past were also considered worthy

as literary subjects. The presence of Neo-Assyrian copies of the Sargon Legend and the Legend of Naram-Sin prove that interest in this type of literature was considerable and stories about historic figures, even those from the distant past, were still very popular.

3. There are orthographic forms employed in the Legend which appear to be of Neo-Assyrian origin. The normal form of the animal name for "wild ass" is *serrēmu*. A variant in our text appears as *sír-ra-mu*,[51] an orthography that von Soden considers Neo-Assyrian.[52] The unusual spelling of the substantive *tiāmtu* "sea" *tiāmat* with the GEME sign is attested outside of the Legend in *Enūma Eliš* and in sources from the first millennium.[53] These forms do not prove that our text was composed during the first millennium but only that the copies are preserved in Neo-Assyrian orthography.

4. Three idiomatic expressions, which are found in the first column of the Legend, are attested only in the late Middle Assyrian or Neo-Assyrian periods. They provide the strongest available evidence that the Sargon Legend was composed in its present form at a much later date than previously thought.

An idiom compounded of *bêlu* and *šapāru* with the meaning "to take over and govern"[54] is first attested in the royal inscriptions of the Neo-Assyrian kings, Aššurnaṣirpal II (883-859), Sargon II (721-705), and Esarhaddon (680-669). The phrase may have arisen in an administrative context and seems to have been used as a formulaic expression in these inscriptions. Its occurrence in a "pseudo-royal inscription" of Sargon of Akkad would not be difficult to explain. The author of the Sargon Legend might well have borrowed elements from the royal inscriptions of his day in constructing an inscription for Sargon. While the root **špr* with the sense "to rule," "to command" is known in older sources, the idiom *bêlu* plus *šapāru* is not attested before the first millennium and seems to be a Neo-Assyrianism (at least in date).

The second idiom preserved in the Sargon Legend is based on the quadriliteral verb *nabalkutu* plus the noun *šadû*. The expression means "to cross mountains," literally "to jump over mountains." An examination of the occurrences of the idiom listed by von Soden's *AHw*[55] and by Heidel's study of the quadriliteral verb[56] indicates that the phrase was used commonly in Assyrian royal inscriptions attested first during the reign of Tiglath-Pileser I (1115-1077) and in the subsequent reigns of Middle and Neo-Assyrian rulers through Sargon II. One finds the idiom employed in another quite different literary form: incantation texts. All occurrences here are in late copies (first millennium). The presence of this idiom in our text would also seem to be an imitation of the style of later royal inscriptions. Assuming that the concept "to jump over mountains" was introduced into the formulary of royal inscriptions during the Middle Assyrian period, we would have a second indication of a late date of composition.[57]

A third phrase that may be of value in assigning a relatively late date of composition reflects the concept of cutting roads through mountainous terrain by the use of copper or bronze picks.[58] This must have been considered a significant undertaking, for it appears in the inscriptions of Tukulti-Ninurta I, Tiglath-Pileser I, Aššur-bel-kala, Aššurnaṣirpal II, Sargon II, and Sennacherib.[59]

Why Was the Text Written?

It might be useful to pause a moment to consider some questions related to the problem of dating the text. Why was the Sargon Legend written? What purpose does it serve? The answers to these questions would go a long way toward solving the problem of dating. The most obvious explanations are:

1. A scholar's interest in the traditions surrounding the figure of Sargon may have led to the composition of a new text based on old sources.
2. Sargon stories were popular; the Legend may have been written simply to satisfy an audience that delighted in such literature.
3. The Sargon Legend may have been inspired by the reign of a powerful and ambitious king whose own conquests evoked comparison with this prototype of Mesopotamian kingship.
4. The Legend may have been written when a new king arose who assumed the illustrious name of Sargon.

Uncovering the *Sitz im Leben* of the Sargon Legend appears as formidable a task as determining its date of origin. Perhaps, if more of the text were preserved including a section with a colophon, we might then be able to deal with these questions with greater confidence. Let us consider each possible "explanation" in our investigation of the origin of the text.

Neither the first nor second of these suggestions appears likely to help in establishing the date of composition, for interest in Sargon of Akkad existed throughout the second millennium and well into the first. Naturally, there were periods of greater literary activity than others, for example, the Old Babylonian period which saw the proliferation of numerous Sargon texts.[60] Yet, original works in the Sargon tradition were also composed during the first millennium.[61]

Considering the third possibility, a number of important kings of Assyria stand out as potential candidates. That we should look toward the northern kingdom as the point of origin of the Sargon Legend seems reasonable. In Assyria the memories of the Akkadian kings were particularly cherished for their prowess as conquerors and empire builders.[62] Two kings of Assyria went so far as to adopt the name of Sargon as their own, perhaps partly in hope of restoring his empire. It should be recalled that Sargon is presented in the Legend as the prototype for kingship, whose greatness derives from his important conquests. Also the Legend would seem to teach that whoever would aspire to the same glory as king must repeat those feats that had made Sargon famous.

Historically, Assyria expressed much more of an interest in "empire" than did her neighbor Babylonia,[63] and the measurement of greatness as revealed in col. i of the Legend fits well in an Assyrian setting. Another consideration concerns the idiomatic expressions that we have singled out for purposes of dating. Outside of the Legend, they are found in the royal inscriptions of Middle and Neo-Assyrian kings.

Therefore, after reflecting upon the correspondences in language between their royal inscriptions and the "pseudo-inscription" of Sargon as well as their own historical record, we may suggest the following kings as most likely to represent the type of ruler envisioned in our third possible explanation: from the Middle Assyrian period, Tukulti-Ninurta I (1244-1208); Tiglath-Pileser I (1115-1077); and Aššur-bel-kala (1074-1057); and from the Neo-Assyrian era, Aššurnaṣirpal II (883-839) and Sargon II (721-705).

Now we shall consider another interesting possibility, that the Sargon Birth Legend was composed during the reign of a king bearing the same name. But what might have prompted the production of a new Sargon text at such a time? A court poet, wishing to honor his sovereign, might have written the tale of the king's namesake for the celebration of a special occasion.[64] On the other hand, the text may have served a political or propagandistic function: to foster an illusion of legitimacy by identifying a usurper with the greatest king in Mesopotamian history whose own origins were questionable. Such a motive would also account for the adoption of the name of Sargon. Finally, the Legend may simply have arisen from a revival of interest in the ancient hero inspired by the appearance of a new "Sargon."

If we knew that the Legend originated under any of these circumstances, we would then be able to limit its date of composition to two periods separated by about a thousand years. Two kings of Assyria are known to have assumed the name *šarrukīn:* Sargon I, son of Ikunum,[65] and Sargon II, possibly a usurper, possibly a son of Tiglath-Pileser III, whose succession was irregular.[66] At first glance the reign of Sargon I would seem a favorable time for the production of a literary work devoted to Sargon of Akkad. The Akkad Dynasty left a strong impression on the Assyrians, who considered themselves their spiritual as well as physical descendants. The Akkadian kings had provided the first model for universal empire, a dream to which Assyria aspired from time to time throughout its history.[67] That interest in the heroes of the Akkad Dynasty was particularly strong in the Old Assyrian period is proved by the fact that two kings took the names of its greatest heroes, namely, Sargon I and his grandson Naram-Sin. The adoption of these names would seem to indicate a desire to reestablish the grandeur of the old days, for Sargon I, according to the Assyrian King List, was not a usurper but a legitimate successor to the throne.

Although very little information is available for the reign of Sargon I, some scholars believe the era marked a high point in the Old Assyrian period, recognized by later generations as a golden age.[68] It is possible that the years of Sargon I were on the whole peaceful and prosperous, so much so that S. Smith believes that Sargon II named himself after his

Old Assyrian ancestor.[69] Whatever his power and prestige, there is no evidence that Sargon I embarked on major campaigns of conquest or ruled over a large empire. This raises the question whether this type of Sargon literature would have been written during his reign. For in view of the challenge laid down in the epilogue for future kings to emulate his accomplishments, one would expect that the Old Assyrian king had done respectably well in matching his namesake. Otherwise, why would he commission a work against whose standards he failed to measure up.[70] Without additional information such as the royal inscriptions of Sargon I, we cannot arrive at a definite conclusion.

Another factor to be considered is how would the composition of the Legend fit what we know of the literary activity of the Old Assyrian period. The nineteenth century was an active period in which many texts were at least copied if not written in Sumerian. Whether Akkadian texts of this literary type were produced in Assyria at this time or even, for that matter, in Babylonia is not known. Although there is very little information on which to base an opinion, it would seem unlikely that the Sargon Legend originated during the reign of Sargon I.

What then is the likelihood that the Legend was composed as late at the eighth century during the era of Sargon II of Assyria? The origins of this Sargon are also in doubt; he has been taken as a usurper or a son of Tiglath-Pileser III. S. Smith tries to reconcile these opposing views by suggesting that the Assyrian may have been a scion of a "junior branch of the royal family" who ascended the throne under somewhat irregular circumstances.[71]

Adopting the name of Sargon would be a shrewd maneuver for someone in such a position, for it would encourage identification with Sargon of Akkad, another usurper, and thus lend credibility to the newcomer's regime. Also implicit in the name is the promise of the revival of the original Sargon's greatness and empire, a dream that must have stirred the hearts of many and muted potential opposition. The commissioning of a text like the Legend would serve both these aims. The Legend does emphasize the obscure origins of Sargon; nearly the entire prologue is devoted to his early "history." The specific image of the hero projected in the text is that of the model king, whose greatness derives from his role as conqueror: he conquered Tilmun; he captured (?) Dêr; he ruled "mankind" 55 years; he besieged the sea land (?) three times. This portrait of the ideal ruler who had challenged others to follow in his footsteps would flatter the later king who also enjoyed a fair degree of military success and wished to be considered a worthy successor.

A possible problem arises over when the Legend was likely to have been written under Sargon II. If its primary motive was to detract from the king's irregular succession, one would expect an early commissioning of the text. But in this case, the apparent correspondences between the feats enumerated in the Legend and those boasted by Sargon II in his still unwritten royal inscriptions should be coincidental.[72] If the Legend was composed for a special occasion such as the dedication of his own inscriptions, or if it grew out of a renewed interest in the king's namesake, a later date would be called for.

What are the apparent similarities between the Sargon Legend and the career of Sargon II that might suggest a possible connection?

1. In the Sargon Legend, one of the principal accomplishments that establishes Sargon's greatness is the conquest of Tilmun. As we have already indicated, the Nippur copies of Sargon's inscriptions do not support this contention, rather they claim merely that Tilmun and the lands to the south sent their ships to Agade. In his royal inscriptions, Sargon II boasts that Uperi, king of Tilmun, sent tribute to him upon hearing of his victories in Elam and the Persian Gulf region.[73] Why should the conquest of Tilmun be considered so significant in the Legend? Following the Larsa period, contacts between Tilmun and Mesopotamia became more and more restricted so that while some trade existed throughout the second millennium, it was extremely limited.[74] Prior to Sargon II's mention of Tilmun, the only known occurrence of Tilmun in Assyrian royal inscriptions comes during the reign of Tukulti-Ninurta I. Although this ruler ascribes to himself the grandiose title "King of Dilmun and Meluḫḫa,"[75] this

probably reflects no more than a vague awareness of Tilmun's ancient ties to Mesopotamia.[76] It is only with Sargon II that we have hard evidence of a resumption of diplomatic contacts with Tilmun. Whether the reference in the Legend reflects the return of Tilmun to the political sphere of the Assyrian empire as well as an ancient recollection of Sargon's dealings with the island remains a possibility that cannot be proved.[77] Interestingly, the tradition that Sargon conquered Tilmun is attested in a Neo-Assyrian text, the Geographical Treatise, which may have originated during the period of Sargon II.[78]

2. Sargon of Akkad, according to the Legend, went up to Dêr and presumably captured it. Sargon II claims to have won an important victory at Dêr over the Elamites and to have "(re)established the freedom of Dêr. . . ."[79]

3. There are similarities between the Sargon Legend and the royal inscriptions of Sargon II in language and style:
   i. Use of the idiom *bêlu* plus *šapāru*[80]
   ii. Use of the idiom *nabalkutu šadâ*[81]
   iii. The concept of using copper picks to build roads through rocky terrain[82]

   Of course these forms are also attested in the royal inscriptions of other Assyrian kings in the Middle and Neo-Assyrian periods.

4. In the Legend, Sargon is called "king of Agade," a city that he built and made into his capital. Following the tradition of founding one's own city, as had other Neo-Assyrian kings, Sargon II constructed Dūr Šarrukīn (Khorsabad) as his royal residence.

These then are the main factors in the argument for a date of composition between 721-705, the reign of Sargon II. Unfortunately, they do not in themselves prove the case. On the other hand, we cannot rule out the possibility despite the fact that it is extremely late and close to the *terminus ante quem* of the text.

If the Legend had been written during the reign of Sargon II, it would probably be a product of his later years. The most likely motive would be to glorify Sargon II by showing that he was a worthy successor to Sargon of Akkad. At the same time, this would help to explain the selective list of exploits attributed to the Akkadian king in the Legend, for at least some of these correspond to the actual experiences of Sargon II.

The Historical Value of the Sargon Legend

In this section we shall attempt to appraise the historical value of the traditions collected in the Sargon Legend. It is self-understood that the text was not composed for the purpose of recording history. Nevertheless, there are statements about Sargon's origins and exploits that purport to be factual. Each "statement" will be classified in the light of the best available evidence, the Old Babylonian copies of Sargon's royal inscriptions and the various traditions preserved in the Sargon Corpus.

Aspects of the Legend corroborated by other Sargon sources:

1. Use of the epithet *šar agade*^{ki} (cf. chap. II, col. i 1.3)[83]
2. Associated with Aqqi, the water drawer/gardener, and with date farming (cf. chap. II, col. i 8, 10.2, 11)[84]
3. Ruled 55 years (cf. chap. II, col. i 13)[85]
4. Took over (and) governed "mankind" (cf. chap. II, col. i 14)[86]
5. Besieged the sea land (?) three times (cf. chap. II, col. i 18)[87]
6. Conquered Tilmun (cf. chap. II, col. i 19)[88]
7. Captured? Dêr (cf. chap. II, col. i 20.2)[89]

Aspects of the Legend that are not corroborated by other sources:

1. Mother is a high priestess (cf. chap. II, col. i 2.1)[90]
2. Father is unknown (cf. chap. II, col. i 2.2)[91]
3. Paternal kin inhabit mountain region (cf. chap. II, (col. i 3.1)
4. City of birth is Azupirānu (cf. chap. II, col. i 4.1)[92]
5. Exposed-hero tale (cf. chap. VI, "The Sargon Legend and the Tale of the Birth of Sargon")[93]
6. Ištar's love for Sargon (cf. chap. II, col. i 12)[94]

Aspects of the Legend that are anachronistic:

1. Use of the epithet *šarru dannu* (cf. chap. II, col. i 1.2)
2. Cutting through mountains with metal picks (cf. chap. II, col. i 15; and the discussion of the idiom under the arguments *For a Late Date* [of composition] no. 4, and nn. 58-59)

One must be cautious in appraising the historical value of the Sargon Birth Legend for the text contains material that originated in very different spheres of interest.

Aside from the traditions that obviously derive from folklore or folk history, little can be dismissed out of hand. Much of the information about Sargon's life and career is based on ancient traditions attested in other sources. Whether these "ancient traditions" are literally true or not is of course another matter. There are claims such as the title "strong king" and the feat of cutting roads through mountains with metal tools which are expressed in language characteristic of a later age. While they seem unlikely to have been used in Sargon's own inscriptions, they accord, in a general way, with his image and presumed activities.

The most reliable information is imparted in the so-called narrative portion of the text. In particular, the conquest of Tilmun and possibly Dêr, as well as the length of Sargon's reign, may not be completely accurate, yet ultimately must rest on historical fact. For example, if Sargon had not actually stormed Tilmun, he must have exercised some influence over its sea trade.

Next in reliability is the brief section on Sargon's origins. These statements concerning his parentage and ethnic identity might represent vestigial memories of historical relationships that had been confused over the centuries. Consider the identification of his mother as an *ēntu*-priestess. We know that Enḫeduanna was a high priestess of Nanna at Ur, and it is not impossible that Sargon had contacts, official and personal, with a priestess of Ištar with whom he may have participated in the sacred marriage rite. Thus, the potential exists for later confusion over the identity of the priestess that he had actually known. At the bottom of the question of his paternity, whether the man's name was known to the tradition or not, is the basic awareness that his position in society was insignificant. The allusion to his paternal kin dwelling in the mountain region is probably no more than the acknowledgment of Sargon's Semitic background.

Of negligible value are the "facts" offered in the folk traditions of the prologue. The story of his exposure and subsequent rise to fame is all too characteristic of the way great heroes are treated in folklore. The narrative of the tale is filled with apparent fairy tale elements such as the city name "Spice Town" (Azupirānu) and the epithetic name of his gardener-father "I poured out" (Aqqi). His alleged affair with the goddess Ištar can be seen as a product of the special status he accorded her or possibly of a relationship to a priestess of Ištar.

The reference to Sargon's early career as gardener may reflect simply his humble origins or may have developed from his role in the sacred marriage since the king was sometimes identified as a gardener.[95] It is also possible that Sargon's identification as gardener arose from his association with the cult of Inanna (Ištar), for the goddess, whose name means "Lady of the Date Cluster," originally "belonged to the pantheon of orchardmen."[96]

To summarize, one has to be selective in evaluating the Sargon Legend in terms of the type of material considered, and while many of the statements that are offered as facts cannot be accepted at face value, they may derive in some way from actual circumstances.

Sargon and the Literary Tradition

With the possible exception of Gilgameš, Sargon of Akkad dominated the literary tradition of Mesopotamia as no other historical figure before or after. His life and career made so great an impression on the popular imagination that Sargon stories were recounted for nearly two thousand years, not only in Mesopotamia but in Anatolia and Egypt as well.[97] Sargon is remembered in tradition first as the great conqueror who built an empire that future kings would continually aspire to re-create. In the eyes of the tradition, Sargon was a heroic figure larger than life, yet subject to the same weaknesses that all men know. His successes were prodigious; his lapses were reportedly nearly ruinous to himself and his people.[98] Sargon's stature seems not to have diminished with the passage of time, although his image varies slightly depending on the period and the outlook of those who fashioned the literary sources.

Third Millennium

From the Old Babylonian copies of Sargon's royal inscriptions, we may gain an insight into the way Sargon wished to be seen. The immediate impression conveyed by these documents is pride in his military accomplishments. He depicts himself as a mighty conqueror, whose empire stretches from the upper to the lower sea.[99] He defeated the Sumerian city states in the south, destroying their walls. Sargon's total dominance is reflected in the formula "Enlil gave him no rival."[100] He portrays himself as the champion of the Semitic population by installing Akkadians as *ensi*'s.[101] Befitting his position, he was a man of wealth and generosity: "5400 men ate bread at his table."[102] Not solely a military man, Sargon was shrewd enough to use his power to economic advantage by securing a share of the lucrative Persian Gulf trade.[103] Finally, Sargon was a pious king, whose success was attributed to the gods. He pays homage to Enlil, Dagan, Ištar, and Ilaba[104] in his inscriptions. While some of the claims made by Sargon may be exaggerated, they are essentially realistic and within the realm of historical possibility.

A short note, included in the Sumerian King List, remembers Sargon as the founder of a new dynasty, the builder of the city Agade, and as one who had arisen from modest beginnings to rule as king for 56 years.

Second Millennium

During the Old Babylonian period, Sargon became the subject of epic literature. As a consequence, his figure is more remote and impersonal. Because of the fragmentary condition of the Sargon-Lugalzagesi Legend, we cannot be completely sure of the picture it draws of Sargon. The text is written in Sumerian and at least a portion of it was devoted to the story of Sargon's overthrow of the ruler of Uruk. One might expect a certain sympathy for Lugalzagesi in a Sumerian text, and it appears that Sargon is viewed as a brash rebel who has taken a woman belonging to Lugalzagesi, perhaps as a provocation.

The Sargon epic published by Nougayrol presents the hero in quite a different light. Here Sargon is depicted as a calm and reflective ruler who allows his advisors to state their arguments before he takes action. Once battle is joined Sargon overwhelms the foe. At the conclusion of the text, Sargon boasts of his previous victories and alternately of his harshness and his mercy.

"The King of Battle Epic" reveals a similar picture of Sargon. He is deliberative, listening to the arguments of the merchants and the soldiers. The king decides to undertake the campaign without concern for the hazardous route. When the city and its ruler, Nur-Dagan, are captured, Sargon first taunts his antagonist and then presumably spares him.[105]

First Millennium

The Chronicle of Early Kings and the Weidner Chronicle reflect different perceptions of the great king. Written from the perspective of the Esagila cult, the Weidner Chronicle considers Sargon an important historical figure, but one who was not superior, at least not morally, to those kings before and after him. Even though Sargon received kingship as a reward for his piety, he eventually sinned against Marduk from pride or arrogance and brought suffering upon himself and his land. Despite the sacrilege, the Chronicle of Early Kings and the Sargon Omens portray the hero in a much better light. Sargon appears as a mighty conqueror, campaigning successfully in the East and West. He is a figure without rival.

The first column of the Sargon Legend emphasizes our hero's rise from obscurity to the position of the greatest king of all time and prototype for rulers to come. The Legend shows that fairy tale elements had surrounded the figure of Sargon, particularly the period of his early years.

The Babylonian World Map portrays Sargon as a semimythical king, who was one of only three mortals to have visited the lands at the edge of the world. Finally, at all periods, the historical omens of Sargon are favorable. Apodoses mentioning Sargon portend success, prosperity, and military supremacy.[106]

The Second Column and the Sargon Legend

Progress has been disappointingly slow in the reading and interpretation of column ii. The reasons for this are (1) only a small portion of the column is preserved on Text B, and (2) there are no apparent points of contact between columns i and ii. Sargon is not mentioned at all in the extant narrative of the column. One wonders whether column ii is in fact part of the same composition as column i. In his treatment of the text, Güterbock admits that one cannot be certain that the narrative of column ii belongs to the story of Sargon.[107] But, at the same time, he raises the possibility of its connection with the traditions of fabulous animals and travels to unknown regions found in the World Map and *šar tamḫāri* epic.[108]

With the identification and publication of the new fragment (Text D), which overlaps B and preserves more of column ii, hopes seemed bright for achieving a breakthrough in our understanding of the Legend. Unfortunately, the reconstructed portion of the second column offers surprisingly little additional information with which to work.

Nevertheless, we may make some observations about Text D and the narrative of the second column. If D does indeed derive from the reverse of A (not a trace of which is preserved),[109] then the likelihood increases that the two columns belong to the same literary work. There is still nothing in column ii that appears to relate to the fragments of column i.[110]

The most interesting feature of column ii is the presence of wild animals. The animal names that can be read with some degree of confidence are the gazelle, the stag, the Qaṭă-bird, the wild ass, the onager, the wolf, and the lion. Less certain are the restored names of the *ḫūqu*-bird and the ewe.

While the significance of the narrative is obscure, the setting is clearly the prairie or steppe.[111] Some of the animals appear to be agitated, although the reason for their activity in unknown.[112] The action does not take place in a totally uninhabited region, for there are apparent references to the house of men (?) (*bīt amē*[*lūti?*]) and to a temple or temples (?) (*bīt* DINGIR[.MEŠ?]). One god is referred to in the narrative, Šamaš.

We cannot detect any indication of a relationship to the traditions of Sargon's travels to unexplored regions or of mythological animals. All the animals found in the reconstructed portion of column ii are real and indigenous to the steppe, an area for which one need look no further than northern Mesopotamia.

It seems likely that significant progress in understanding column ii and the Legend as a whole will not come before the discovery of new fragments or copies containing at least the lost portions of the first and second columns.[113]

NOTES

CHAPTER III

[1]H. G. Güterbock introduced the term "*narû*-Literatur" in "Die historische Tradition und ihre literarische Gestaltung bei Babyloniern und Hethitern bis 1200," *ZA* 42 (1934). See his discussion on pp. 19-21 and 62-86.

[2]Grayson and Lambert, "Akkadian Prophecies," *JCS* 18 (1964), p. 8.

[3]See Grayson's *Babylonian Historical-Literary Texts* (Toronto, 1975), pp. 7-9, and *Assyrian and Babylonian Chronicles*, TCS V (Locust Valley, 1975), pp. 2-3.

[4]Grayson, *BHLT*, p. 8.

[5]See Gurney's edition of the text in "The Sultantepe Tablets IV. The Cuthaean Legend of Naram-Sin," *Anatolian Studies* 5 (1955), pp. 93-113. Cf. M. Astour, "Ezekiel's Prophecy of Gog and the Cuthean Legend of Naram-Sin," *JBL* 95 (1976), pp. 567-79.

[6]And the Sargon Legend may not even be a text of the same genre as the Cuthean Legend; see the discussion below.

[7]Confusion over Naram-Sin's relationship to Sargon already existed in the Old Babylonian period. Cf. the Old Babylonian copy of a Naram-Sin epic concerning the revolt of Kiš (see chap. IV, *IV* 3).

[8]The impression given here is that a ruler was morally obligated to leave a record of his reign for the edification of future generations. In this text Naram-Sin seems to blame his errors on Enmerkar's failure to provide him with the proper guidance.

[9]Grayson, *BHLT*, p. 8.

[10]Gurney, "Cuthaean Legend of Naram-Sin," p. 96.

[11]See J. J. Finkelstein, "The So-Called 'Old Babylonian Kutha Legend,'" *JCS* 11 (1957), pp. 83-84. According to Finkelstein, the Old Babylonian version, which may have been twice as long as the Neo-Assyrian text, contained material that is not found in the younger text. This makes its exact relationship to the Neo-Assyrian version difficult to assess (p. 88). On the relationship between versions, cf. J. S. Cooper, "Symmetry and Repetition in Akkadian Narrative," *JAOS* 97 (1977), esp. pp. 510-12.

[12]Cf. Brinkman's reconstruction of the Elamite campaign(s) of Nebuchadnezzar I based, in part, on this text, in *A Political History of Post-Kassite Babylonia*, AnOr XLIII (Rome, 1968), pp. 105-6 and nn. 571, 575.

[13]H. Tadmor, "Historical Implications of the Correct Reading of Akkadian *dâku*," *JNES* 17 (1958), esp. pp. 137-39.

[14]Ibid., p. 139 r. 6.

[15]Ibid., p. 137.

[16]Ibid., p. 137; cf. Grayson, *BHLT*, p. 8, n. 11c.

[17]Because the fragment is from a Neo-Assyrian copy, we can establish the *terminus ante quem* as the seventh century.

[18]A. Clay edited the fragment and published a copy in *BRM* IV no. 4. It was identified as a *narû*-literary text by Güterbock ("Historische Tradition," p. 64 n. 3) and was listed as such by Grayson (*BHLT* p. 8 n. 11b and *ABC* p. 2 n. 14). Note, however, the resemblance of the incipit of the Sargon text to the opening lines of two compositions that are assigned to another subcategory of historical-literary texts known as "prophecies" or "apocalypses." Cf. the Šulgi Prophecy--"I (am) Šulgi, beloved of Enlil and Ninlil, the hero-god Šamaš has spoken to me" (see Borger, "Gott Marduk und Gott-König Šulgi als Propheten," *BiOr* 28 [1971], p. 14 I 1-3) and the Marduk Prophecy--"I (am) Marduk, the great lord, the traveler (?), the explorer, who roams the mountains" (ibid. p. 5 I 7-8). In view of the mutilated condition of the Sargon tablet, it may become necessary one day, should additional fragments come to light, to reconsider the literary classification of the text as a pseudo-autobiography and also, for that matter, the premise that prophecy and pseudo-autobiography are two distinct genres.

[19]Now published by Grayson and Sollberger in "L'insurrection générale contre Narām-Suen," *RA* 70 (1976), pp. 103-28, as text *L*; see esp. p. 106.

[20]See Tadmor's treatment of the text, "The 'Sin of Sargon,'" *Eretz Israel* 5 (1958), pp. 150-63, 93*. This is of course Sargon II.

[21]Ibid., p. 93* and p. 162.

[22]Güterbock, "Historische Tradition," p. 19.

[23]The question of the date of composition of the text will be discussed below.

[24]Note that the portion of col. i that conforms to the "epilogue" of *narû*-literature (lines 22-30?) does not contain an explicit blessing oracle or curse formula. There is, however, a challenge addressed to future kings, which implicitly promises the blessing of Sargon's greatness to any ruler who is able to repeat his achievements. Whether this section included an additional message, blessing oracle, or curse formula is unknown, for the text is mutilated after line 30.

[25]Cf. the epilogues of the Laws of Hammurabi (*ANET*[3] pp. 177-80); and the Laws of Lipit-Ištar (ibid. p. 160).

[26]As represented by Text A (K 3401 = col. i).

[27]A rough estimate based on the curve of the edge of the tablet. Perhaps a bit more than half of the original length of K 3401 is preserved.

[28]See J. J. Finkelstein, "Ammiṣaduqa's Edict and the Babylonian 'Law Codes,'" *JCS* 15 (1961), pp. 91-104, esp. p. 103.

[29]So that they may be blessed with equal fame and success? Or, should we look upon this as a message--to obtain greatness follow Sargon's example?

[30]Lines 2-4.

[31]Noun + possessive pronoun = X (predicate, predicate nominative).

[32]Lines 10-11; see Scheil, "Nouveaux renseignements sur Šarrukin," p. 176. Cf. chap. IV, *III* 6.

[33]Güterbock, "Historische Tradition," p. 38.

[34]We are assuming that the Sargon Legend, in its present form, is a relatively late composition which may have been based on older written sources. This problem will be discussed in detail below.

[35]Jacobsen, *The Sumerian King List*, p. 111 32.

[36]Cf. ibid., n. 238.

[37]The exposed-hero tale will be studied and its components analyzed in Chapter VI.

[38]See chap. II, commentary to the text, col. i 12.

[39]See King, *CCEBK* II, pp. 3-9; and most recently Grayson, *ABC*, pp. 152-54.

[40]Unless Nougayrol's restoration of line 21 to read [*ka*]-*zal-lu* is correct (*RA* 45 [1951],p. 172), in which case we would have an episode in common with the Chronicle of Early Kings (line 9) and the Sargon Omens (line 31). See my discussion of the restoration in the commentary to the text, chap. II col. i 21.

[41]See chap. I *Publication of the Text*.

[42]Assuming that the genre has been correctly identified and defined. Cf. n. 18. For some of the difficulties with the classification of the Sargon Legend as a pseudo-autobiography, see above *The Sargon Legend and the Pseudo-autobiography*.

[43]Cf. chap. IV, sub *III* 10.

[44]See the discussion of this problem in Chapter II, col. i 1.2.

[45]Both these points may be reduced slightly. Because the epithet originated in Sumerian (it replaced Sumerian n i t a k a l a - g a) and is not attested in its Akkadian version until the reign of the next king Šu-Sin (2037-2029), it is likely that the Legend was written after Šu-Sin and most probably is not a third millennium composition. One may also assume a date earlier than the end of Assurbanipal's reign to allow for circulation of the text, catalogue entries, and its spread to the south (the Neo-Babylonian practice tablet).

[46]These texts are listed as part of the Sargon Corpus in Chapter IV, *III*.

[47]Although the earliest copies are from Assyria in the late second millennium, the description of foundling adoption might well reflect ancient practice.

[48]Jacobsen, *The Sumerian King List*, pp. 145-47.

[49]See above n. 11. Despite discrepancies in length and content, the episode common to both the Neo-Assyrian and Old Babylonian versions of the text was written in the first person narrative style of a *narû*-literary text.

[50]Unless the restored form [*m*]*a-ti ti-amat* (lines 18, 28) represents as Malamat has suggested in *AS* XVI, p. 366, n. 9 an archaic *status constructus*. But, if that were the case, should we not expect an archaic form of the genitive or at least one that includes the proper case ending and mimation? Cf. chap. II, commentary to the text, col. i 18.1.

[51]See Text D line 8.

[52]See von Soden, *AHw* p. 1038, s.v. *serrēmu*.

[53]See chap. II, col. i 18.2.

[54]See my discussion of the idiom in Chapter II, the commentary, col. i 14.

[55]S.v. *nabalkutu(m)* II, pp. 694-96.

[56]A. Heidel, *The System of the Quadriliteral Verb in Akkadian*, AS XIII (Chicago, 1940).

[57]The idiom compounded of *nabalkutu* plus *šadû* is found in the royal inscriptions of the following Middle and Neo-Assyrian kings: Tiglath-Pileser I (1115-1077) *AKA* 36 72-73; *KAH* II, no. 75 11; Aššur-bel-kala (1074-1057) *AfO* 6 82 34; Adad-nirari II (911-891) *KAH* II, no. 84 31; Aššurnaṣirpal II (883-859) *MAOG* 6/1 12 26; *AKA* 230 14; Shalmaneser III (858-824) III *R* 7 ii 14; ibid. 8 31 40; *WO* 2 30 7; ibid. 222 132; *WO* 1 462 10; Šamši-Adad V (823-811) *AfO* 9 92 19.24; Sargon II (721-705) *TCL* III 8 29; ibid. 44 280; and in an inscription of the Neo-Babylonian king Nebuchadnezzar II (604-562) *CT* XXXVII 6 13. The idiom is also attested in these first millennium copies of incantation texts: *Maqlû* VI 118 201; ibid. 127 29; ibid. 138 47; *TuL* 142 21; *RA* 13 109 4; *ArOr* 17 204 18; and *BA* X, 68 14.

[58]See *CAD* Vol. A, pt. 1, p. 276 b under *akkullu*. This idiom occurs in the inscriptions of Tukulti-Ninurta I (1244-1208) *ITN* no. 16 44; ibid. no. 18 7; Tiglath-Pileser I (1115-1077) *AKA* 39 9; ibid. 65 67; Aššur-bel-kala (1074-1057) *KAH* II, no. 74 9; ibid. 75 10; Aššurnaṣirpal II (883-859) *AKA* 230 12; ibid. 322 77; ibid. 331 96; Shalmaneser III (858-824) III *R* 7 i 19; ibid. 8 ii 42; Sargon II (721-705) *TCL* III 6 24; ibid. 50 329; and Sennacherib (704-681) *OIP* II 124 42; ibid. 114 37.

[59]Cf. *CAH*³ Vol. I, pt. 2, pp. 738-39; H. Lewy interprets these references as an indication that the later kings of Assyria were aware of the challenges laid down in the Sargon Legend and were declaring their adherence to its principles. This, of course, assumes an early date of composition for the Legend. We would suggest the opposite, that the expressions alluded to above which are not attested before the late Middle Assyrian period, were probably taken from these royal inscriptions in the preparation of a pseudo-inscription for Sargon.

[60]See chap. IV, *III*.

[61]As an example, we cite the Geographical Treatise (VAT 8006), which is attested in a Neo-Assyrian copy from Assur. The text was discovered, according to Weidner, among remains from the period of the Sargonids (Sargon II to Sin-šar-iškun). Concerning the date of composition, Weidner states "Zwar haben wir kaum das Original dieser Kommentararbeit vor uns, es dürfte aber wohl in nicht viel früherer Zeit entstanden sein." (E. Weidner, "Das Reich Sargons von Akkad," *AfO* 16 [1952-53], p. 3; and cf. p. 1). Note that Grayson is also of the opinion that the text was either composed or largely reedited about the time of Sargon II (see A. K. Grayson, "The Empire of Sargon of Akkad," *AfO* 25 (1974-77), p. 57.

[62]Cf. *CAH*³ Vol. I, pt. 2, pp. 734-39.

[63]*CAH*³ Vol. I, pt. 2, p. 736.

[64]For example, at the dedication of the king's own inscriptions. Note that at least part of our text purports to be an inscription of Sargon of Akkad. If this were the case, we might expect to see some similarities between Sargon II's royal inscriptions and the Sargon Legend. There are in fact some correspondences in language and content which will be discussed presently.

[65]Cf. I. J. Gelb, "Two Assyrian King Lists," *JNES* 13 (1954), p. 212 31.

[66]See S. Smith's discussion of Sargon II's origins in *CAH*¹ Vol. III, pp. 44-45. Cf. E. Unger who argues that Sargon was a legitimate son and successor of Tiglath-Pileser III in *Sargon II von Assyrien, des Sohn Tiglath-pilesers III*, İstanbul Asarıatika Müzelerinesriyatı, IX (Istanbul, 1933), pp. 18-21.

[67]Cf. *CAH*³ Vol. I, pt. 2, p. 735.

[68]Ibid.; speaking of Sargon I, H. Lewy says, "This king's reign must have been remembered by posterity as the apogee of the Old Assyrian period representing an age of wealth and power for the country" (p. 761).

[69]See *CAH*[1] Vol. III, p. 46; cf. Lewy, of Sargon II, ". . . an ambitious young king chose the name Sargon the Younger in hopes of bringing back the golden age of his older namesakes" (*CAH*[3] Vol. I, pt. 2, p. 761).

[70]Such a text would only serve to embarrass the king by stressing his inadequacy.

[71]Cf. n. 66.

[72]It would also be difficult to explain why the exploits listed in the Legend were selected out of all of Sargon's achievements.

[73]See D. Luckenbill, *Ancient Records of Assyria and Babylonia*, Vol. II (Chicago, 1927), p. 21 41 (=Winckler, *Die Keilschrifttexte Sargons* [Leipzig, 1889], pp. 60-63, 369-71,and passim in the Annals).

[74]Cf. A. L. Oppenheim, "The Seafaring Merchants of Ur," *JAOS* 74 (1954), pp. 6-17, esp. p. 15.

[75]Luckenbill, *ARAB* I, p. 59 170 (=*KAH* II, no. 61 15). Cf. Weidner, "Reich Sargons von Akkad," p. 8 13.

[76]Cf. Oppenheim, "Seafaring Merchants of Ur," p. 16, who likens this reference to the "antiquarian reminiscence" of Esarhaddon's boast "king of kings of Telmun, Makkan, Meluḫḫa (K 2801:28f. = *BA* III, 287 ff.) at the end of his titulary."

[77]It would serve to show that Sargon II was following in the path of his illustrious namesake.

[78]Since, according to Weidner, the Geographical Treatise was found among remains dated to the period of the Sargonids and was probably composed not long before the date of this particular copy. Cf. n. 61.

[79]D. Luckenbill, *ARAB* II, p. 40 78 (=Winckler, *Keilschrifttexte Sargons* I, pp. 80-81 4).

[80]See Winckler, *Keilschrifttexte Sargons* I, pp. 38-40 236 7.

[81]See F. Thureau-Dangin, *Une relation de la huitième campagne de Sargon*, TCL III (Paris, 1912), p. 8 29, p. 44 280.

[82]Ibid., p. 6 24.

[83]The royal title *šar agade*[ki] appears in the Sumerian and Akkadian versions of the Nippur copies of Sargon's royal inscriptions. See Hirsch, "Inschriften der Könige von Agade," p. 34 b 1 2-3 and passim in the inscriptions and in the other Sargon sources.

[84]Sargon's connection with someone in the gardening profession is corroborated by an ancient tradition embedded in the King List (see Jacobsen, *Sumerian King List*, p. 111 31-32). Whether Sargon had ever engaged in date farming is unknown.

[85]The figure given as the length of Sargon's reign may be fairly accurate in terms of his entire career from the time that he emerged independent of Ur-Zababa until his death. The figure of 55 years rests on an ancient tradition preserved in the Sumerian King List.

[86]There are many references in Sargon literature to his success as conqueror and empire builder. For example, the Old Babylonian copies of the royal inscriptions claim an empire extending from the Mediterranean to the Persian Gulf (see Hirsch, "Inschriften der Könige von Agade," p. 36 7-10 and passim). Also cf. the Geographical Treatise which outlines the extent of Sargon's empire (Weidner, "Reich Sargons von Akkad," pp. 4-5).

[87]It is difficult to evaluate this tradition because of the mutilated condition of the text and the obscurity of the reference. For possible connections with other traditions, see the Geographical Treatise (ibid., p. 5 43-44); the Chronicle of Early Kings (*CCEBK* II, p. 4 3); and the Neo-Assyrian Omen version (ibid., p. 31 24). If the reference is to the Sea Land of southern Babylonia, then we have confirmation from the Old Babylonian inscriptions and the Geographical Treatise that the area was part of Sargon's empire, since he controlled the lands around the lower sea.

[88]This claim is supported by another tradition preserved in the Geographical Treatise "Tilmun, Makan, the lands beyond the lower sea . . . Sargon, the king of the world, conquered three times" (Weidner, "Reich Sargons von Akkad," p. 5 42-44). The Nippur inscriptions make a much more modest claim, namely, that ships from Tilmun, Makan, and Meluḫḫa docked at the quay of Agade (see Hirsch, "Inschriften der Könige von Agade," pp. 37-38 11-15). In this case of conflicting claims, it is fairly certain that the older source (the inscriptions) is more reliable. If Sargon had actually conquered Tilmun, he surely would have boasted of the deed in his royal inscriptions.

[89]If Nougayrol's restoration of ⌈*ka*⌉-*zal-lu ú-naq-qir-ma* is correct, which we think unlikely for reasons of space (cf. chap. II, col. i 21), then the tradition of the destruction of Kazallu should be listed here. References to this tradition are found in the Chronicle of Early Kings (*CCEBK* II, p. 5 9); the Omen versions (ibid., p. 33 31-32, p. 41 2-3); and perhaps the Old Babylonian Sargon epic published by Nougayrol (*RA* 45 ⌈1951⌉, p. 179, n. 2).

[90]The claim that Sargon's mother was an *ēntu*-priestess is not impossible, although it is not supported by any other tradition. The Sargon-Lugalzagesi Legend first published by Scheil (*RA* 13 [1916], pp. 175-79) might have established the antiquity of this assertion or else refuted it, for it too has a passage about Sargon's ancestry. This Sumerian composition gives the name of Sargon's father as Laibum and is about to identify his mother when the column is broken off. Whether the text gave a personal name or perhaps the title n i n - d i n g i r cannot be determined, and the answer must await the discovery of additional fragments or copies.

[91]This tradition is contradicted by the Sargon-Lugalzagesi Legend, which shows that early in the second millennium the father of Sargon was identified as Laibum. This is a Semitic name that Landsberger has explained as "one who is stricken with the *li'bu* sickness," (see Güterbock, "Historische Tradition," p. 37, n. 6). An attempt to account for the apparent contradiction as a misunderstanding of the name *la-'i-bu* → *la i-ši* and *ul i-di* has been dismissed by Güterbock (ibid., n. 2).

[92]The portion of the Sargon-Lugalzagesi text that preserved the name of Sargon's city is destroyed. Note that, in Güterbock's opinion, the available space does not permit the restoration of a name as long as Azupirānu.

[93]This account of the birth of Sargon is not corroborated in any other source except in the nonessential detail that Sargon was related to a date farmer.

[94]Of course references to Ištar of a nonsexual nature occur frequently in Sargon Literature, such as the Nippur inscriptions, the Old Babylonian Sargon *narû*, the Chronicle of Early Kings, and Sargon omens, etc.

[95]Cf. Hallo and van Dijk, *Exaltation of Inanna*, p. 6 ". . . 'gardener,' an epithet apparently applied to kings or their substitutes in the 'sacred marriage' of the New Years' Ritual. . . ."

[96]T. Jacobsen, *Toward the Image of Tammuz*, Harvard Semitic Series, XXI (Cambridge, 1970), p. 27.

[97]Fragments of a Hittite version of "the King of Battle Epic" have been found at Boğazköy. For a list of all relevant Sargon material from Boğazköy, see chap. IV, *VII*. The most important fragment of the Akkadian version of this text was discovered at El Amarna.

[98]A tradition preserved in the Chronicle of Early Kings, the Sargon Omens, and the Weidner Chronicle maintains that Sargon committed a sacrilege with respect to the city of Babylon and was punished with famine, revolt, and restlessness.

[99]Hirsch, "Inschriften der Könige von Agade," p. 36, col. ii 7-12 and passim.

[100] Ibid., p. 36, col. ii 4-6 and passim.

[101] Ibid., p. 36, col. ii 16-19 and passim.

[102] Ibid., p. 38, col. ii 41-44.

[103] Ibid., pp. 37-38, col. ii 11-16.

[104] On the reading of the divine name Ilaba, see J. J. M. Roberts, *The Earliest Semitic Pantheon* (Baltimore and London, 1972), p. 34 and p. 96 n. 238.

[105] This we infer from the World Map which states that Utnapištim, Sargon, and Nur-Dagan were the only mortals to venture to the remote *nagû*-regions (cf. chap. IV, *VI* 4).

[106] For a list of the apodoses of the individual Sargon omens, see chap. IV, *V* 1-28.

[107] Güterbock, "Historische Tradition," p. 64 "Es lässt sich weder mit Bestimmtheit sagen, dass diese Erzählung zur Geschichte Sargons gehört, noch sind die erhaltenen Tiernamen charakteristisch für eine märchenhafte oder entlegene Gegend."

[108] Ibid. "Immerhin darf an die Weltkarte und an den *šar tamḫāri* erinnert werden, die Sargon mit fernen, von seltenen Tieren belebten Gegenden in Beziehung bringen." Cf. chap. IV, *VI* 4 and III 5 for bibliographical material on the World Map and *šar tamḫāri*.

[109] See chap. II, n. 2.

[110] It is quite possible that the missing portion of column i provided the transition to the narrative found at the beginning of column ii.

[111] The words used in the text are *ṣēru* and *namû*. Cf. *CAD* Vol. Ṣ, p. 138 under *ṣēru* A 3; and *AHw* p. 771, s.v. *nawû(m)* I.

[112] Note such phrases as "the wild ass ran about, " "the Qaṭā-bird which was crying out," "of a swift (or galloping) onager," and cf. "the wolf did not escape."

[113] W. G. Lambert has called my attention to an unidentified fragment (K 6497) for consideration as possibly belonging to the Sargon Legend. The text was published by K. D. Macmillan in *BA* V/5, p. 691 as no. 44. (Cf. *CAD* Vol. Ṣ, p. 43 a, which suggests an identification with Gilgameš.) I am unable to see any connection with the Legend, but the possibility remains open.

CHAPTER IV

CLASSIFICATION OF LITERATURE CONCERNING SARGON

That Sargon of Akkad had achieved a preeminent position in Mesopotamian historical tradition is clear from the great amount of literature devoted to his exploits. When we assume that only a portion of this literature has survived, then the accounts of his figure must have been all the more imposing. Sargon traditions are reflected in a wide range of material including inscriptions, date names, historical-literary texts, omens,and miscellaneous documents. Literature about Sargon was written in Sumerian, Akkadian, Hittite, and perhaps Hurrian[1] over a span of more than fifteen hundred years, from the third millennium (original inscriptions) to the middle of the first millennium (the Babylonian World Map).

We offer now a sketch of the corpus of texts concerning Sargon.[2] The sources are arranged according to the following categories:

I. Inscriptions: original, copies, Sargon family inscriptions

II. Date Names

III. Historical-Literary Texts Featuring Sargon: chronicles, epics, other literary texts

IV. Historical-Literary Texts Mentioning Sargon: king lists, epics

V. Omens: collected, individual

VI. Miscellaneous Texts

VII. Boğazköy Texts: Hittite, Hurrian

I. Inscriptions

Original

1. Inscription on a fragment of a victory stele found at Susa. Three fragments are preserved depicting a battle scene, the detention of captives in a large net, and a figure (a deity?) seated on a throne. A cartouche bearing the legend *šar-ru*-GI LUGAL identifies the monument. The stele was treated by V. Scheil, "Inscription de *Šarru-ukîn*" in *MDP* X,

pp. 4-8, pl. 2, nos. 3-4 and E. Nassouhi, "La stèle de Sargon l'Ancien," *RA* 21 (1924), pp. 65-74, figs. 1 and 5. Cf. H. Hirsch, "Inschriften der Könige von Agade," p. 2, n. 6 (hereafter referred to as Hirsch) and A. Spycket, "Illustration d'un texte hépatoscopique concernant Sargon d'Agade (?)," *RA* 40 (1945-46), pp. 151-56.

2. Inscription on a fragment of a calcite vase which may be restored in part [*šar*]-*ru*-GI [LUG]AL [K]IŠ. The text was published by E. Sollberger in *UET* VIII, no. 10, pl. 2 (U. 17843 = BM 123122) and edited by W. Nagel and E. Strommenger, "Reichsakkadische Glyptic und Plastik im Rahmen der mesopotamisch-elamischen Geschichte," *Berliner Jahrbuch für Vor- und Frühgeschichte* 8 (1968), p. 172.[3]
3. A mutilated Akkadian inscription (from a macehead) ascribed to Sargon by C. J. Gadd on the basis of the reference to the conquest of Ur and Uruk. See *UET* I, no. 6 and Hirsch, p. 2 2.

Old Babylonian Copies from Nippur

A. Sumerian

1. A fragment of a copy of what may have been a Sargon inscription. Only a small portion of the closing curse formula is preserved. Cf. Hirsch b 3, p. 39.
2. A fragment of a Sumerian inscription listed by Hirsch as b 5 on p. 40. The mutilated text apparently mentioned Ilaba[4] and a weapon given to Sargon by Enlil.

B. Bilingual

1. An inscription in Sumerian and Akkadian copied from the pedestal of a statue that included notes on the figures who were presumably depicted: Sargon, Lugalzagesi, and Mes-e. The text appears as b 1 in Hirsch, pp. 34-37; cf. p. 2, n. 9. The inscription records the assault and destruction of Uruk, Ur, Eninmar, and Umma; the capture of Lugalzagesi; the subjugation of Elam and Mari; the appointment of Akkadians to governorships; and the rise of Sargon to absolute power (Enlil gave him no rival). The inscription ends with a standard curse formula and scribal note.

2. A bilingual inscription taken from a Sargon statue whose pedestal was not inscribed. See Hirsch b 2, pp. 37-39 and p. 3, n. 10. This text commemorates 34 victorious battles; the destruction of city walls as far as the sea (Persian Gulf); control of the sea trade--ships of Meluḫḫa, Makan, and Tilmun dock at the quay of Agade; and the acquisition of the upper lands including Mari, Jarmuti, and Ebla as far as the Cedar Forest and Silver Mountains. The inscription concludes with a scribal note identifying its source as a statue.

C. Akkadian

1. An inscription possibly copied from a Sargon statue. The text appears in Hirsch as b 4 on pp. 39-40; see also p. 3, n. 12. The inscription begins with the declaration that Ilaba is Sargon's (protective) deity. It recounts the conquest of Uruk, the capture of 50 e n s i 's and the king, and the defeat of Lagaš and Umma. The scribal note recording the source of the inscription is partially destroyed.
2. An inscription taken from the base of a Sargon statue. See Hirsch b 6, pp. 40-44 and p. 3, n. 14. This inscription is similar to the bilingual text B 1, recording the conquest of Uruk, Ur, Eninmar, Lagaš, and Umma; the capture of Lugalzagesi with fifty e n s i 's; the subjugation of Mari and Elam; the installation of Akkadian governors; and the unrivaled power of Sargon.
3. A poorly preserved Akkadian inscription copied from a Sargon monument on which had been inscribed a picture of Lugalzagesi with epigraph. Hirsch lists this as b 7 on pp. 44-45. For the interpretation of the Lugalzagesi reference as part of a Sargon monument rather than a copy of an original Lugalzagesi inscription, see W. Hallo, *Titles*, p. 28. The text contains a list of Sargon's epithets. It also describes the conquest of Uruk as Enlil's judgment, the purification of Nippur, and the unchallenged rule of Sargon. A scribal note separates the inscription from the Lugalzagesi note.
4. An inscription taken from a statue of Sargon. The text,

in fragmentary condition, appears as b 8 in Hirsch, pp. 45-46; cf. p. 4, n. 17. It retells in part the defeat of Uruk, and the capture of fifty e n s i's and the king. The curse formula concluding the inscription is similar to that in C 3.

5. An inscription from the base of a Sargon monument which included an extensive postscript on an Elamite campaign. Hirsch gives this text on pp. 46-47 as b 9. This inscription commemorates the conquest of Elam and Barahsi and concludes with a curse formula and source identification. A long note follows the actual inscription naming important cities and individuals encountered on the expedition.
6. A fragmentary inscription whose source is unknown. See Hirsch b 10, pp. 47-48 and n. 19 on p. 4. The little that remains of the text appears to attribute Sargon's success to the will of Enlil.
7. A poorly preserved inscription of the same type as C 1 and A 2. For Hirsch's treatment see b 11 on p. 48.
8. Almost totally destroyed, this Akkadian inscription does not seem to resemble any of the others. See Hirsch b 12, pp. 48-49 and n. 21 on p. 4. The text, broken at the beginning and the end, mentions rebellious cities.
9. A Sargon inscription with Lugalzagesi postscript that duplicates part of B 2. See Hirsch, p. 4, n. 22; the text is given on pp. 49-50. For the contents cf. B 2 column vi.
10. An inscription copied from a Sargon statue. The text, which is poorly preserved, appears as b 14 on pp. 50-51 in Hirsch.
11. A short inscription similar to C 5; cf. Hirsch b 15 on p. 51. This text recalls the conquest of Elam and Barahsi and concludes with a curse formula.
12. Part of an inscription copied from the base of a statue; the beginning is not preserved. It is similar to the second part of C 5. This inscription appears as b 16 in Hirsch, pp. 51-52. Cf. C 5 for contents.

Inscriptions of Sargon's Family

1. A Sumerian votive inscription of Ašlultum, the wife of Sargon, on a fragment of an alabaster object (see *YOS* I, no.

7, p. 7). Cf. Hirsch, p. 9 1 and n. 75. For a reading of the name as Tašlultum (ÁŠ = *tàš*), see Gelb *MAD* II p. 212, sub p. 93, n. 192.

2. An Akkadian inscription of Maništušu, the son of Sargon, from an Old Akkadian monument found at Susa. The inscription, which mentions Sargon in C col. xiii 25, was edited by V. Scheil, "Obélisque de Maništu-Irba" in *MDP* II, pp. 1-52, pl. 1-10. Cf. Hirsch, pp. 9 3 and 14-15 3.
3. A Sumerian inscription of Enḫeduanna, the daughter of Sargon and high priestess of Nanna, found on an alabaster disk at Ur (*UET* I, no. 23). Cf. Hirsch, p. 9 2 and n. 76; and E. Sollberger, *RA* 63 (1969), p. 180, n. 16, who restores the entire inscription based on an Old Babylonian copy published originally in *UET* I, no. 289.
4. An inscription in Sumerian of Dingir-igi-DU, servant of Enḫeduanna, from a lapis lazuli cylinder seal found at Ur. The text was published in *UET* I, no. 271. See Hirsch, p. 9 2b and nn. 79-80.
5. A Sumerian inscription of Kitušdug?, scribe of Enḫeduanna, from a cylinder seal excavated at Ur (*UE* II, pl. 191, U. 11684:3 = pl. 212, no. 309 = *UE* III, pl. 31, no. 537). Cf. Hirsch, p. 9 2c and n. 83.
6. A granite cylinder seal inscription of Adda, steward of Enḫeduanna, published in *UET* I, no. 272. Cf. Hirsch, p. 9 2a and n. 78.

II. Date Names

1. A Sumerian economic text containing a Sargon date name commemorating "the year when Sargon raided Elam." The text has been edited by A. Westenholz in *Early Cuneiform Texts in Jena* (Copenhagen, 1975), p. 53, no. 85 and pl. 3. An autograph copy was published by A. Pohl, *TMH* V 85 r. iv 1-3.
2. A Sumerian economic text containing a date name that commemorates "the year when Sargon raided Urua" (see Westenholz, *ECTJ*, pp. 89-90, no. 181 and pl. 6). Cf. Pohl, *TMH* V 181 r. 9-10.[5]
3. A Sumerian economic text containing a Sargon date name

commemorating "the year Sargon made a campaign against Simurrum" (see Westenholz, *ECTJ*, p. 76, no. 151 and pl. 21). Cf. Pohl, *TMH* V 151 r. 10-12.[6]

III. Historical-Literary Texts Featuring Sargon

Chronicles

1. The Weidner Chronicle (Assur 13955) also known as "the Chronicle of Esagila"[7] was first edited by H. G. Güterbock in "Historische Tradition," pp. 47-57 (treatment includes cuneiform copy and photo). In addition to the Neo-Assyrian copy, two Neo-Babylonian fragments exist duplicating part of the reverse of the text. See A. Boissier, "Fragment de chronique en caractères néo-babyloniens" in *Babyloniaca* 9 (1926), pp. 23-27; and A. Falkenstein, "Episch-literarischer Text" in *Literarische Keilschrifttexte aus Uruk* (Berlin, 1931), no. 41 (VAT 14515). Also note the emendations offered by Güterbock and Weidner in *AfO* 13 (1939-40), pp. 50-51. The Chronicle deals with Sargon in lines 13-19b while relating the reasons for the succession of dynasties that had ruled the land. The text imposes a certain interpretation on the historical traditions explaining the rise and fall of various figures as a function of their piety to Marduk and the cult of Esagila. Sargon's elevation from cupbearer of Ur-Zababa to king of the four quarters is understood as a reward for refusing to carry out his master's demands to reduce the fish offering of Esagila. By removing soil from the foundation pits of Babylon in order to build a new city opposite Agade, Sargon also sinned against Marduk. As punishment for this sacrilege, the god stirred revolt in Sargon's realm so that he found no rest.
2. The Chronicle of Early Kings (BM 26472) also known as "the Sargon--Naram-Sin Chronicle," preserves traditions about a number of early Babylonian rulers. The text is written in Neo-Babylonian script; its provenience is unknown. L. W. King published the first edition of the text in *CCEBK* II, pp. 3-14, 113-19.[8] The tablet begins with Sargon and devotes twenty-four lines to the founder of the dynasty of

Akkad. Most of the material relating to Sargon with the exception of lines 20-23 is paralleled in the historical omens of Sargon and Naram-Sin, of which two versions (a Neo-Assyrian and a Neo-Babylonian) exist.[9] The similarities between the Sargon traditions found in the Chronicle and those preserved in the omen versions are so great that some kind of genetic relationship must be assumed.[10] The Chronicle records Sargon's rise during the heavenly reign of Ištar (*palê ištar*); campaigns in the East (to the Persian Gulf) and the West (as far as the Mediterranean); the settlement of his court officials (*mārē ekallīšu*); the utter destruction of Kazalla; the suppression of a large scale revolt in his old age; the defeat in ambush of Subartu; the sacrilegious removal of soil from the *essû*-pits[11] of Babylon in order to build a replica of the city before Agade; and finally, the punishment imposed by Marduk for the sin--famine, revolt, and restlessness.

Epics

3. An Old Babylonian Sargon epic (AO 6702) dated by Nougayrol to the period of the First Dynasty of Babylon; its provenience is unknown. The poor condition of the text creates great difficulties in its interpretation. The tablet had preserved 123 lines of poetic narrative arranged in three and one-fourth columns. J. Nougayrol has treated the epic in "Un chef-d'oeuvre inédit de la littérature babylonienne," *RA* 45 (1951), pp. 169-80, pl. 1. Some improvements in the reading were suggested by von Soden in *OR* N.S. 26 (1957), pp. 319-20. The composition focuses on the undertaking of a campaign against a rebellious city[12] and the city's eventual destruction. At the beginning of the text, the commander of the army speaks first to the troops and then to the king (Sargon) urging action against the city. Next, the more cautious advice of the vizier is related. Finally, Sargon agrees and through some incident the city is captured seemingly without a direct assault. The destruction of the city effectively ends the rebellion. In the concluding section, Sargon enumerates his most memorable victories and

challenges future kings to follow in his footsteps.

4. An Old Babylonian Sargon epic (IM 52684 + IM 52305), which is, in some manner, related to the preceding Nougayrol text (see above). Although some passages seem to be parallel,[13] there are many differences. J. van Dijk has published an autograph copy of the text in "Textes du Musée de Baghdad," *Sumer* 13 (1957), pp. 99-105, pl. 16-19.[14] K. Hecker has referred to the epic in his *Untersuchungen zur akkadischen Epik*, AOATS VIII (Neukirchen-Vluyn, 1974), pp. 37-38, n. 10. There has been some suggestion that this text (and the Nougayrol work) is connected with *šar tamḫāri*, "the King of Battle Epic";[15] nevertheless, van Dijk could find no direct reference to *šar tamḫāri* in his text. At present the text is unedited.

5. "The King of Battle Epic" (*šar tamḫāri*) first known from a copy discovered at El Amarna by the *Deutsche Orient-Gesellschaft*. The script is the so-called Hittite style commonly employed at the Egyptian court. O. Schroeder published an autograph copy in *VS* XII, no. 193. Additional fragments of the composition have turned up at Assur, Kujunjik, Amarna, and Boğazköy.[16] The most recent treatment of the text appeared in A. F. Rainey's *El Amarna Tablets*, AOAT VIII (Neukirchen-Vluyn, 1970), no. 359, pp. 6-11. According to its colophon, the Amarna copy represents Tablet I of the composition. The text, which is poorly preserved, tells of a military expedition to Asia Minor undertaken by Sargon at the request of merchants suffering harassment from the king of Puršaḫanda (Nur-Dagan). The merchants persuade Sargon to make the campaign despite the warnings of his soldiers that the way is long and hazardous. After traversing mysterious regions, Sargon captures the city with little resistance. The tablet ends after a sojourn of three years with the army anxious to return home.

Other Literary Texts

6. A fragment from an Old Babylonian copy of a Sumerian literary text (AO 7673) which dealt, at least in part, with Sargon and Lugalzagesi. The text was published by

V. Scheil (transliteration, translation, and copy) as "Nouveaux renseignements sur Šarrukin d'après un texte sumérien," *RA* 13 (1916), pp. 175-79. A new autograph copy, prepared by de Genouillac, appeared in *TCL* XVI, p. 142 as no. 73. The most recent treatment remains Güterbock's in "Historische Tradition," pp. 37-38. According to Scheil and Güterbock,[17] the tablet had originally contained two columns on each face; the extant fragment, from a corner of the tablet, preserves parts of the first and fourth columns. Column i began by describing the decline of the dynasty of Kiš from prosperity to ruin (at the hands of Lugalzagesi of Uruk?). After its overthrow, Sargon was appointed by Enlil as the legitimate successor. Sargon's origins were then recounted in terms reminiscent of the opening lines of the Sargon Legend.[18] After a gap of two columns, the reverse tells of a woman of Lugalzagesi's taken by Sargon in marriage or concubinage, and the rude reception given Sargon's messenger at the court of Lugalzagesi. The rest of the text, which has not survived, must have continued with the story of the quarrel and its ultimate resolution.

7. A fragment of an Old Babylonian text in Sumerian described by de Genouillac as a hymn. Gelb classifies the text as a late Sargon legend (see *MAD* II, p. 194, no. 8). A cuneiform copy of the fragment appeared in de Genouillac's *Fouilles francaises de El'Akhymer premières recherches archéologiques à Kich*, Vol. II, (Paris, 1925), p. 37, pl. 11 C 55. The reverse ends with the words LUGAL *šar-ru-ki-in*.

8. The beginning of an Old Babylonian Sargon composition, thought to be a pseudo-autobiography.[19] Only the first few lines are preserved: "I (am) Sargon, beloved of Ištar, who roams the entire world." A transliteration, translation, and copy were published by A. Clay, *BRM* IV, no. 4, p. 11. Cf. Hirsch, nn. 46-47 on p. 6.

9. A Sargon text which resembles a pseudo-autobiography and is known as "the Sargon Legend" or "the Sargon Birth Legend." There are four manuscripts of the text, three are written

in Neo-Assyrian and one in Neo-Babylonian script. The composition most likely consisted of from two to four columns; about half of the first column is preserved and a much smaller portion of the second. The beginning of column i relates Sargon's origins and rise to power. L. W. King had published the most comprehensive treatment of the text in *CCEBK* II, pp. 87-94. A new edition of the Legend appears in Chapter II of this work; for a short history of the study of the Legend see Chapter I.

10. The existence of two additional Sargon compositions has been assumed on the basis of two incipits present in a catalogue of titles of literary works found among the Kujunjik collection.[20] The titles begin with the words LUGAL.GI.NA *šu-pu-u* "Sargon, the glorious" and LUGAL.GI.NA MAN *dan-nu* "Sargon, strong king."[21] This inventory list (Rm 618) was published by C. Bezold, *Catalogue of the Cuneiform Tablets in the Kouyunjik Collection*, Vol. IV (London, 1896), p. 1627, see lines 4 and 21. W. G. Lambert has recently published a similar catalogue (K 13684 + Sm 2137) in the *Kramer Anniversary Volume*, AOAT XXV (Neukirchen-Vluyn, 1976), pp. 313-18. Line 6' has the partially preserved incipit LUGAL.GI.NA *šu-pu-*[. . .], which Lambert suggests may be the Neo-Assyrian version of *šar tamḫāri*. He also identifies a second title LUGAL.GI.NA LUGAL̆[. . .] as the incipit of the Sargon Legend.

IV. Historical-Literary Texts Mentioning Sargon

King Lists

1. The Sumerian King List preserves an historical anecdote which identifies Sargon as the successor of Lugalzagesi (after kingship had passed from Uruk); the former cupbearer of Ur-Zababa; the founder of Agade; the adopted son? of a date farmer,[22] and ruler for fifty-six years. For a transliteration, translation, and commentary see T. Jacobsen, *The Sumerian King List*, AS XI (Chicago, 1939), pp. 110-11.

Epics

2. The Sumerian epic "the Curse of Agade," which, in its

introduction, relates how Sargon had received kingship from Enlil after the god had smitten Kiš and Uruk. The most recent edition of the text was published by A. Falkenstein, "Fluch über Agade," *ZA* 57 (1965), pp. 42-124.[23] Cf. Kramer's translation in *ANET*, pp. 646-51; Hirsch, p. 6 2, 24 b 1; and Güterbock, "Historische Tradition," pp. 24-37.

3. An Old Babylonian copy of a Naram-Sin epic which deals with the revolt of Kiš against the rule of Agade. In lines i 16-26, Sargon is identified as the father of Naram-Sin (he is in fact his grandfather), who had freed Kiš by removing the yoke of Uruk and to whom Kiš had sworn eternal friendship. The latest discussion of the epic is by A. K. Grayson and E. Sollberger, "L'insurrection générale contre Narām-Suen," *RA* 70 (1976), pp. 103-28. Cf. A. Boissier, "Inscription de Narâm-Sin," *RA* 16 (1919), pp. 157-64; and A. Poebel, "The 'Schachtelsatz' Construction of the Naram-Sin Text *RA* XVI (1919), pp. 157f." in *Miscellaneous Studies*, AS XIV (Chicago, 1947), pp. 23-42.

V. Omens

Collected Omens

1. The collected omens of Sargon and Naram-Sin were edited by L. W. King in *CCEBK* II, pp. 25-37, 40-44.[24] These liver omens are preserved in two versions: a Neo-Assyrian copy from Kujunjik (K 2130) and a Neo-Babylonian fragment (BM 67404) from Sippar. As far as the latter is preserved, it maintains the same order of material found in the Neo-Assyrian version as well as the same association of phenomenon with historical event. In both texts the omens are separated from each other by horizontal lines; however, the two copies differ in that the Neo-Babylonian, unlike the Neo-Assyrian version, divides the protases and the apodoses into individual boxes. From this fact King concluded that while the versions ultimately go back to a common ancestor they have different lines of descent.[25] The omens dealing with Sargon preserve the following traditions: the conquest of Elam; a campaign against the Amurru; the construction of a new Babylon near Agade[26]; Sargon's rise to power during the reign of Ištar; the conquest of the Land of the West; the expansion of the

palace; the destruction of Kazalla; the suppression of a revolt in his old age; and the defeat of Subartu.

Individual Omens[27]

1. A clay liver model from Mari (early Old Babylonian) inscribed *a-mu-ut* KIŠ^{ki} *sá! šar-ru-ki-in* "the Kiš omen of Sargon." The liver inscription was published by M. Rutten, "Trente-deux modèles de foie en argile provenant de Tell-Hariri (Mari)," *RA* 35 (1938), p. 53, no. 1, pl. 1; cf. Hirsch, p. 7 1 and nn. 56-57; Nougayrol, p. 12, no. 38; and Goetze, p. 255 sub 10.
2. An Old Babylonian liver omen from the Likhachev collection: *ǎ-mu-ut šar-rum-ki-in ša ek-le-tam i-iḫ-bu-tu-ma nu-ra-am i-mu-ru* "omen of Sargon who made an incursion during darkness and saw a luminous phenomenon."[28] W. Schileico published the omen in "Ein Omentext Sargons von Akkad und sein Nachklang bei römischen Dictern," *AfO* 5 (1928-29), pp. 215-16 8. Cf. Hirsch, p. 7 2; Nougayrol, p. 15, no. 55; and Goetze, p. 256, no. 12.
3. An Old Babylonian omen whose apodosis reads *a-mu-ut šar-ru-ki-in ša ma-ḫi-ra-am la-aš-šu-ú* "omen of Sargon who had no rival." The text appears in V. Scheil's, "Nouveaux présages tirés du foie," *RA* 27 (1930), p. 149 4. Cf. Hirsch, p. 7; Nougayrol, p. 16, no. 59; and Goetze, p. 255, no. 8.[29]
4. An Old Babylonian omen published by Scheil, ibid., p. 149 16-17: *a-mu-ut* [*šar-r*]*u-ki-in ša ek-le-tam il$_5$-li-ku-ma nu-ru-um ú-ṣi-aš-šu-um* "omen of Sargon who marched during darkness and to whom a luminous phenomenon appeared."[30]
5. A birth omen from the Old Babylonian version of *šumma izbu* whose apodosis is simply *a-mu-ut šar-ru-ki-in* "omen of Sargon." A. Goetze published it in *YOS* X, 56 iii 31-32; cf. Hirsch pp. 7-8; Goetze (*JCS* 1), p. 254, no. 2; and Leichty, p. 207 (50), 31-32.
6. An Old Babylonian liver omen; its apodosis is ^{giš}TUKUL (*kakki*)[31] *šar-ru-ki-in* "mark of Sargon." See *YOS* X, 31 i 1-4; cf. Hirsch, p. 8; and Goetze, p. 254, no. 3.
7. An Old Babylonian liver omen: ^{giš}TUKUL (*kakki*) *šar-ru*-GI "mark of Sargon," *YOS* X, 31 i 5-8; cf. Hirsch, p. 8 and

Goetze, p. 254, no. 4.

8. An Old Babylonian omen of Sargon: ^{giš}TUKUL *(kakki) šar-ru-*GI "mark of Sargon," *YOS* X, 31 iii 1-5; cf. Hirsch, p. 8; and Goetze, p. 255, no. 5.
9. An Old Babylonian omen: ^{giš}TUKUL *(kakki) šar-ru-ki-in* "mark of Sargon," *YOS* X, 31 x 4-7; cf. Hirsch, p. 8; and Goetze, p. 255, no. 6.
10. An Old Babylonian omen: ^{giš}TUKUL *(kakki) šar-ru-ki-in* "mark of Sargon," *YOS* X, 31 xiii 42-45; cf. Hirsch, p. 8; and Goetze, p. 255, no. 7.
11. An Old Babylonian liver omen: *a-mu-ut šar-ru-ki-in ša ki-ša-tam i-be-lu* "omen of Sargon who ruled the entire world," *YOS* X, 59 r. 7-9; cf. Hirsch, p. 8; and Goetze, p. 255, no. 9.[32]
12. An Old Babylonian liver omen whose apodosis reads [*a-m*]*u-ut šar-ru-ki-in ša ki-iš-*[*ša-tam*] [*i*]*-bi-*[*e*]*-lu* "omen of Sargon who ruled the entire world," *YOS* X, 13 5; cf. Hirsch, p. 8; and Goetze, p. 255, no. 10.
13. A Sargon omen from a Middle Babylonian text (BE 36404 = Photo Babylon 1554)[33] dated by Weidner to the middle Kassite period. The text is discussed but not edited by Weidner in "Keilschrifttexte aus Babylon," *AfO* 16 (1952-53), p. 74. The apodosis reads *amūt*[34] LUGAL.GI.NA "omen of Sargon"; cf. Hirsch, p. 8 sub 3.
14. A Middle Assyrian birth omen (VAT 10168) from the library of Tiglath-Pileser I at Assur: BÀ-*ut (amūt)* LUGAL-*ki-en* "omen of Sargon." A copy of the omen was published by E. Ebeling in *KAR* 152 r. 20; cf. Hirsch, p. 8 sub 3; Weidner, p. 231 c; and Nougayrol, p. 6, no. 3.
15. A Neo-Assyrian copy of a liver omen (Rm II, 112 9-10)[35]: BÀ-*ut (amūt)* LUGAL.GI.NA *šá* ERIN-*šú (ummānšu) ra-a-du i-si-ru-ma til-li-šú-nu ana a-ḫa-meš uš-pi-lu* "omen of Sargon whose troops a rainstorm immobilized [literally: hemmed in] with the result that they exchanged weapons among themselves."[36] The text appears in *CT* XX, pl. 2 r. 9 and passim. Cf. Hirsch, p. 8 sub 3; Weidner, p. 230 b; and Nougayrol, p. 8, no. 20.
16. From the series *šumma izbu*, a partially destroyed omen text (K 8265) published in *CT* XXVII, pl. 23 19, 23; the text

has LUGAL.GI.NA *šá kiš-šú-ta* x "Sargon who ruled all"; BÀ-*ut (amūt)* LUGAL.GI.NA "omen of Sargon"; and MU.MEŠ *(šanāt)* LUGAL.GI.[NA][37] "years of Sargon." Cf. Hirsch, p. 8 sub 3; and Leichty, p. 77, tablet V, 43, 44, and 47.

17. A Neo-Assyrian text (K 3843) which appears to be a late version of the Old Babylonian omens (see above, 2 and 4).[38] The apodosis reads *šá ina ek-le-ti* GIN *(illiku)* . . . "who marched into the darkness"; the text was published in *CT* XXX, pl. 9, 2-3. Cf. Hirsch's remarks, p. 8 sub 3; and Nougayrol, p. 17, no. 66.

18. An astrological omen concerning Sargon (K 2065:1f. and duplicates) whose apodosis reads: GEMÉ-*ut (amūt)* LUGAL.GI.NA LUGAL *(šar)* UB.DA.LIMMÚ.BA *(kibrāt erbetti) ina* MU.BI *(têrti šâti)* KUR *(mātāti)* DÙ.A.BI-*ši-na (kališina) be-lu*₄ "omen of Sargon, king of the four quarters, who in this sign was the ruler of all lands."[39]

19. An astrological omen of Sargon restored on the basis of K 2065:6 (only partially preserved) and duplicates (complete): GEMÉ-*ut (amūt)* LUGAL.GI.NA[40] *ša ina* UR.SAG.MEŠ-*šú (qurādīšu)* KUR ŠÚ-*tú be-lu*₄ "omen of Sargon, who with his warriors was the ruler of the world." Cf. the variant . . . *ša* UR.SAG.ME *(qurādī)* TUK-*ma (iršûma)* ŠÚ-[*tú be-lu*₄].[41]

20. A Neo-Assyrian commentary on the astrological series *Enūma Anu-Enlil* (K 4336): LUGAL *(šar) a-ga-dè*[ki]: LUGAL. GIN:GI:*ta-ra-ṣa* "king of Agade--Sargon."[42] See Weidner, "Die astrologische Serie Enûma Anu Enlil," *AfO* 14 (1941-44), pp. 172-95 Tf. VII, v. 1 3; cf. Hirsch, p. 8 sub 3; and Weidner (*MAOG* 4), p. 231 e.

21. A fragment of a Neo-Assyrian omen text (K 16302:3) which mentions Sargon: BÀ-*ut (amūt)* LUGAL.GI.NA "omen of Sargon." See L. W. King, *Catalogue of the Cuneiform Tablets in the Kouyunjik Collection, Supplement* (London, 1914), p. 211, no. 2834; cf. Nougayrol, p. 25, no. 106.

22. An omen from a Neo-Assyrian copy of *šumma izbu* (K 5929 and duplicates): BÀ-*ut (amūt)* LUGAL.GI.NA *šá* ŠÚ-*ti (kiššati)* [*i-be-lu*] "omen of Sargon who ruled the world." See Leichty, p. 81, tablet V, 87.

23. A Neo-Assyrian omen from the series *šumma izbu:* BAL *(palê)* [d]EN.LÍL *(enlil)* MU.MEŠ *(šanāt)* LUGAL.GI.NA *ina* KUR *(māti)*

ú-šab-šá TUR.BI *(tarbāṣu šū)* DAGAL *(irappiš)* KIMIN *(šumma)* LUGAL *(šarru) ina šal-ma-at* BAL-*šú (palêšu) ú-l*[*ab-bar*] "reign of Enlil, he will cause the years of Sargon in the land; that oxfold will increase; ditto (same protasis) the king will reign peacefully into his old age." See Leichty, p. 82, tablet V, 94.

24. A Sargon omen from the series *šumma izbu* (K 8265, dupl. BM 75209): ^{giš}TUKUL *(kakki)* LUGAL.GI.NA NUN *(rubû)* LUGAL *(šarrūt)* ŠÚ-*ti (kiššati)* DAB_5-*bat (iṣabbat)* "mark of Sargon; the prince will seize universal kingship"; see Leichty, p. 76, tablet V, 33.

25. An omen from *šumma izbu* whose apodosis reads ^{giš}TUKUL *(kakki)* LUGAL.GI.NA KUR *(māt)* NUN *(rubê)* DAGAL-*iš (irappiš)* ^{giš}TUKUL *(kakkū)* KALAG.ME-*ma (idanninūma)* LUGAL *(šarru)* GABA.RI *(māḫira)* NU *(ul)* TUK-*ši (iraššі)* "mark of Sargon, the land of the prince will expand, the weapons will be strong,and the king will have no opponent." See Leichty, p. 117, tablet IX, 32'.

26. A poorly preserved omen from the series *šumma izbu* (MLC 1875, 81-2-4, 505): ^{giš}TUKUL *(kakki)* LUGAL.GI.NA "mark of Sargon." The omen appears in Leichty, p. 117, tablet IX, 34'.

27. A Neo-Babylonian model of the face of Ḫuwawa (BM 116624). The apodosis of the omen is BÀ-*ut (amūt) šar-ru-ki-in ša* KUR-*ta (māta) i-be-lu* "omen of Sargon who ruled the world." S. Smith edited the omen in "The Face of Humbaba," *AAA* 11 (1924), pp. 107-14. Cf. Hirsch, p. 8 sub 3; Goetze, p. 255 sub 10 and n. 15; and Nougayrol, p. 7, no. 12. For a discussion of the omen and the previous attempts at dating it, see C. Wilcke, "Ḫuwawa/Ḫumbaba" in *RLA* IV (1975), pp. 534-35; and cf. M. Stol, *BiOr* 33 (1976), p. 150 b.

28. A Neo-Babylonian omen text from Uruk (AO 6452:65 = K 10599, v. 1): BÀ-*ut (amūt)* LUGAL.GI.NA *šá ana* ^{kur}*mar-ḫa-ši* GIN-*ma (illikuma)* ^{d}15 *(ištar) ina* MU-*iḫ (nipiḫ)* ZALAG-*šú (nūrīšu)* È *(ūṣi)* "omen of Sargon who marched to the land of Marḫaši and (to whom) Ištar appeared in a burst? of light."[43] Thureau-Dangin published the text in *TCL* VI 1 r. 1. Note the variant readings by Goetze, p. 256;

Nougayrol, p. 15, no. 54; Weidner, p. 230 a; and Hirsch, p. 8 sub 3, nn. 67-68.[44]

VI. Miscellaneous Texts

1. A fragmentary school boy's copy of a letter from Sargon to eight individuals preserved on an Old Babylonian practice tablet. An autograph copy was published by O. Gurney in *UET* VII, no. 73 i, 1-17; the text is as yet unedited.
2. A fragmentary copy of a Sargon letter addressed to a number of individuals whose names have not survived. The letter is preserved on the obverse of an Old Babylonian Proto-LÚ (*MSL* XII 25-73) and was used there as manuscript D_3 (ibid., p. 32). The Sargon letter (CBS 15217) was discovered by S. J. Lieberman who will also publish it.
3. A Neo-Assyrian copy of a geographical text (Assur 13955 eb = VAT 8006) which purports to sketch the limits of the empire of Sargon naming its important cities and geographical divisions. O. Schroeder published an autograph copy of the text in *KAV* as no. 92. A transliteration, translation, and commentary were offered by W. F. Albright in "A Babylonian Geographical Treatise on Sargon of Akkad's Empire," *JAOS* 45 (1925), pp. 193-245. The most recent edition is E. Weidner's "Das Reich Sargons von Akkad," *AfO* 16 (1952-53), pp. 1-24, Tf. I; cf. Hirsch, p. 7 9.[45]
4. The Babylonian World Map (BM 92687) found at Sippar. This Neo-Babylonian tablet contains a map of the world with Babylon at the center and has an accompanying text which described in some detail the seven *nagû*-districts that lay at the extremities of the world. The text of the World Map preserves the tradition that only three heroes had ever visited these mysterious regions--Utnapištim, Sargon, and Nur-Dagan. On the basis of the common motif of Sargon's travel to unknown lands and his association with Nur-Dagan, some scholars[46] have suggested a connection with the *šar tamḫāri* epic. Aside from an awareness of these traditions, we can detect no evidence to justify connecting the two works. A copy of the World Map was published by R. C. Thompson in *CT* XXII, pl. 48,

while a good photo of the obverse may be found in M. A. Beek's *Atlas of Mesopotamia* (London, 1962), p. 75, no. 155. The most recent transliteration and translation remains E. Unger's treatment in *Babylon* (Berlin and Leipzig, 1931), pp. 254-58. Cf. Hirsch, p. 7 6 and n. 49; and *ZA* 59 (1969), p. 325; and J. T. Milik, *The Books of Enoch* (Oxford, 1976) pp. 15-17. The text of the obverse, which is badly damaged, contains references to ruined gods and cities as well as animals, real and mythological, that were created by Marduk. The reverse is in worse condition than the obverse and gives a confusing picture of the distant *nagû*.[47]

VII. Boǧazköy Texts

1. A Hittite version of "the King of Battle Epic" which is based on a number of fragments found at Boǧazköy. The largest fragment, Bo. 68/28, was discovered in 1968;[48] H. G. Güterbock has edited the text in "Ein neues Bruckstuck der Sargon-Erzählung 'König der Schlacht,'" *MDOG* 101 (1969), pp. 14-26.[49] The other Hittite copies are published in *KBo* III, 9 (Bo. 2400); *KBo* III, 10 (Bo. 7333); *KBo* XII, 1 (110/t); and *KBo* XIII, 46 II (624/u). The Hittite version does not represent an exact translation of the Akkadian epic, but rather, as Güterbock says, a paraphrase. It does, however, establish certain important points that are unclear in the Amarna copy, namely, that Nur-Dagan was the ruler of the city Purušḫanda and that Sargon had been content to dwell in the city until his soldiers took action to compel their return home. Perhaps, the most interesting addition to the narrative supplied by the Hittite copies is the previously unknown role of dreams. Ištar appeared to Sargon in a dream promising him victory should he undertake the perilous expedition, while, at the same time, Enlil visited Nur-Dagan offering him false assurances of his success.
2. The Bilingual Annals of Hattušili I (ca. 1640) mention Sargon of Akkad. A copy of the Annals, which were written in Hittite and Akkadian, appeared in *KBo* X, 2 and

1 respectively. The relevant paragraphs of the text were treated by Güterbock in "Sargon of Akkad Mentioned by Hattušili I of Hatti," JCS 18 (1964), pp. 1-6[50] In his Annals, King Tabarna (Hattušili I) sees fit to compare his accomplishments to those of Sargon, noting that like Sargon before him, he too crossed the Mala river[51] and defeated the armies of Ḫaḫḫa. But, unlike his predecessor, he destroyed the city and burned it.

3. Sargon is referred to in two Hurrian texts from Boğazköy, *KUB* XXXI, 3 6, 10 and *KUB* XXVII, 38 iii 9, iv 23 (see n. 2 above).

NOTES

CHAPTER IV

[1]Sargon is at least mentioned in a Hurrian text *KUB* XXXI 3 6,10 (Bo. 4178); cf. also the fragments of a Hurrian text containing ritual and historical-mythological material, in which Sargon's name occurs *KUB* XXVII 38 iii 19, iv 23 (Bo. 2359 + Bo. 3054). For a discussion of these sources, see Güterbock, *ZA* 44 (1938), p. 81; and E. A. Speiser, *Introduction to Hurrian*, AASOR XX (New Haven, 1940-41), p. 5, n. 18.

[2]Much of this chapter is based on the fine survey of Sargon literature by H. Hirsch, "Die Inschriften der Könige von Agade," *AfO* 20 (1963), pp. 1-9.

[3]Nagel's suggestion that the inscription contained at least another line is not justified by Sollberger's copy which clearly shows the bottom edge of the inscription (after the line with KIŠ).

[4]Cf. chap. III, n. 104.

[5]For a simple variant of this date name, see Westenholz, *ECTJ*, p. 53, no. 86.

[6]Another date name assigned to Sargon by Westenholz is "the year when Mari was raided." See *ECTJ*, p. 50, no. 80.

[7]The title used by Labat in his translation of the text in *Les religions du Proche-Orient asiatique* (Paris, 1970), pp. 315-16. The most recent treatment is that of A. K. Grayson in his *Assyrian and Babylonian Chronicles*, TCS V (Locust Valley, 1975), pp. 43-45; 145-51.

[8]Includes cuneiform copy and photo (see frontispiece); for other references to this text see Hirsch, p. 5, n. 34. Cf. Grayson, *ABC*, pp. 45-49, 152-56.

[9]Also published by King in *CCEBK* II, pp. 25-39 (Neo-Assyrian version) and pp. 40-45 (Neo-Babylonian version).

[10]That the omen collections preceded the composition of the Chronicle and served as source material for the section dealing with Sargon and Naram-Sin has been argued by Grayson in *ABC*, pp. 45-47 and in "Divination and the Babylonian Chronicles," *La divination en Mésopotamie ancienne et dans les régions voisines* (Paris, 1966), esp. pp. 71-73. Cf. King, *CCEBK* I, p. 53 and chapter two; and Güterbock, "Historische Tradition," pp. 57-61.

[11]Line 18 reads: *e-pi-ir e-si-e šá* KÁ.DINGIR.RA[ki] *is-suḫ-ma*. Cf. the parallel passage in the Weidner Chronicle *ZA*

42 (1934), p. 52 r. 17; Güterbock *AfO* 13 (1939-40), p. 50; and in the Sargon Omens, *CCEBK* II, p. 28 9. For the latest interpretation of *essû* and the difficulties inherent in these passages, see H. Weiss, "Kish, Akkad and Agade" in *JAOS* 95 (1975), pp. 447-51. Weiss interprets *essû* as "clay rich watery depression" and uses the term in support of his localization of Agade as Išan al-Mizyad.

[12]Identified by Nougayrol as Kazallu (see *RA* 45 [1951], p. 179, n. 2). On Nougayrol's proposed reading of [*ka*]-*zal-lu û-naq-qir-ma* in the Sargon Legend, see our discussion in the commentary to the text (col. i, 21).

[13]For example, r. 1 3-15 = AO 6702 30-71 (*Sumer* 13, p. 66); and according to K. Hecker (*AOATS* VIII, p. 35), r. 2 9'-12' = AO 6702 57-64.

[14]Now republished by van Dijk in *TIM* IX as no. 48, pls. 36-39.

[15]Hecker, *AOATS* VIII, p. 37.

[16]A list of fragments and previous literature is given by Hirsch on p. 6, n. 48; cf. Rainey, *AOAT* VIII, pp. 6-7. The copies of *šar tamḫāri* from Boğazköy appear below under *VII. Boğazköy Texts*.

[17]See Scheil, "Nouveaux renseignements sur Šarrukin," p. 175; and Güterbock, "Historische Tradition," p. 37.

[18]For a discussion of the relationship between these texts, see chap. III, sub The Sargon Legend: Source Analysis; and cf. Güterbock, "Historische Tradition," p. 38.

[19]Cf. Grayson, *BHLT*, p. 8 n. 11b; and chap. III, n. 18.

[20]See Hirsch, "Inschriften der Könige von Agade," p. 7 10; and Güterbock, "Historische Tradition," p. 64, n. 3.

[21]Oddly neither Hirsch nor Güterbock has considered the possibility that the second title may refer to the Sargon Legend. The difference in orthography--MAN *dan-nu* in place of LUGAL *dan-nu*--does not rule out the identification. The publication of another catalogue by Lambert (see below) with LUGAL.GI.NA LUGAL[. . .] would seem to support the identification. Lambert also believes this is the Sargon Legend.

[22]See chap. II, p. 54.

[23]A new edition of the text by J. S. Cooper is now in preparation.

[24]A comparison of the omen versions along with a discussion of their relationship to the Chronicle appears in King, *CCEBK* I, Chapter III. See above *III* 2 and n. 10.

[25]King, *CCEBK* I, p. 30; cf. n. 24 above.

[26]For a recent treatment of the variant traditions found in the Chronicle of Early Kings, the Sargon Omens, and the Weidner Chronicle, see H. Weiss, "Kish, Akkad and Agade," pp. 447-48.

[27]The individual omens of Sargon have been treated in these earlier collections: E. Weidner, "Historisches Material in der babylonischen Omina-Literatur," *MAOG* 4 (1928), pp. 230-31 (hereafter designated as Weidner); A. Goetze, "Historical Allusions in Old Babylonian Omen Texts," *JCS* 1 (1947), pp. 253-56 (hereafter Goetze); J. Nougayrol, "Note sur la place des 'présages historiques' dans l'extispicine babylonienne," *Annuaire de l'École Pratique des Hautes Etudes* (1944-45), pp. 5-41 (hereafter Nougayrol); H. Hirsch, "Die Inschriften der Könige von Agade," *AfO* 20 (1963), pp. 7-8 (Hirsch); and E. Leichty, *The Omen Series summa izbu*, TCS IV (Locust Valley, 1970), passim (hereafter Leichty).

[28]*CAD* translates this omen in Vol. Ḫ, p. 12 under *ḫabātu* D.

[29]See now K. Riemschneider, "Ein altbabylonischer Gallenomentext," *ZA* 57 (1965), p. 128 4.

[30]Ibid. p. 130 16-17.

[31]For an interpretation of *kakku* as the name of the grapheme GAG used to describe a specific phenomenon present on various parts of the liver, see S. J. Lieberman, "The Names of the Cuneiform Graphemes in Old-Babylonian Akkadian," *Essays on the Ancient Near East in Memory of Jacob Joel Finkelstein*, ed. Maria De Jong Ellis, Memoirs of the Connecticut Academy of Arts and Sciences, XIX (Hamden, Connecticut, 1977), pp. 147-54, esp. p. 149.

[32]See *CAD* Vol. B, p. 199 under *bêlu* 1 a'.

[33]A late duplicate of this text from Uruk was published by A. Clay, *BRM* IV, 13. The copy, which dates from the Seleucid era, is apparently corrupt preserving BÀ-*ut (amūt)* LUGAL.IM.GI "omen of a usurper" against *amūt* LUGAL.GI.NA

"omen of Sargon" (see above). An interpretation of LUGAL.IM. GI as a variant emphasizing Sargon's role as usurper rather than some other type of error in transmission is also possible. Cf. C. Wilcke, "Ḫuwawa/Ḫumbaba," *RLA* IV (1975), pp. 534-35.

[34] Weidner does not indicate how *amūt* is written.

[35] This omen is duplicated in *CT* XX, pl. 8 (80-7-19), 157, v. 5-6; ibid. (K 3671), pl. 3 a 1-2; and *Bezold Catalogue, Supp.* (K 15100) 5ff.

[36] See *CAD* Vol. E, p. 334 under *esēru* B 2'.

[37] Cf. *CT* XXVII, pl. 22 r. 10 MU.MEŠ (*šanāt*) LUGAL.GI.NA *ina* KUR (*māti*) *ú-šab-ša* (K 3970).

[38] On the relationship, see Nougayrol, *RA* 38 (1941), p. 76; Hirsch, p. 8; and *CAD* Vol. I/J under *ikletu*, p. 60 a.

[39] See E. Reiner, "New Light on Some Historical Omens" in *Anatolian Studies Presented to Hans Gustav Güterbock on the Occasion of his 65th Birthday*, ed. K. Bittel (Istanbul, 1974), pp. 257-61, esp. pp. 258-59. An incomplete version of the omen (Rm 103) was published by C. Virolleaud, *L'astrologie chaldêene* Fasc. 3 (Paris, 1908), Ištar II 41-42. Cf. Hirsch, p. 8 sub 3; and Weidner, p. 231 d.

[40] According to Reiner, "New Light on Some Historical Omens," p. 259 n. 22, one of the duplicates preserves the spelling MAN.GI.NA. Until now this orthography was known only in reference to Sargon II. See the Appendix sub Sargon II 8.

[41] Reiner, ibid. p. 259.

[42] See chap. II, p. 32.

[43] See *CAD* Vol. Ḫ, p. 12 under *ḫabātu* D.

[44] Probably to be excluded from this list of Sargon omens are K 59:46 (Boissier, *Documents assyriens relatifs aux présages* [Paris, 1894], p. 228; cf. Nougayrol, p. 24, nos. 92 and 98); and K 209, K 12534 (Leichty, p. 87, no. 26; cf. *CAD* Vol. K, p. 161 1 c BALA LUGAL GI.NA).

[45] A Neo-Babylonian exemplar of the Sargon geography was discovered by A. K. Grayson who has now edited it in "The Empire of Sargon of Akkad," *AfO* 25 (1974-77), pp. 56-64.

[46]See K. Hecker, *Untersuchungen zur akkadischen Epik*, p. 37.

[47]We would suggest the following improvements in the reading of the text: obv. 9--restore *ib-nu-šu-[nu-ti]*. From the context and the grammar a plural pronoun suffix would seem to be indicated. The antecedent is *umāmu* "Getier," "beasts" often used as a collective, cf. *umām* EDIN *šadê kalašunu ina ālija . . . lu akṣur* "in my city (Calah) I put (into cages) every (kind of) beast of the open country and the mountains" (*AKA* 203 46 Asn.) *CAD* Vol. Ṣ, p. 144 2'. Rev. 21--collation confirms the restoration of the first part of the line as ⸢*a*⸣-*š*⸢*ar*⸣ GUD *qar-nu šak-nu* "where the horned bull lies."

[48]Another Hittite fragment of the epic (Bo. 3715), which duplicates Bo. 68/28, has recently been published in *KUB* XLVIII as no. 98.

[49]Güterbock's article presents a valuable review of the development of our knowledge of the epic both in its Akkadian and Hittite versions. Included are a transliteration, translation, commentary, and photo of the new Hittite fragment. Cf. P. Meriggi, "Die hethitischen Fragmente vom *šar tamḫâri*," *Innsbrucker Beiträge zur Kulturwissenschaft* Bd. XIV, Gedenkschrift für Wilhelm Brandenstein (Innsbruck, 1968), pp. 259-67. For a list of the Hittite fragments of *šar tamḫāri*, see now Grayson, *ABC* p. 57, n. 60.

[50]Cf. Goetze's review of the text in *JCS* 16 (1962), pp. 24-30.

[51]The Akkadian version has *Purattu* for the Euphrates.

CHAPTER V

THE SARGON LEGEND: LITERARY MOTIFS

The Infant-Exposure Motif

The first column of the Sargon Legend preserves an account of the hero's origins expressed in a literary form that has been recognized as an example of the Infant-Exposure Motif.[1] From the beginning of the study of the Akkadian text, attention has focused on the presence of the motif as well as the similarities to the story of the exposure of Moses in the second chapter of Exodus. In 1872, in the first published treatments of the Legend, George Smith and H. F. Talbot[2] already discussed the apparent connections. Smith wrote, "There is a striking parallel between some points in this story, and the account in Exodus ii, of the concealment of the infant Moses."[3] Talbot, likewise, pointed out the similarity between the two accounts in the construction of the vessel and the materials used. Furthermore, he was the first to recognize that the Sargon Legend belonged to a category of ancient stories relating the births of "other great lawgivers or founders of nations"[4] such as Romulus, Cyrus, and the god Dionysus.

The initial interest in the Sargon Legend, demonstrated by the numerous treatments that appeared during the last quarter of the nineteenth century,[5] rested, to a large degree, on the presence of the exposure motif and its correspondence to the biblical narrative. So impressed were scholars with this feature that they came to refer to the composition as "the Sargon Birth Legend,"[6] despite the fact that the exposure story occupies only a small portion of the extant text.

The motif of the infant cast away at birth has been applied to gods, kings, and culture heroes. The popularity of the theme, attested by numerous occurrences in the traditions of cultures, ancient and modern, is largely explained by an intrinsic curiosity in the origins of those who rise above the crowd to shape the lives and thought of the common man. What is more natural than to attribute to great individuals an unusual birth foreshadowing their future destiny? Such traditions, which exert a strong hold on the popular fancy, clearly belong to the realm of folklore and are frequently embellished with elements of the marvelous.

In dealing with material of this type, we shall follow the terminology and methodology developed by folklore scholarship for the classification, analysis, and interpretation of folk literature.[7] Thus, the term "motif," which we have repeatedly used, is understood as "the smallest element in a tale having a power to persist in tradition."[8] The motif of the future hero exposed in a boat or basket is familiar to scholars of folklore. In his *Motif-Index of Folk-Literature*, Stith Thompson lists this theme under the broad category of "Reversal of Fortune" as L 111.2.1.[9]

But how does one break down for analysis "the smallest element in a tale?" Will focusing on the motif profit our study of the Sargon exposure in relation to Exodus II and the other examples of infant exposure? Very little work has been done in the field of folklore studies below the level of the motif; rather, attention has been lavished on the analysis of a larger unit of tradition known as the "tale." A study of the Sargon Legend and the collection of folk material that appears below indicates that we are dealing not merely with a motif, but with a (tale) "type." A type is a complete tale made up of one or more motifs in a relatively fixed order and combination. A traditional tale has an independent existence and does not depend on any other tale for its meaning.[10] An index of tale types has been assembled by A. Aarne and S. Thompson under the title *The Types of the Folk-Tale*.[11] The type that concerns our study, however, is not represented in the Aarne-Thompson index.[12] This is not too surprising because, in general, folklorists have neglected the traditions of the peoples of the ancient Near East and the classical world in favor of the study of the European folktale. Thompson's *Motif-Index*, which attempts to be a representative collection of motifs of folk narratives from around the world, also fails to mention Sargon as an example of the exposed hero.[13]

While it may prove impossible to determine the origin of our tale type, one may arrive at a rough estimate of the age of the various occurrences by dating the sources in which they are preserved. On this basis, we can state that the tale of the hero cast away at birth is attested in written sources from the first half of the second millennium up to the present. The exposure tale of Sargon, as preserved in the Legend text, certainly ranks among the earliest versions.[14]

The rest of this chapter will be devoted to a collection of versions of the type. In Chapter VI, we shall undertake a componential analysis of the tale, a reconstruction of the hypothetical archetype, and a discussion of the Sargon account and its position vis-à-vis the biblical story of the birth of Moses.

The Tale of the Hero Who Was Exposed at Birth

Our list of versions of the tale of the hero who was exposed at birth is arranged according to the language of the written source in which it is found.[15] Furthermore, the languages are arranged according to language family: Semitic, Indo-European, and miscellaneous groups. An exception is made, however, in the case of (D.) Indian, for the large variety of languages and dialects indigenous to the subcontinent is more conveniently treated under a general cultural heading than under separate linguistic classifications. In addition, tales that presumably originated in an Indo-European dialect of India but are now preserved in a non-Indo-European language are included under the heading of Indian.

Within each language category, an attempt is made to arrange the sources according to their approximate chronological order. The tales are listed by the name(s) of the hero(es) when present. If the hero is unnamed or the name is not preserved, the tale is designated with a descriptive title that usually includes the names of the parents.

Because there is an enormous amount of folk tradition incorporating varying elements of the exposed-hero tale, it is virtually impossible to compile a "definitive list." Realizing that selection of versions is, in the end, subjective, we have tried to be guided by the following considerations:

1. Does the exposure tale involve infants rather than older children?
2. Does the version follow the pattern of the structure of the type as set forth below?[16]
3. Does the version belong to the exposed-hero tale or to some other tale type that has borrowed the exposure motif. Examples of such types are "the Slandered Queen" and "the Maiden Without Hands."[17]

List of Versions

A. Akkadian[18]

1. Sargon: The Sargon Birth Legend. (Thirteenth-Eighth centuries B.C.)
   An unidentified high priestess became pregnant despite the prohibition of her office against having children. Fearing the punishment for such an offence, the priestess concealed her condition, giving birth to a son in secrecy. In order to dispose of her "problem," while also offering her infant a chance for survival, she placed him inside a reed basket that she had made watertight with bitumen. The basket was abandoned on the river Euphrates and floated along until it reached a gardener named Aqqi, who lifted it out with his water bucket. Aqqi adopted the infant and later introduced him to the gardening profession. During his career as a gardener, Sargon formed a liaison with the goddess Ištar, resulting in his elevation to the throne and the establishment of his empire.

B. Hebrew

2. Moses: Exodus II. 1-10. (First millennium B.C.)[19]
   A Levite took to wife a daughter of the tribe of Levi. The woman conceived and gave birth to a son. She hid the infant for three months (because Pharaoh had decreed death for all Hebrew male children). When she could no longer conceal him, she took a basket of bulrushes, caulked it with pitch and bitumen, and placed the babe inside. The basket was set adrift by the river bank as the infant's sister watched to learn of his fate. The daughter of

Pharaoh, who was bathing at the river, caught sight of the basket and commanded her servants to fetch it. The princess opened it and discovered a beautiful Hebrew boy inside. Surmising the circumstances of his abandonment, she took pity on him and decided to keep him. The boy's sister approached to offer her services in locating a nurse for the child. In this way the child's natural mother was hired as his nurse. Later the child was brought to the princess, who raised him as her son. She named him "Moses" because "she had drawn him out of the waters."

3. Moses: Babylonian Talmud, Sotah 12a-13b. (Third-Fifth centuries A.D.)[20]

In response to Pharaoh's decree that all Hebrew male infants be slain, Amram, the greatest of his generation, divorced his wife in order to prevent conception. Soon all Hebrews had followed his example. But Amram was rebuked by his daughter over the injustice done to the potential female offspring by his decision. So Amram re-married Jochebed, who miraculously regained her youthful appearance and conceived. Jochebed experienced an unusual pregnancy free of pain or discomfort. As the infant Moses came into the world, the house was filled with his radiance. For three months the couple successfully concealed their son. When it was no longer possible to do so, the mother took an ark of bulrushes and caulked it with pitch on the outside and slime on the inside so that the infant would not smell the fetid odor. The ark was placed in the reeds by the bank of the river as the infant's sister stood watch. Soon Pharaoh's daughter came to the river to bathe and, spying the ark, commanded her servants to fetch it. When they refused, her hand miraculously lengthened allowing her to grasp the vessel. The princess was filled with compassion by the sight of the beautiful infant within and sent immediately for a nurse. After the infant had refused the Egyptian breast, Miriam, the boy's sister, drew near to offer to find a nurse from among the Hebrew women. Thus Jochebed was retained to suckle her own son. Shortly afterwards, Pharaoh ended the drowning of Hebrew male infants.

4. Joshua ben Nun: *Rab̲ Pe'alim* 12a. (Second millennium A.D.)[21]

A man and a woman lived in a district of Jerusalem. The man used to pray to God because his wife could not produce children. When the woman finally did conceive, the husband fasted and wept instead of rejoicing. Questioned about his behavior, he confided that he had been informed by heaven that his son would one day slay him. Therefore, knowing her husband to be a truthful man, the mother fashioned a little chest and sealed it with clay and pitch. She placed her newborn son within and cast it into the river. The Lord sent a great fish which swallowed up the chest with the infant inside. Now it happened that the king had prepared a feast for his nobles and that same fish had been caught for the occasion. When they cut the fish open, all were surprised to find a baby weeping. The king sent for a nurse for the foundling, who grew up in the palace. Years later the lad was appointed royal executioner. One day the father of young Joshua wronged the king and was sentenced to death. According to the law of the land, the wife, children, and property of the condemned went to the royal executioner. After Joshua had performed his duty, he approached the man's wife to have relations with her (unaware that she was his mother). But miraculously, milk began to flow from her breasts. Joshua was horrified and, believing her guilty of witchcraft, was about to slay her too when words sent by the spirit of her dead husband apprised them of their true relationship. After learning the story of his birth, Joshua made atonement for his father's execution. Since people remembered the episode of the fish, which in Aramaic is *nun*, Joshua came to be called "the son of Nun."

5. Abraham: Rabbi Elijah ha-Cohen from Smyrna, *Shevet Musar* chapter 52. (Eighteenth century A.D.)[22]

Terah, a prince in the household of King Nimrod, married Emtelai, the daugher of Karnabo. Now the king was a wicked man who did not recognize the true god and held himself up as a deity before his people. When Nimrod read in the stars that a child would be born who would put an end to his conceit, he sought the counsel of his wisemen. On their advice he caused to be built a great maternity house, where all females had to go to deliver. All male children were put to death, while female offspring were spared and given gifts. Meanwhile, the wife of Terah conceived and after three months her condition was apparent. Nevertheless, with the help of a miracle, she concealed her pregnancy from her husband. At the end of her term, Emtelai fled the city to a cave lying near a valley. There a child was born whose radiance illuminated the entire cave. Fearing for his safety and not wishing to witness his execution, she wrapped the boy in a blanket and abandoned him to providence. When the deserted infant cried, the angel Gabriel appeared to nourish him. Gabriel enabled milk to flow from the babe's little finger, so that he was able to nurse himself. After ten days Abraham could walk and talk. Soon he came to the recognition of the true God. In sorrow and guilt the mother returned for her abandoned child and found Abraham, whom she did not recognize. Chiding her for the exposure of her infant, Abraham finally revealed his identity and later on the knowledge of the true God.

C. Arabic

6. Nimrod: *Sīrat 'Antar* I 13. (Eighth-Twelfth centuries A.D.)[23]
Kena'an had a disturbing dream which was interpreted to mean that a son born to him and his wife Sulkha would one day cause his death. Soon afterwards, his wife conceived and gave birth to a boy. Because Kena'an wanted to slay the infant, his wife secretly delivered her child to a herdsman. When the herdsman's flock began to scatter at the sight of the ugly infant, the herder's wife threw him into the river. The waves carried him to shore, where he was suckled by a tigress (whence comes the name Nimrod, **nmr*). The lad grew up, became the leader of a band of thieves, and slew Kena'an one day without realizing his identity. Later he married Sulkha and became lord of the whole world.

D. Hittite

7. The Sons of the Queen of Kaneš: Boğazköy Archives. (Sixteenth century B.C.)[24]

The queen of Kaneš gave birth to thirty sons in one year. Ashamed of such an unusual birth, she filled a vessel with excrement, placed her children within, and abandoned them on the river. The river carried them to the sea by the land of Zalpuwa. There the gods rescued them from the sea and brought them up. Some years passed and the queen again gave birth, this time to thirty daughters. The girls, however, she raised herself. As her sons, now grown, were on their way to Neša, they stopped at a place called Tamarmara. There they engaged in conversation with the men of the city and revealed to them the extraordinary nature of their birth. The men of the city then told them that their queen of Kaneš had once delivered thirty daughters. Realizing that they had finally discovered the identity of their mother, the sons immediately set out for Neša. But the gods changed their appearance so that their mother did not recognize them. Consequently, the queen gave her daughters in marriage to her own sons. The boys, except for the youngest, did not recognize their sisters. The youngest warned the others that they should not commit so great a sin as sleeping with their sisters. (The text breaks off at this point.)

8. The Sun God and the Cow: Boğazköy Archives. (ca. Thirteenth century B.C.)[25]

While looking down from heaven, the sun god beheld a cow ravenously grazing in a meadow. He descended to earth to find out why she was consuming so much grass. After listening to her explanation, he impregnated her in a flash of light. Nine months passed and the animal gave birth to a human child, whose appearance so surprised and frightened her that she was about to kill her own offspring. Fortunately, the sun god intervened and chased the cow away. He then provided nourishment for the infant, who was bathed by the waters of a stream. The servant of the god was sent to place the child on a ledge overlooking another stream. There a fisherman spotted the infant near where he had earlier left his basket. Being without children of his own, he joyfully took up the foundling to return to his wife. As soon as the fisherman reached home, he shrewdly ordered his wife to withdraw to their bedroom and scream out as if in labor. After the wife had carried out the instructions, the neighbors, believing her about to give birth, brought many presents to the couple. (The end of the text is destroyed.)

E. Greek

9. Iamus: Pindar, *Olympian Ode* VI 25-55. (Fifth century B.C.)[26]

Pitane had a daughter Euadne by the god Poseidon. After attempting to conceal her pregnancy, Pitane sent her infant daughter to be raised by King Aepytus. The girl grew up and had an affair with Apollo that left her pregnant. Euadne also tried to keep her condition secret but was unsuccessful. Aepytus found out and sent to the oracle for instructions. Meanwhile Euadne gave birth to a son, whom she exposed on the ground among the rushes in the canebrake. Now the king returned and asked about the child born to his ward. His anger had been assuaged by the oracle which had informed him that the child, fathered by Apollo, was destined to become a great prophet of a great race. No one, however, knew that the infant had been exposed. By the will of the gods, the child survived, for two serpents had watched over him and fed him with honey. Because the boy had lain among the pansy flowers, his name became Iamus and he did in fact grow up to become a great prophet.

10. Oedipus: Sophocles, *Oedipus The King*. (Fifth century B.C.)[27]

Laius, the king of Thebes, was warned by an oracle that a son born to him and his queen Jocasta would grow up to slay his father and marry his mother. So when the child was born, Laius had the infant's legs bound together and exposed him to die on Mt. Cithaeron. But a shepherd found the babe and delivered him to another shepherd; he in turn took the infant to his master Polybus, the king of Corinth. Since Polybus was childless, he adopted the boy, who grew up unaware of his real identity. Later when he began to doubt his parentage, Oedipus inquired of the oracle and learned the terrible prophecy. Immediately he fled what he believed was his father's house. On his way, he met and slew his natural father Laius. After solving the riddle of the Sphinx, Oedipus was made king of Thebes and took the widowed queen Jocasta as his wife. When their true relationship was revealed, Oedipus blinded himself and Jocasta committed suicide.[28]

11. Cyrus: Herodotus, *The Histories* Book I, 107-22. (Fifth century B.C.)[29]

King Astyages, ruler of the Medes, had a daughter Mandane. One night the king dreamed that enough water flowed from his daughter to fill his city and overflow all of Asia. After summoning the Magi interpreters, Astyages was informed that a son to be born to Mandane would conquer Asia and do away with him. To forestall the prophecy, he decided to give his daughter not to a noble Median but to a Persian of lower social standing. After a year of marriage had passed, Astyages had a second dream in which a vine grew from the girl and covered Asia. Now the king sent for Mandane in order to slay her unborn child. When the child was born, the king commanded his steward Harpagus to take the infant home and kill him. Thinking it unwise to perform the deed himself, Harpagus sent for the royal cowherd and ordered him in the name of the king to slay the child. The herder returned home with the babe to find that his wife had just delivered a stillborn infant. The disconsolate woman urged her husband to keep the living child and expose the dead one in his place. The peasant agreed and placed the infant's body in Cyrus's casket.[30] Years passed as the child grew up in the home of his adoptive parents. One day after he had inflicted injuries on a nobleman's son during a game of "king," Cyrus was brought before his grandfather for punishment. Astyages recognized him and soon discovered the means of his escape. Convinced that the old prophecy had been fulfilled in the game of play-king, he allowed Cyrus to return to his real parents. Eventually, Cyrus lead a revolt that culminated in his elevation to the throne of Astyages.

12. Ion: Euripides, *Ion*. Athens (Fifth century B.C.)[31]

In a grotto near the Athenian acropolis, Apollo mated with Creusa, the daughter of King Erechtheus. The girl conceived and bore a son whom she abandoned in a basket in the same grotto. Creusa hoped that Apollo would not allow his own son to perish. Apollo sent Hermes to transport the infant to Delphi where he was left on the threshold. The next morning Pythia, the prophetess of the temple, discovered the foundling and decided to raise him herself. While the lad was growing up, Creusa was given in marriage to Xuthus, but the union produced no children. In order to solve their problem, the couple sought the counsel of the oracle. Thus Xuthus was advised that the first person he would meet after leaving the temple would be his son. As Xuthus rushed out, whom should he encounter but the cast-away son of Creusa. He immediately greeted the lad as his son, naming him Ion "walker." Suspecting that the youth was actually Xuthus' illegitimate son, Creusa refused to accept him and even tried to poison him. Fortunately, her plot failed and, as she was about to be slain by an angry Ion, Apollo intervened revealing the entire situation to Pythia. The prophetess then showed Creusa the basket in which Ion had been found. Creusa recognized her son and explained to him the circumstances of his birth. Later on Ion married the daughter of the king of the Aegialeans and inherited the throne. He also became king of Athens.

13. Dionysus: Euripides, *Bacchanals*. Athens (Fifth century B.C.)[32]

Semele, a mortal maid, was taken to wife by Zeus. Out of jealousy Hera tricked Semele into obtaining a binding request from Zeus. He was to appear before her in all his divine splendor. The god unhappily acceded to her demand, although he was aware of the tragic consequences. As he revealed his glory, Semele was consumed by the flashing lightning of his form. The god, however, snatched up the unborn child that she was carrying and implanted him in his thigh. When Dionysus was born, Zeus hid his son from Hera until he was grown. Later Dionysus traveled the earth distributing the gift of wine.[33]

14. Charisius and Pamphila: Menander, *The Arbitrants.* Athens (Fourth-Third centuries B.C.)[34]

    In the course of a festival celebration, Charisius raped Pamphila, the daughter of Smicrines. During the struggle, the girl got possession of his ring but failed to see her attacker clearly. Later on the couple met and married, unaware of their previous contact. When Pamphila found herself pregnant from her attacker, she decided to rid herself of the child. With the help of her nurse, she exposed the infant on Mt. Parnes. Certain birth tokens were left with the infant including the ring of his unknown father. A shepherd found the babe in a thicket and brought him home. Not wishing to raise the child himself, he gave him to a charcoalman whose wife had recently lost a baby. The charcoalman, learning of the existence of valuable birth gifts, demanded them from the shepherd as the right of the adoptive parent. He cited the example of Pelias and Neleus, exposed twins who were able to discover their true identities because they had retained their birth tokens. The dispute was brought to arbitration before a passing nobleman who happened to be Smicrines, the grandfather of the infant. Smicrines decided in favor of the charcoalman. Meanwhile, Charisius had separated from his wife following the disclosure of her abandonment of the child. When the charcoalman and his wife had to go to pay their taxes, a slave of Charisius saw the ring and in this way the identity of the child became known to the master. Eventually Charisius and Pamphila reconciled after learning the full story of the abandoned infant.

15. Semiramis: Diodorus, *Library of History* Book II 4.1-6.10. Rome (First century B.C.)[35]

    The Syrian goddess Derceto, whose cult was centered at Ashkalon, incurred the wrath of Aphrodite. Derceto was stricken with an uncontrollable desire for one of her votaries. This led to an affair that left the goddess pregnant. After giving birth to a daughter, Derceto was so humiliated that she slew her lover and exposed the infant in a desolate area. To punish herself she dove into a lake and was immediately transformed into a creature with the head of a woman and the body of a fish. The abandoned babe was warmed by the wings of doves. The birds also fed her with milk and bits of cheese stolen from local cowherds. After becoming aware of the pilfering, the herdsmen discovered the beautiful infant girl. They turned the child over to the royal cowherd Simmas, who adopted her because he was without children of his own. Simmas gave the girl the name Semiramis which is said to mean "doves." Years passed and Onnes, the governor of Syria and second in rank to the king, fell madly in love with the maiden. He married Semiramis and fathered two children. In the company of her husband, Semiramis began to demonstrate exceptional abilities such as the capture of a city during a military campaign. Unfortunately for Onnes, King Ninus fell in love with Semiramis and demanded that she be given to him. Placed in an impossible situation, Onnes committed suicide freeing his wife to marry the king and become queen of Assyria.

16. Telephus: Diodorus, *Library of History* Book IV 33.7-12. Rome (First century B.C.)[36]

Returning to Arcadia, Hercules stopped at the home of King Aleos. There he lay with the king's daughter Auge, impregnated her, and continued on his way. When Aleos discovered his daughter's condition, he refused to believe her explanation that Hercules had violated her. So the king commanded Nauplius to drown Auge at sea. During the journey to the coast, the girl gave birth to a boy in the vicinity of Mt. Parthenium and abandoned him there in the bushes. After they reached the sea, the servant of the king decided not to slay Auge and gave her instead to Teuthras, king of Mysia. Meanwhile, the herdsmen of Corythus had found the infant being nursed by a deer. They quickly brought him to their master, who adopted the foundling and named him Telephus after the episode with the deer. When Telephus had grown up, he set out to locate his mother on the advice of the Delphian oracle. He discovered her at the court of Teuthras in Mysia and there learned the circumstances of his birth. Since Teuthras was without male issue, he gave the lad his daughter in marriage and appointed him his successor.

17. Heracles (Hercules) Diodorus, *Library of History* Book IV 9.1-10.1. Rome (First century B.C.)[37]

Zeus, taking the form of Amphitryon, king of Thebes, lay with Alcmene, his queen. The lovemaking lasted a length of three normal nights in order to procreate a special child. Later Zeus announced to the assembly of gods that a child to be born that day would become the ruler of the descendants of Perseus. Out of jealousy, Hera, the divine wife of Zeus, conspired to delay the birth of Heracles so that another child would assume that destiny. When Alcmene had finally delivered her infant, she decided to expose him from fear of Hera. The child was abandoned in what became known as the field of Heracles. There Hera and Athena unwittingly came upon the babe, and Athena prevailed upon her companion to suckle the child. But the infant nursed with such force that Hera cast him to the ground in pain. Athena picked up the child and brought him to Alcmene to nurse and raise as an adopted son. Later Hera sent two serpents to kill the boy, but the youth strangled them. Consequently, the people of Argos named him Heracles because he had gained glory by the aid of Hera.

18. Cybele: Diodorus, *Library of History* Book III 58.1-3. Rome (First century B.C.)[38]

King Meïon ruled over Phrygia and Lydia. He married a woman named Dindyme and sired by her a female child. Not wishing to bring up a girl, he exposed her on a mountain named Cybelus. There leopards and other wild beasts nursed the infant until shepherdesses found her, took her up, and named her Cybele after the mountain. As the child grew, she excelled in beauty, virtue, and intelligence. Cybele was responsible for many inventions including the pipe, cymbals, and medical treatments for people and animals. She came to be called the Mother of the Mountain and the Mother Goddess.

19. Agathocles: Diodorus, *Library of History* Book XIX 2.2-7. Rome (First century B.C.)[39]
An exile from Rhegium named Carcinus settled in Therma and soon developed a relationship with a local woman. When the woman became pregnant, Carcinus began to suffer from disquieting dreams about the expected child. Therefore, he sent for clarification to the oracle at Delphi. In this manner he learned that the child was destined to bring misfortune upon Carthaginians and all of Sicily. Carcinus, fearing the prophecy, had the infant exposed in a public place to die and posted his agents nearby to watch. A few days passed, but the infant did not die. Meanwhile, the guards became negligent allowing the mother to steal the boy. She then entrusted her son to her brother's care. The lad named Agathocles grew up in the house of his uncle and developed into a strong, handsome youth. On the occasion of a festival celebrated at the home of the uncle, Carcinus took notice of the impressive qualities of Agathocles. Reminded of his own son, he began to grieve over the exposure of the babe. Realizing that he had had a change of heart, the wife revealed to Carcinus the secret of the boy's escape. Carcinus readily accepted the youth as his son, but still fearing the prophecy, he moved his family to Syracuse. Agathocles later became tyrant of Syracuse.

20. Moses: Josephus, *Jewish Antiquities* Book II 210-29. Rome (First century A.D.)[40]
On the basis of a prophecy that the Israelites would bring forth a deliverer who would humiliate Egypt, Pharaoh decreed the execution of all Hebrew male infants. Amarames, a Hebrew of noble birth, was informed in a dream that his pregnant wife Jochebed would bear the redeemer. After a miraculously easy delivery, the child was reared for three months. Fearing the wrath of Pharaoh and trusting in the Lord, Amarames decided to expose the infant. A basket of papyrus reed was fashioned into a cradle and then caulked with pitch. The child was placed inside, and the vessel was launched on the river.

The current carried the vessel along as Miriame, the boy's sister, watched from the shore. Now Pharaoh's daughter Thermutis happened to be by the river, saw the basket, and had it brought to her. Enchanted by the beautiful child found within, she decided to raise him as her own. She sent for a nurse to suckle the infant, but the babe refused to take the Egyptian breast. Miriame then drew near and offered to bring a kinswoman to serve as nurse. She returned with the boy's natural mother, who was entrusted with his care. When he was weaned, Thermutis adopted the boy as her son since she was childless. Because of the circumstances of his birth, the lad was named Mouses from *mou* "water" and *eses* "those who are saved."

21. Jesus: Luke I.26-II.21 (First century A.D.)[41]
An angel of God was sent to the Virgin Mary in Nazereth to announce that Mary would conceive a son of the Holy Spirit. The child would be named Jesus and was destined to inherit the throne of David. Joseph and his betrothed went up to Bethlehem for the purpose of a census as Mary was nearing the end of her term. Because there was no room for them in the inn, Mary gave birth in a barn, placing her infant son in a trough. Hearing of the birth, local shepherds sought out the child and found him in the manger surrounded by Joseph and Mary.

22. Romulus and Remus: Plutarch, *The Lives* Romulus III.1-IX.1. (First-Second centuries A.D.)[42]
Two brothers, Numitor and Amulius, descendants of Aeneas, were in the line of succession to the throne of Alba. Through cunning Amulius took possession of the land and its wealth. He shrewdly appointed his niece a vestal priestess so that she would bear no future rival. Despite the rules of her office, she was soon with child by Mars. Amulius placed her in solitary confinement, where she gave birth to extremely beautiful twin boys. Perceiving the potential danger, the uncle ordered a servant to dispose of the children. The servant placed the twins in a trough and headed for the river. Since the river was swollen at that time, he abandoned the trough by the river

bank. The flood waters lifted up the vessel and carried it to a spot called Kermalus, where a wolf and a woodpecker nursed Romulus and Remus. Finally, a swineherd discovered the infants and brought them home. He and his wife raised the foundlings, providing them with an education suitable to those of noble birth. One day Remus, who had gotten into a scrape, was brought before Numitor. From this chance encounter with his grandfather, he learned the secret of his birth. The swineherd then informed Romulus of the same facts and urged him to go to the aid of his brother. Eventually, the twins led a revolt that resulted in the death of Amulius. The heroes later founded a city (Rome), which Romulus ruled after slaying Remus.

23. Romulus and Remus: Plutarch, *The Lives* Romulus II.3-6. (First-Second centuries A.D.)[43]

The cruel ruler of Alba, King Tarchetius, was plagued by an apparition of a phallus that appeared over his hearth for many days. In Tuscany, an oracle advised the king to offer a virgin to the spirit and that she would bear a son who would become famous for his strength and valor. So the king ordered one of his daughters to comply. But, not fully appreciating the opportunity, the princess sent her maidservant in her place. When the king learned of her disobedience, he commanded that both females be imprisoned and executed. Fortunately, the goddess Hestia intervened forbidding Tarchetius to carry out the sentence. But the king decreed that they remain in jail until they completed sewing a certain piece of cloth. Secretly, Tarchetius sent his servants each night to undo the day's work. In prison the maidservant gave birth to handsome twin sons, whom the king ordered to be cast away. A servant of the king brought the infants to the bank of the river and abandoned them there. But a she-wolf came to nurse them, while birds brought crumbs to nourish them. A cowherd eventually found the twins and raised them. Upon reaching maturity, the heroes slew Tarchetius.

24. Perseus: Apollodorus, *The Library* Book II iv 1-4. (First-Second centuries A.D.)[44]

Being without male issue, King Acrisius consulted an oracle in hopes of obtaining a son. In this way he was warned that his daughter Danae would bear a son destined to slay him. The king was greatly troubled and had Danae imprisoned in a specially built subterranean cave. There he and his twin brother Proeteus guarded her. Now Zeus, it is said, had intercourse with the girl in the form of a golden stream that poured through the roof into her lap. Acrisius, learning that his daughter had become pregnant, refused to believe that Zeus was responsible. Therefore, he placed mother and child in a chest and cast it into the sea. The chest washed ashore on Seriphus where a fisherman named Dictys took up the infant and raised him. Later the king of the island fell in love with the beautiful Danae, but his advances were thwarted by the now-grown Perseus. So the king conceived a plot to be rid of the youth by sending him off on a seemingly impossible task. Nevertheless, Perseus succeeded in his mission to slay the Gorgon Medusa and before returning home he saved the life of Andromeda whom he then married. Back on Seriphus he displayed the Gorgon's head at court turning the king and his retinue into stone. Soon afterwards, while competing in an athletic contest sponsored by the king of Larissa, Perseus threw a quoit that accidentally struck and killed Acrisius. Not wishing to take over the rule of Argos under these circumstances, he exchanged his grandfather's kingdom for the realm of Tiryns.

25. Amphion and Zethus: Apollodorus, *The Library* Book III v. 15. (First-Second centuries A.D.)[45]

Zeus had relations with Antiope, the daughter of Nycteus. As a consequence, the girl conceived and faced the threat of punishment for her indiscretion. Fearing for her life, Antiope fled, making her way to Epopeus of Sicyon. Epopeus kindly took her in and married her. In a state of despair over the incident, Nycteus took his life, but before he died he made his brother Lycus promise to avenge him. So Lycus traveled to Sicyon, where he slew King Epopeus and brought back poor Antiope in chains. During the long journey home, Antiope stopped at Eleurethea to give birth to twin boys, Amphion and Zethus. But her cruel uncle exposed the children on the mountain. There the infants were found and raised by a local cowherd. Given a lyre by Hermes, Amphion grew up to become a superb musician. Zethus, on the other hand, became a herdsman. Meanwhile, Antiope had been imprisoned and tortured by Lycus's wife Dirce. Somehow she managed to escape and was reunited with her grown sons. Intent on avenging their mother, the brothers slew Lycus and Dirce, taking over the rule of his city.

26 Paris/Alexander: Apollodorus, *The Library* Book III xii. 5. (First-Second centuries A.D.)[46]

As Hecuba was about to bear King Priam of Troy a second son, she was visited with a terrible dream in which she delivered a firebrand that consumed the entire city. Priam, when informed of the dream, consulted with Aesacus, who was skilled in dream interpretation. Thus he was advised that the child to be born would be the ruin of his country and should be exposed to die. So Priam gave the newborn boy to his servant Agelaus to abandon on Mt. Ida. There the infant was kept alive by a she-bear that nursed him for five days. When Agelaus returned and found the child still alive, he decided to bring him home to raise as his own son. Thus the boy grew up with Agelaus and was named Paris. He reached maturity endowed with great strength and beauty. Paris acquired the name Alexander after he had driven off robbers who were plundering his flocks. Eventually he discovered the identity of his natural parents and was reunited with them.

27. Pelias and Neleus: Apollodorus, *The Library* Book I ix. 8-9. (First-Second centuries A.D.)[47]

Tyro, the daughter of Salmoneus, was raised by her uncle after her father's death. The maiden fell in love with the river Enipeus, spending much time by its banks. Poseidon, disguised as the river god, lay with her and begat twin sons. In secret Tyro gave birth to the boys and exposed them shortly after. As they lay abandoned, a passing mare kicked one of the babes in the face leaving a permanent mark. A horse-keeper found the children and brought them up. One child he named Pelias on account of the mark on his face, the other he named Neleus. When the lads were grown, they were reunited with their mother who had long suffered abuse from her stepmother Sidero. As loyal sons, Pelias and Neleus slew Sidero in revenge. Later, the brothers quarreled and went their separate ways.

28. Atalanta: Apollodorus, *The Library* Book III ix. 2. (First-Second centuries A.D.)[48]
Iasus and Clymene had a daughter Atalanta, who was exposed because her father wanted only male offspring. A she-bear saved the infant's life by nursing her until hunters came upon the child in the wilderness and brought her up. When the girl had reached maturity, she became a great hunter and wrestler. Eventually Atalanta discovered the identity of her natural parents. When her father wished her to wed against her will, she ran off.

29. Dionysus: Pausanias, *Description of Greece* Book III xxiv. 3-5. (Second century A.D.)[49]
Semele, the daughter of Prince Cadmus, gave birth to a child born out of wedlock to Zeus. When her father discovered the situation, he placed her and the child in a chest and threw it into the sea. The chest was washed ashore on the island of the Laconians. When the box was opened, it was found that only the infant had survived. The townfolk gave Semele a suitable funeral and brought up the infant Dionysus. To commemorate the washing ashore of the chest, the people changed the name of the town to Brasiae. During her travels, Ino, the sister of Semele, stopped in the land and agreed to nurse Dionysus. Later a local plain situated near the town was named after Dionysus.

30. Attis: Pausanias, *Description of Greece* Book VII xvii. 10-12. (Second century A.D.)[50]
Agdistis, the hermaphrodite offspring of Zeus, created such fear in the gods that they mutilated him, depriving him of his male organ. From his severed member grew an almond tree. Nana, the daughter of the river god, ate the fruit of this tree, conceived, and gave birth to a

son. Shortly after the birth, she exposed the infant to die. The wild goats of the forest cared for the infant until shepherds found him. The lad grew up to become so beautiful that Agdistis fell in love with him. The relatives of the youth sent him away to marry the daughter of the king of Pessinus. During the wedding ceremony, an enraged Agdistis appeared and caused both the king and Attis to go mad and emasculate themselves. Regretting his foul deed, Agdistis prayed to Zeus that the moribund body of Attis neither rot nor decay. Zeus complied with the request, and a tomb was set up to Attis on Mt. Dindymus in the sanctuary of Agdistis.

31. Asclepius: Pausanias, *Description of Greece* Book II xxvi. 3-5. (Second century A.D.)[51]
Secretly carrying the child of Apollo, Coronis accompanied her father on a trip to spy out Pelopennesus. While in the land of the Epidaurians, she gave birth to a son, Asclepius, whom she exposed on Mt. Myrtium. The helpless infant was nursed by a goat and protected by the watchdog of a goatherd. When the herder sensed something amiss and went to investigate, he found the abandoned child. As he was about to pick up the baby, lightning issued forth from the infant frightening the peasant away. As an adult, Asclepius went about discovering remedies and cures in all lands. But when he succeeded in reviving the dead, Zeus slew him.

32. Gilgameš: Aelian, *Characteristics of Animals* Book XII 21. (Second-Third centuries A.D.)[52]
Seuechorus, the king of the Babylonians, was warned by his Chaldean fortunetellers that one day his daughter would bear a son who would depose him. Fearful of the prophecy, the king had his daughter watched carefully so that she would have no opportunity to fulfill the prediction. Nevertheless, the girl conceived a child in secret by a man of no distinction. The guardians of the princess, who had neglected their responsibility, removed the newborn child and threw him from the citadel of the prison. Miraculously, an eagle happened to spot the falling infant and caught him on its back. Flying the child to safety,

the eagle deposited him in the midst of a garden. There the gardener found the child, took a fancy to him, and decided to raise him. The boy was named Gilgameš and grew up to become ruler of Babylon, fulfilling the prophecy.

33. Daphnis and Chloe: Longus, *Daphnis and Chloe*. Lesbos (Second-Sixth centuries A.D.)[53]

A goatherd on the isle of Lesbos came upon a goat nursing an infant boy in the wilderness. Drawing near he saw that the foundling was accoutred with rich trappings such as a purple mantle and gold dagger. Picking up the babe and his belongings, he returned home to his wife and showed her everything. The couple hid the items and raised the boy as a son, bestowing upon him a good shepherd's name, Daphnis. Two years later, another herder had a similar experience. While searching for a wandering sheep, he found the animal inside of a cave nursing a baby girl. He took up the child with her possessions and brought them home to his wife. The couple raised the girl naming her Chloe. When these foundlings had grown, they happened to meet and fall in love. After numerous adventures and mishaps, their story reached a conclusion when Daphnis learned that his natural parents were the rulers of the land. His father had exposed him because he felt that he had enough children. Chloe also found out that her father, now a great noble, had abandoned her out of poverty. In the end both sets of parents accepted their cast-away children and gave them in marriage to each other.

34. Charicleia: Heliodorus, *Aethiopica*. (Third century A.D.)[54]

After ten years of married life had produced no children, King Hydaspes of Ethiopia, inspired by a dream, slept again with his wife. This time a child was conceived leading to public celebrations that continued throughout her pregnancy. But when the time came to give birth, the queen, to her great consternation, delivered a white daughter. (The reason was that during the act of procreation, the queen had looked upon a picture of the white Andromeda depicted in a scene with Perseus.) Since the

Ethiopians were a dark-skinned race, she feared she would be branded an adulteress and put to death. So the queen informed her husband that the child had been stillborn, while she prepared to expose the baby and leave her to providence. She laid the girl out with great riches, which were to serve as a reward to any finder, and a letter explaining the reasons for her abandonment. Sisimathes found the infant, took her up, and raised her for seven years. On assuming an ambassadorship, he turned the girl over to Charicles, who made her a priestess in the temple of Apollo. The maiden learned the secret of her birth, and after many trials and tribulations with her fiancé Theagenes, she returned home to reveal her identity. Her royal parents acknowledged their daughter and permitted her to marry her sweetheart.

35. Miletus: Antoninus Liberalis, *Metamorphoses* XXX Byblis 1-2. (Third century A.D.)[55]

On the island of Crete, Apollo begat a son with the daughter of King Minos. Fearing the wrath of her father, the princess exposed her child in a forest where she-wolves sent by Apollo fed and watched over the babe. Later some cowherds found the infant and raised him among themselves. The lad grew into a handsome and vigorous young man. Forced to flee from the unnatural attentions of his grandfather, he traveled by ship to the land of the Carians.[56] There he married the daughter of the king and founded the town of Milet.

36. Ptolemy Soter: Suda λ 25 (Tenth century A.D.)[57]

King Lagos married Arsinoe, who was the mother of Ptolemy Soter. The king exposed the infant on a bronze shield as if he were not related to him. From Macedonia comes the story that an eagle protected the child from the sun and rain by spreading his wings over him. In addition, the bird tore quails asunder giving the blood to Ptolemy as nourishing milk.

F. Latin

37. Cyrus: Justinus, *Universal History* Book I iv-vi. (Third century A.D.)[58]

King Astyages had a dream in which he saw a vine growing from the bosom of his only daughter. The vine grew sprouts and cast a shadow over Asia. The king's interpreters explained that the dream portended the birth of an illustrious grandson, who would depose the king. To forestall the prophecy, Astyages gave his daughter in marriage to a lowly Persian. But the girl conceived, and shortly before she was to give birth, the king summoned her in order to slay her infant. After the child was born, Harpagus, the king's servant, was commanded to dispose of him. Fearing the mother's revenge, Harpagus delivered the babe to the royal herder to expose. The herder carried out the order at the same time that his own wife gave birth. When the woman implored her husband to fetch back the royal child that had been abandoned, the herder returned to the woods to find a bitch nursing the boy and protecting him from other animals. The herder's wife became so enamored of the noble infant that she persuaded her husband to expose their own son in his place, and the herder and his wife raised Cyrus as their son.

38. Hieron: Justin, *Universal History* Book XXIII iv. (Third century A.D.)[59]

Hieron was the son of Hierocles, a man of high rank; his mother was a slave girl. Ashamed of the infant's maternal line, Hierocles decided to expose his infant son. Fortunately, bees kept the child alive by feeding him honey. The father, meanwhile, was informed by an omen that his son was destined to rule over an empire. Therefore, he set out to retrieve the boy and prepare him for his role. The child's early years were marked by marvelous occurrences, such as the times when an owl perched on his lance and an eagle alighted on his shield. Often challenged to combat, Hieron always emerged victorious. He grew up with beauty, strength, and propriety. Later when Pyrrhus left Sicily, dominion passed to him, and all gladly agreed to his rule.

39. Habis: Justin, *Universal History* Book XLIV iv. (Third century A.D.)[60]

Gargoris, the ancient king of Cunetes, had a daughter whose indiscretion resulted in the birth of a grandson. The king was filled with shame and desired to rid himself of the embarrassment. He ordered that the child be exposed to die. After a few days, his servants went to seek the body. Instead they found the infant in good health, for wild animals had nursed him in the wilderness. The child was brought back to the palace only to be placed upon a narrow path frequented by large beasts. The king's desire was again thwarted when the child was not injured. Next, the infant was given up to wild dogs and pigs specially starved for the occasion, but instead of devouring him, the animals nursed him. In desperation, Gargoris had him cast into the sea. This scheme also failed as the waters conveyed him to shore as if he were contained in a vessel. On shore a bitch drew near and suckled the young hero. Growing up on such nourishment, the lad became a remarkably swift runner who used to roam with a herd of deer. Caught one day and brought before the king, the boy was recognized from certain birth marks as the grandson of the king. Ultimately, Gargoris accepted the youth, gave him the name Habis, and designated him as his successor. After ascending the throne, Habis displayed great abilities including the introduction of cultural improvements. Kingship resided in his family for several generations.

40. Aegisthus: Hyginus, *Fabulae* LXXXVII-III.
(Fourth-Fifth centuries A.D.)[61]
Thyestes fled to Sicyon after a heinous crime was perpetrated against him by his brother. In disguise he raped his own daughter Pelopia to fulfill a prophecy that he could avenge himself on Atreus, his brother, through a son sired by him with his daughter. Afterwards, Atreus unwittingly married his niece , unaware that she was pregnant by her own father. When Aegisthus was born, his mother exposed him, but shepherds discovered the infant and provided a she-goat to nurse him.[62] Atreus had the boy found and raised at home. Years later when Atreus had imprisoned his brother Thyestes, he ordered Aegisthus

to slay him. But Thyestes, recognizing Aegisthus' sword as the sword he had lost when ravishing Pelopia, had the youth's mother summoned. After Pelopia had explained how she came in possession of the sword, their true relationships became apparent. Pelopia slew herself, and Aegisthus slew Atreus before returning to his father's kingdom.

41. Aeolus and Boeotus: Hyginus, *Fabulae* CLXXXVI. (Fourth-Fifth centuries A.D.)[63]

Neptune seduced the beautiful Melanippe, who conceived and gave birth to twins. When the girl's father Desmontes found out, he had his daughter blinded and ordered that the children be thrown to the beasts. The infants were exposed instead, but were nursed by a cow in the wilderness. Some cowherds witnessed this and picked up the twins in order to raise them. Meanwhile, a ruler named Metapontus, angry at his wife's inability to have children, threatened her to produce offspring or be gone. The clever wife sent to the cowherds for an infant to pass off as her own. So the two little boys were sent to her, and her husband, the king, accepted and loved them. Time passed and the queen bore two sons of her own. Now she began to fear that the two older boys would inherit in the place of her natural sons. For this reason, she advised her sons to slay their foster brothers. But in a battle with the twins Aeolus and Boeotus, it was the queen's natural sons who were slain, since Neptune secretly intervened on the side of his children. The queen then killed herself, and the twins returned to live with the cowherds. One day Neptune revealed to the youths the secret of their origin and the fact that their mother was languishing in prison. The loyal sons set out to slay Desmontes and free their mother. When this was accomplished, Melanippe's sight was miraculously restored by Neptune. All three returned to King Metapontes, who married Melanippe and adopted Aeolus and Boeotus as his legal heirs. Two cities named after the twins were founded in Prepontis.

42. Hippothous: Hyginus, *Fabulae* CLXXXVII. (Fourth-Fifth centuries A.D.)[64]

Neptune fell in love with the beautiful daughter of King Cercyon. The god embraced Alope, who became pregnant and bore a son. Because she did not know the identity of the father, Alope had her nurse expose the child. After the babe was abandoned, a mare came to suckle it. Later a shepherd, following the mare, discovered the foundling and brought him home. Another shepherd saw the infant and asked for the child. The first shepherd agreed to give him the boy but kept the child's royal garments for himself. A quarrel arose over possession of the clothes, and the two peasants decided to bring their case before the king for adjudication. Cercyon recognized the garments as belonging to his daughter and flew into a rage. After learning the truth from Alope's nurse, he ordered Alope imprisoned and sentenced her to death. He had the child exposed a second time, but the infant was saved again by a mare and found by a shepherd. This time the boy grew up among the herders, who named him Hippothous. One day Theseus passed through the kingdom and slew King Cercyon. Hippothous, by then a young man, requested that the realm be given to him as his rightful inheritance. When Theseus learned that Hippothous was in fact a son of Neptune, he complied with the request. Meanwhile, the body of Alope was turned into a spring bearing the same name.

43. Lamissio: Paul the Deacon, *History of the Langobards* Book I 15. (Eighth century A.D.)[65]

A cruel prostitute once gave birth to seven boys. Not wanting to care for them, she threw them all into a fish pond to drown. The ruler of the Langobards, King Agelmund, happened to pass by and saw the plight of the infants. Turning the children about by the end of his spear, the king was astounded when one child grabbed it firmly in his hand. Pitying him and interpreting this as a sign that the babe was destined for greatness, he had him pulled out of the water and placed in the care of a nurse. He named the boy Lamissio from the word for the fish pond whence he came--*lama*. The boy grew up to be a strong lad skilled in the military arts. After the death of his foster father, Lamissio directed the affairs of his people and eventually became their king.

44. Judas: *The Golden Legend*. (Thirteenth century A.D.)[66] Reuben Simeon, a Jerusalemite, married a woman named Cyborea. One night Cyborea dreamed that she gave birth to a son destined to be the ruin of his family. Upon awakening, she told her husband about the dream and was comforted by him. But when Cyborea realized that she had in fact conceived that same night, she and Reuben began to fear the portent of the dream. A son was born to the couple, and not wishing to slay him with their own hands, they placed him in an ark and launched it into the sea. The waves carried the vessel to the isle of Iscariot, where the childless queen of the land found it and adopted the boy as her son. Soon she bore her own child and one day when both had grown up, Judas slew his foster brother in a jealous rage. Fleeing to Jerusalem, Judas fell in with the Roman governor Pilate and quickly rose in his service. One day while swiping some apples for his master, Judas was accosted by the irate landowner. In the ensuing quarrel, Judas, not knowing that he was his real father, slew the man. Pilate then rewarded Judas by giving him the property and wife of the dead man. Later, while listening to his new wife bemoan the vicissitudes of her life including the episode of the infant that she had long ago cast away, Judas realized that he had married his mother. Filled with remorse, he confessed his sins to Jesus, who permitted him to join the apostles. Eventually, he betrayed his new master for thirty pieces of silver.

G. Indian

45. Karna: *Mahabharata* Vana Parva CCCIV-VIII. (ca. 400 B.C.-A.D. 400)[67]
After capriciously summoning the sun god Surya through the recitation of the proper mantras, Princess Kunti was faced with a difficult choice. She had either to submit to the god's desire and bear him a son or have her entire family cursed. Finally, the princess acquiesced to his demands when Surya promised that she would remain a virgin and

that the child would become a great hero. Aware of the impropriety of bearing a child out of wedlock and concerned for the feelings of her parents, Kunti and her nurse acted to expose the infant immediately after birth. They placed him in a large wicker basket that had been sealed with wax and fitted with pillows and sheets. The box was conveyed to the river and after prayers for his safety were said, Karna was set adrift on the water. The waves carried the box to the Ganges and finally to the city of Champa, where a charioteer and his wife spotted it while walking by the shore. Opening the box, they found a beautiful infant boy inside. Since they had no children of their own, the couple accepted the child as a gift of the gods and raised him as their own son. Later the child was schooled in the military arts and became a famous bowman. One day Karna challenged Arjuna, another son of Kunti, to combat at a tournament. Karna was anointed king, enabling him to compete with the royal Arjuna. Kunti tried to prevent the fight by disclosing to Karna the secret of his birth, but the hero did not believe her, fought Arjuna, and was slain.

46. Eḷakamara: Kuṇāla-Jātaka Book XXI 536. (Fifth century A.D.)[68]

Brahmadatta overthrew the kingdom of Kosala, slaying its king and capturing his pregnant wife. Despite her condition, Brahmadatta made her his royal consort. In time she gave birth to a son who was like an image of gold. Now the queen began to fear for the life of her infant, thinking that her new husband would seek one day to destroy the son of his former enemy. Therefore, she ordered her nurse to cover him with cloth and abandon him in a cemetery. In the meanwhile, the infant's dead father assumed the form of a guardian angel in order to look after his son. The spirit sent a she-goat to nurse the abandoned babe. Afterwards, a goatherd discovered the child, took a fancy to him, and brought him home to his barren wife to raise. Unable to nurse the child herself, the wife had the goats nourish him. But when the goats began to die mysteriously, the goatherd decided to dispose of the foundling. He placed him in an earthenware vessel, covered him with cloth, and threw him into the river. There the vessel drifted until it came to rest by a river bank where a mender and his wife spotted it. They pulled the infant out of the vessel and adopted him since they were also childless. Years passed and the lad, now fully grown, used to accompany his parents to the palace to do mending work. There he met the beautiful daughter of the king and the royal consort. The two fell in love and embarked on an illicit relationship. The king learned of the affair and sentenced the mender's son to death. But the guardian angel entered the body of his former wife and made her confess that the lad was her own son, whom she had exposed at birth. After the story was verified, the king was so pleased that the youth was of noble blood that he gave him his daughter in marriage. Then he sent his son-in-law with an army to recapture his father's old kingdom of Kosala. The hero's name was Eḷakamara, which means "Goatsbane," and he was a Bodhisattva.

47. Nigrodha: Nigrodha-Jātaka Book X 445. (Fifth century A.D.)[69]

A merchant in Ragagaha brought home a country merchant's daughter to be his son's wife. When the girl produced no offspring, she became increasingly scorned by the family until one day she decided to play a trick on them by pretending that she was pregnant. With the help of her nurse, she carried out this ruse for nine months. Finally, she told her in-laws that she wished to travel to her father's house to have her child. With their permission she set out. Now it happened that a caravan was traveling on the same road at a distance ahead so that each morning the girl and her company would reach the spot where the caravan had camped for the night. One night a poor woman traveling with the caravan had given birth to a son underneath a banyon tree. Fearing that they would leave without her, she abandoned the child under the tree with the intention of possibly returning for him later. A tree spirit watched over and protected the newborn babe. When the young girl arrived at the spot in the morning, she saw the infant and immediately cried out that she was in labor. In this way she acquired a baby to pass off as her own. Thereupon she returned to the home of her husband's family where the infant was accepted as her child. The boy was named Nigrodhakumara or "Master Banyon" after the banyon tree under which he had been found. Years later he ate the fat of a magic rooster, an act which destined him for kingship, and soon, he did become king.

48. Ghosaka: *Dhammapada-Aṭṭhakatha* I-V. (Fifth century A.D.)[70] Ghosaka was reincarnated in the womb of a courtesan at Kosambi. When told that she had given birth to a boy, she ordered that he be placed in a basket and thrown onto a dust heap, for courtesans kept only their female offspring. Now a merchant in the town learned from an astrologer that a boy was born who would become the foremost merchant in the city. Immediately he sent a servant to locate and obtain that child. Since his wife was about to give birth, he planned to wed the boy to his daughter should his wife have a girl, or slay him should she have a boy. The merchant's wife had a son, whereupon the husband commanded his servant to expose the foundling on the floor of a cow pen to be trampled. But the plan was frustrated when the lead bull stood over the infant to protect him. The keeper of the cow herd spotted the child and brought him home with him. The evil merchant had to buy the infant back before plotting to dispose of him again. He tried to kill the boy by exposing him on a cart track and in a cemetery, then by ordering that he be thrown off a mountain--all to no avail. The child always escaped injury. Years later the merchant again conspired to slay his foster son. He paid a potter to slay the youth, cut him into pieces, and bake him in a jar. The next day the merchant sent Ghosaka to the potter with a message to carry out the prearranged instructions. But that day, the merchant's natural son saw Ghosaka and volunteered to carry the message for him. So he became the victim of his father's evil plot. After additional attempts on his life, Ghosaka was dispatched with a death letter to a servant of the merchant. On the way he met

another merchant whose daughter changed the letter, ordering the servant to marry the youth to the merchant's daughter instead of slaying him.

49. Vikramaditya: *The History of Ardshi-Bordshi Chan* chap. 6. (Fifth century A.D.)[71]
King Gandharva married a beautiful princess named Udsesskülengtu. Unfortunately, the union produced no children. Despairing of ever having an heir, the king frequently would implore the aid of Buddha and the heavenly gods in obtaining a son. Aware of her husband's unhappiness, the queen urged him to beget a son with a second wife. Gandharva took the queen's advice and chose a new wife, who soon conceived and gave birth to a son. The queen, meanwhile, seeing the favors and attention paid to the second wife, became distressed and sought out the assistance of a hermit. The hermit gave her a handful of earth and instructed her to cook it in water and eat it, and then she would be able to conceive. Miraculously, the queen did become pregnant in this manner and delivered a son amid marvelous signs in nature. The king sent a delegation to the hermit to inquire of the child's destiny. A cryptic answer was returned to Gandharva, which he interpreted as an evil omen. About to slay his own son, the king was persuaded by a minister to expose him instead. As the infant was left to die, he spoke and revealed the riddle as in fact an auspicious omen. While the king's servant returned to inform his master, the infant was attended and nourished by princes of the serpent dragon in the wilderness. The king hurried out to acknowledge the child as his son and a Bodhisattva. He brought him home, bestowing on him the name Vikramaditya.

50. The Thousand Sons: Fa-hien, *A Record of Buddhist Kingdoms.* (Fifth century A.D.)[72]
An inferior wife of the King of Vaisali gave birth to a malformed fetus. The principal wife, who had always been envious of her rival, warned that this was an evil omen and that the fetus should be placed in a box and thrown into the Ganges. This being done, the box floated until it reached the coast of a neighboring kingdom. There the

local king sighted it and opened the box to discover a thousand beautiful infants inside. He raised the boys to be valiant young warriors. Time passed and one day the king and his thousand sons set out to conquer the city where the sons had been conceived. As the king of Vaisali sat troubled by the approach of the invaders, his inferior wife asked the reason for his anxiety. After he had explained, she asked him to construct a high tower from which she would stop the invaders. When the thousand warriors drew near, she announced her identity as their mother and pressed her breasts causing a thousand drops of milk to squirt into their mouths. Immediately the warriors dropped their arms and the invasion was over. In later centuries, a commemorative tower was built on the site of the original tower.

51. Aghaṭa: *Aghaṭakumarakatha*. (First millennium A.D.)[73]
In the royal city of Ujjayini, a court priest begat a son by a slave girl. The slave gave birth to a male child Aghata, who bore birth marks signifying royalty. For this reason, the father-priest prophesied that the child was destined for absolute kingship. The current ruler, Sughatita, wanted to rid himself of a future rival so he ordered two soldiers to murder the infant. Instead they took pity on him and exposed him by a stream. In this location the child of destiny was surrounded by a mysterious light as all nature bloomed about him. A gardener and his wife found the infant in this radiant state and brought him home to raise. The suspicion of the king grew, and he sent a third hired killer to slay the boy. But this murderer also took pity on the child and did not harm him. A Yaksha took an interest in the lad, protecting him as a father. When the boy was grown, he and the Yaksha came in contact with the king. This time Sughatita sent Aghaṭa with a death letter to his son, the prince. But the Yaksha removed the letter from Aghaṭa's pocket while he was sleeping and replaced it with another that directed the prince to give the bearer of the letter the king's daughter in marriage. Thus the king's plan was thwarted. Aghaṭa married a princess and eventually became

the great ruler that he was destined to be.

52. Candagutta: *Vaṃsatthappakasinī*. (Seventh-Thirteenth centuries A.D.)[74]

When the father of the yet unborn Candagutta was overthrown and murdered by a neighboring king, his pregnant wife fled to Pushpapura where she gave birth to a son. Thinking that she would entrust his safety to a Deva, she placed the infant in a vessel and abandoned him in a cow shed. There a cow named Canda watched over the child until a shepherd found him and brought him home. The shepherd named the boy Candagutta after the cow Canda. Later the lad was given to a hunter friend with whom he then lived. One day while taking part in a game of play-king with the other youths of the village, Candagutta, in the role of the king, commanded that the hands and feet of offending boys be cut off. After this was actually done, the severed limbs were miraculously rejoined to the bodies at his spoken word. Canakka, who had witnessed this astonishing event, purchased the lad from the hunter and took him home. There he discovered his true identity as a Maurya. The lad reached maturity and became a great king and founder of the Maurya dynasty.

53. Kuberadatta: *Hēmacandras Parisiṣtaparvan* II 224-315. (Eleventh-Twelfth centuries A.D.)[75]

A beautiful courtesan named Kuberasena lived in the city of Mathura. Before giving birth to twins, a boy Kuberadatta and a girl Kuberadattā, she suffered great pain. When the infants were born, Kuberasena's mother ordered that the babies be cast away as was customary for courtesans. Kuberasena was permitted to keep them for ten days during which she nursed them and placed rings on their fingers. Then she had a chest built and filled it with jewels. The infants were placed inside and set adrift on the river. The next day two sons of a rich merchant found the chest and removed it from the water. The twins grew up in their home and years later married each other. Before the marriage was consummated, they discovered their true relationship as brother and sister. The girl left to become a student at a monastery, while her brother continued in his profession as a merchant. It happened that Kuberadatta met his mother and unwittingly married her. After the scandal was known, the mother, son, and daughter all lived chaste lives.

54. Trakhan: Folklore of Gilgit. (ca. A.D. 1600-1900)[76]
A Ra (king) of ancient Gilgit married a wealthy woman with seven brothers. The king loved to play polo and often went to compete with his brothers-in-law. On one occasion they decided that whoever would lose the day's contest would forfeit his life. The Ra prevailed and executed the others according to the agreement. Outraged at the news of her brothers' fate, the queen planned to poison her husband for revenge. A month after the king's death had been accomplished, the queen gave birth to his son. Still incensed by the Ra's atrocity, she placed his infant son Trakhan in a box and threw it into the river. The current brought him to a village in the Chilias district, where two brothers from a poor family recovered the vessel and brought it home to their mother. Discovering the handsome infant within, she raised him as one of the family. From that day on, the fortunes of the family began to improve. Trakhan learned the circumstances of his discovery at age six. At twelve he set out with his brothers to see far away Gilgit. They encamped on a hill called Baldas just north of the city. The queen of Gilgit (Trakhan's mother) was now very ill and since she had no other children, the people were looking about for a successor. One morning at cock's crow the village was astonished when the roosters crowed "There is a king at Baldas." Men were sent to fetch any newcomers at Baldas, and they brought back the three youths to the queen. Interrogated about his country and birth, Trakhan revealed his identity and was acknowledged by the queen as her son and heir.

55. Palihar: North Indian popular tale. (Nineteenth century A.D.)[77]
On the island of Lanka, the very beautiful Princess Sona was bathing when a demon approached her leaving her pregnant. Nine months later the princess delivered a baby boy. Sona, afraid of her parents' reaction, enclosed the

infant in a casket and set him adrift on the ocean. Now the Rani Madodari, who was a childless widow, discovered the casket while walking by the coast. The queen adopted the child and named him Palihar. The foundling grew up to be a giant, famous for his skill as a wrestler. One day he stood on a mountain and challenged the whole world to face him. At the palace of Ghazi Miyan, all trembled in fear of Palihar except Ajab Salar, a twelve-year-old. He alone stepped forward to accept the giant's challenge.

56. Sassi: Hasham Shah, *Sassi and Punnun*. (Nineteenth century A.D.)[78]

The king of Bhambor had a daughter named Sassi. The royal astrologers foretold that she would one day fall in love with a man from outside her tribe and bring disgrace upon her family. For this reason, the king had the infant placed in an ark and launched down the Indus river. A washerwoman found the vessel and brought up the child as a daughter. When grown, the maiden was exceptionally beautiful and turned down all proposals offered by the young washermen, claiming that she was a king's daughter. News of a beautiful daughter of a washerwoman reached the king, who desired to make her his wife. When Sassi appeared before him, he recognized her identity from an amulet that she wore around her neck and sent her back to the house of her foster mother. Soon after, she saw a picture of Punnun, a prince of a neighboring kingdom. Sassi fell in love with his picture, and when he came to meet her, the couple began to live together. Refusing to leave his beloved Sassi, Punnun was carried away forcibly by his friends. Sassi tried to follow him but died in the desert en route.

H. Persian

57. Zarathustra: *Denkhart* Book VII iii. 1-16. (Ninth century A.D.)[78]

The parents of Zarathustra were imbued with three divine elements that made them fit to conceive the future prophet. Most important of these was kingly glory, which descended from the deity Ahura Mazda and entered into the body of the mother. Wondrous signs were seen on the occasion of Zarathustra's birth, and the baby was born laughing, not crying. Learning of his birth, Durasropo, the most powerful of the sorcerors, conspired with other fiends to slay the child. First he attempted to crush the baby's head in the cradle but failed. Next he cast a spell over the father of Zarathustra so that he sought the death of his own son. Various attempts on his life were made. The infant was placed on an ox path to be trampled. Later, they abandoned him at a watering hole frequented by horses. In both cases, the lead animal of the herd protected Zarathustra. Finally, the child was exposed in the den of a wolf, whose cubs had been murdered. When the wolf returned to take her revenge on the infant, she was miraculously struck dumb. Zarathustra survived and grew up to become the great religious leader of his people.

58. Faridun: Firdausi, *Shah Namah* vv. 37-63. (ca. A.D. 1000)[80]

King Zahhak of Iran was troubled by a dream in which three men of noble bearing approached him. The youngest of the three carried a bull's head club and drew near to smite the king. The interpreters identified the young man as Faridun, who would soon be born and who was destined to grow up and slay the king. Zahhak was greatly alarmed and sought to kill Faridun to avert the prophecy. Abtin, the father of Faridun, tried to conceal his infant son from the danger. Later, he fled for his own life but was slain. Meanwhile, the child's mother spirited him away placing him in the care of a forester, whose cow nursed the infant. Three years later, the mother returned to fetch Faridun and bring him to a hermit on Mt. Alburz. After following their trail, Zahhak found the forester, put him to death, and slaughtered his cow. On his sixteenth birthday, Faridun learned the secret of his birth. Accompanied by two older brothers, he fashioned a club from the head of a bull in honor of the cow that had suckled him. Eventually, he found Zahhak and slew him with the club, fulfilling the prophecy.

59. Zal: Firdausi, *Shah Namah* vv. 131-148. (ca. A.D. 1000)[81]
Sam, the mighty Pahliva, prospered in all ways but one: he was without an heir. Finally, a son was born to him, beautiful and without blemish, but with white hair like an old man. Fearing his reaction, the women of the palace kept the news from him for eight days. When Sam was told finally, he examined the child himself and decided to cast out the infant from fear of the taunts of his enemies. Thus the white-haired babe was exposed at the foot of Mt. Alburz. Nesting at the summit was a wondrous bird called a simurgh. The bird took pity on the child, brought him up to her nest, and cared for him as one of her fledglings. When the child had grown, his prowess and beauty were known throughout the land. In a dream Sam was informed of the fate of the son he had long ago abandoned and was chided for his misconduct in the episode. He immediately set off with his army to seek his son and effect a reconciliation. Spying the youth with his foster parent at the top of the unassailable mountain, Sam cried out to God for help. The simurgh recognized Sam down below and informed Zal of the presence of the man who was his real father. At first reluctant to leave the kind bird, Zal was reunited with his repentant father. Before returning home, they stopped at the palace of the Shah, where Sam was rewarded with a throne, crown, and treasure. Zal was named crown prince and eventually inherited his father's realm.

60. Kai Khusrau: Firdausi, *Shah Namah* vv. 564-1396, (ca. A.D. 1000)[82]
King Afrasiyab of Turan had a dream during his invasion of Iran that portended the ultimate destruction of the Turks through Siyawush, the son of the Iranian king. Afrasiyab wisely made peace with Siyawush, creating a split between him and his father. The prince received Afrasiyab's daughter in marriage despite a prophecy that a child would result who would bring calamity on the king. Now the king's brother was envious of Siyawush's position and incited Afrasiyab to slay his son-in-law, but not before Siyawush had impregnated his wife. A general in

Afrasiyab's army aided the wife to escape and then named her newborn son Kai Khusrau. Furthermore, he received the king's permission to spare the child. The only condition was that the infant be given to shepherds to raise in the mountains, with no knowledge of his true identity. When grown to maturity, Kai Khusrau was summoned to court to face the anxious king. He shrewdly played the simpleton and was again spared. In the end, Kai Khusrau succeeded to the throne of his grandfather and avenged his father by decapitating Afrasiyab.

61. Darab (Darius): Firdausi, *Shah Namah* vv. 1756-1774. (ca. A.D. 1000)[83]

King Behman had a son, Sasan, and a daughter, Humai. Now Humai was exceedingly beautiful and the king took her to wife as was customary. She conceived, but shortly before she was to deliver, the king fell mortally ill. Assembling his court, Behman named Humai as regent with sovereignty to pass to the as yet unborn child. When Humai assumed the throne, she decided to bear her child in secret. Enlisting the aid of a noblewoman as nurse, she had her put out the report that the infant had died. After eight months had passed, the queen commanded a carpenter to fashion an elaborate casket, covered with bitumen, musk,[84] wax, and varnish on the outside, and spread with linen and jewels within. One evening at midnight the nurse put the infant inside and launched the casket on the Euphrates. Two servants were posted to report on the fate of the infant. The box floated downstream until it was stopped by a stone placed in the water by a launderer. The washerman saw the casket, opened it, and brought the infant home. Since he and his wife had recently lost a baby, they welcomed him with an open heart, and the woman nursed him herself. The boy, whom they named Darab, grew into a fine sturdy youth, who had no peer in wrestling or in tests of strength. The boy refused to be trained as a launderer and demanded a scholarly education. Later, he became a horseman and learned the military arts. The time came when Darab rather ungratefully demanded to know the secret of his birth from his foster parents. Thereupon, he set out to join the queen's army which was engaged in a campaign. Informed of the young man's exploits and his true identity (the commander of the army sent the queen a jewel belonging to Darab that had been placed in his casket), Humai acknowledged her son and made him heir to the throne.

62. Zarathustra: *Zaratush Namah*. (Thirteenth century A.D.)[85] The mother of the prophet gave birth to her son following a dream that predicted the birth and greatness of the child. The infant, who was of unsurpassed beauty, emerged from the womb laughing. Fearing his power, the magicians and demons moved quickly to destroy him. The Shah of the sorcerors, Duransarun, tried to stab the infant, but his hands became withered. Next, they carried him off to burn him in the desert, but this plan also failed. Then they exposed Zarathustra on an ox path, hoping to see him trampled. This time the infant was saved when the lead animal stood over him. The fiends exposed him again on a horse path with similar lack of success. Finally, they abandoned Zarathustra in a wolf den after slaughtering the wolf's cubs in an attempt to incite her to mangle the infant. But the wolf became miraculously docile when encountering Zarathustra. Two cows then appeared in the den and nursed the infant.

I. German

63. Gregorius: Hartmann von Aue, *Gregorius*. (Twelfth century A.D.)[86] The wife of the king of Aquitania died giving birth to twins, a boy and a girl. The children, who were orphaned at an early age, grew up to be very close and loving. But the devil turned the boy's brotherly love into lust so that one night he raped his sister leaving her pregnant. On the advice of their most trusted counselor, the brother departed on a pilgrimage, while his sister delivered her child in secret. Deciding to trust in providence, the girl and her advisor prepared a strong chest in which to expose the infant. The boy was placed inside and covered with silk. Gold was put in the chest as well as a tablet explaining the circumstances of his abandonment. Thus the

infant was consigned to the sea. But he did not die, for God nursed him until his chest floated to shore. There two fishermen discovered the receptacle and brought it to the local abbot. He opened the chest to find a beautiful baby boy within. Before entrusting him to the care of a fisherman for a period of six years, the cleric baptized the infant Gregorius and officially adopted him. Later the boy was raised in the monastery and grew into a fine youth. One day Gregorius learned that his birth was obscure and set out to find his parents. In the process he accomplished a great feat and unwittingly married his mother. When their true relationship was discovered, they separated, and Gregorius went off to do penance for seventeen years chained to a rock. Finally, he was forgiven by God and selected to be the next pope.

J. Icelandic

64. Tristan: Arnason, *The Folktales and Fairy Tales of Iceland*. (Nineteenth century A.D.)[87]
A king, disturbed by his wife's inability to produce offspring, threatened to put her to death if she did not present him with a child on his return from a journey. In disguise she followed his entourage and was brought to his quarters, unrecognized, as the fairest of three ladies chosen for the king's enjoyment. In this way, the queen conceived a child by the king and returned home to bear a daughter, whom she named Isol shortly before her death. Some years passed and the young Isol was walking by the seashore when she spied a small box with an infant inside. Isol rescued the lad, named him Tristan, and pledged herself to him for the future. Meanwhile, the king took a second wife who was a sorceress. During a trip when both the king and Tristan were away, the new queen tried to poison Isol so that her own daughter Isota might marry Tristan. After Tristan returned, the sorceress gave him a potion that made him forget Isol and accept Isota. Disguised as a peasant girl, Isol was made to stand in for Isota during the marriage procession because the latter had to give birth to a child out of wedlock. Forbidden to

speak to Tristan, Isol disregarded the command and said something to jar his memory. That night Tristan asked Isota to explain the remarks "she" had made earlier that day. When Isota could not, she went to Isol for an explanation. Tristan found out and the plot was uncovered.

K. English

65 Superman: Siegel and Schuster, *Detective Comics* 1 (Twentieth century A.D.)[88]
A scientist named Jor-el, certain of the impending destruction of his planet Krypton, decided to save the life of his infant son. He and his wife placed the child in a space ship which blasted off as the planet began to explode. The capsule reached Earth, landing safely in the countryside around Smallville U.S.A. A local citizen and his wife were traveling through the area when they sighted the vessel and the baby inside. They took the infant to a nearby orphanage, where he soon began to exhibit many unique powers. The Kents, who had no children of their own, began to long for the foundling that they had left at the orphanage. Finally, they returned to the institution and adopted him. The lad grew up to become the mighty man of steel, Superman.

L. Irish

66. Lugh: O'Donovan, *Annals of the Kingdom of Ireland.* (Nineteenth century A.D.)[89]
On an island off the coast of Ireland there lived a famous robber named Balor. Balor, a cyclops, was warned by a Druid that he would die at the hands of a son of his only daughter Ethnea. In order to forestall the prophecy, Balor had the girl imprisoned in a lofty tower guarded by twelve matrons; thus, he hoped to remove any opportunity for her to conceive. Soon after, he stole the magic cow of Mac Kineely, the lord of the district. Learning that the cow could only be recovered after Balor's death, Mac Kineely, who was also aware of the Druid's prophecy, disguised himself as a woman and was transported to Balor's island with the help of a fairy friend. There they

received shelter and were gone by morning, their mission accomplished. In due course, Ethnea gave birth to three sons, to the great distress of her father. Balor wrapped the infants in a blanket and threw them into the ocean. One infant escaped with the assistance of Balor's fairy friend. The babe, named Lugh, was raised by his uncle and grew up to be a famous smith. Years later Balor slew Mac Kineely and was himself slain when Lugh thrust a burning iron into his eye.

M. Albanian

67. The Jealous Sisters: Dozen, *Contes albanais*. (Nineteenth century A.D.)[90]

Three daughters of a recently deceased king were overheard by his successor, discussing what they would give as a gift if married to the king. The two older girls spoke of material presents; the youngest promised to give her husband a son with a star on his forehead and a daughter with a crescent on her shoulder. The king decided to marry all three sisters and received the gifts pledged by the first two girls. When the youngest became pregnant and was about to give birth, her jealous sisters conspired to expose her children. The king, who had just returned from a long journey, was told that his wife had delivered a cat and mouse. In a rage, he ordered that the wife be exposed on the staircase where all who passed by would spit upon her. Meanwhile, the sisters placed her babies in a chest and had it thrown into the sea. A strong wind carried the chest to shore where an old man and his wife discovered it. They opened the box, found the infants, and brought them home. When the children had grown, the foster father sent the lad to fetch a magic bridle that had once belonged to him. With this bridle, the boy conjured up two horses to transport him and his sister to the land of their natural parents. After numerous adventures, provoked by the evil aunts, the lad acquired a beautiful wife. He then attended a dinner at his father's palace and revealed his identity to the king. After the king had learned of the circumstances of his abandonment, he had the two sisters slain. The mother was restored and the lad named heir to the throne.

N. Turkish

68. Abu'l Giwaliq: Suhaili, Folklore of Turkey. (Seventeenth century A.D.)[91]
A rich man slew a female slave who had given birth to his son; he exposed the child in the wilderness. Somehow the infant survived and after a few years the father found the lad alive. This time he threw the boy into the sea from fear of his current wife. But a fisherman saved the youth by pulling him out of the sea in a sack. Thereby, the lad received the name Abu'l Giwaliq "father of the sack." Years passed and one day the father came to the fisherman and recognized his son who was now grown up. Determined to be rid of him at last, he sent the boy to his wife with a death letter. His daughter, however, found out about the letter and thwarted the evil plan by changing the death letter into a marriage contract. Since the couple was married without delay, the only course left to the father was to hire a murderer. When the young wife warned her husband about her father's plot, the father fell victim to his own scheme.

69. The Children of Ahmed Aga: Kunos, *Turkische Volksmärchen aus Stambul*. (Nineteenth century A.D.)[92]
Once upon a time there was a rich man, Ahmed Aga, who lived with his wife. The couple lacked nothing in life except children. One night, in a dream, the wife beheld a mermaid emerging from the sea with a jar. The mermaid said that Allah had granted her husband's wish and that she was to fetch him hither. The couple awoke and the dream was recounted to Ahmed Aga. The next morning, urged by his wife, Ahmed went to the seashore and saw a jar tossing on the waves. Opening the vessel, he found two babies, a boy and a girl. Ahmed returned home with the children and happily began to raise them. In another town a rich man, who was also childless, had bought a maiden to serve as his second wife. This act had stirred the jealousy and enmity of his first wife. When the young girl

had become pregnant, the older wife had conspired with a sorceress to protect her position. The sorceress, posing as a midwife, had replaced the girl's twin babies (a girl and a boy) with a dead snake. The infants were those placed in a jar and thrown into the sea, eventually to be recovered by Ahmed Aga. Appalled by the "offspring" presented to him, the husband had sent his new wife away. Fortunately, the girl was taken in by a shepherd and his wife and was herself adopted. In time, Aga's adopted son grew up possessed of enormous strength. He and his sister had a similar dream in which they saw their natural mother residing with the shepherd and his wife, and thus learned the nature of their origins. The lad was inspired to locate his mother, and his quest, following several adventures, was finally successful. He and his mother returned to the home of Ahmed Aga and all lived happily ever after.

O. Chinese

70. Kun-bok: Communication from Tsiang Kien to the Emperor. (Second century B.C.)[93]

The father of Kun-bok ruled a small kingdom bordering another dominated by Hung-ho. The neighboring king slew the father of Kun-bok and cast away his infant son in the wilderness, where a wolf came and nursed him. Another nomadic ruler, Tan-hu, found Kun-bok, took him home, and brought him up. Later he appointed him leader of his warriors and placed him in command of his father's former people. Kun-bok conquered the nearby cities building up a large force of bowmen. When Tan-hu died, Kun-bok made himself king and declared his independence of Hung-ho. The latter sent his troops against the upstart but could not prevail militarily. Kun-bok was considered divine and there were no more attempts to defeat him.

P. Malayan

71. Raden Paku: The Legend of Raden Paku. (Fifteenth century A.D.)[94]

A Muslim preacher named Sheikh Isak came to live as an ascetic in the mountains of a Hindu kingdom in Java. The king of the land had a daughter who fell critically ill. When no one seemed able to heal her, the king sent for the Muslim. Sheikh Isak agreed to cure the girl on one condition, that the king would promise to convert to Islam after his daughter had recovered. The Muslim saved the princess's life as promised, and as a reward he was given her hand in marriage. Isak then had to return to his own land, but not before he had impregnated his bride. The princess gave birth to a beautiful son at the same time that a plague broke out in the land. The royal astrologers said that the king should never have sent for the Muslim and that, to be rid of the disease, he had to cast the child into the sea. A waterproof chest was constructed and the infant placed inside. They threw the chest into the water, and it floated until it reached the kingdom of Gersik. One night the crew of a small boat found it, pulled the chest out of the water, and returned with it to their lady, the owner of the boat. She opened the box to discover a handsome infant within. The lady raised the child herself and educated him in the best Muslim school in Java. The lad began to exhibit marvelous qualities and acquired the name Raden Paku when leaving school. Some time later, the lady conceived a passion for Raden and bared her breasts before him. As he sucked from her breasts, milk was miraculously produced because of his saintly virtue. This designated her as the proper mother of Raden, a role she fulfilled with every care and attention.

Q. Palaung

72. Udibwa and Min Rama: Scott, *Indo-Chinese Mythology*. (Nineteenth-Twentieth centuries A.D.)[95]
Prince Hsuriya, the son of the solar deity, became involved with a serpent maiden, Princess Thusandi, who conceived and delivered three eggs. When Hsuriya was summoned home by his father, he had to leave his lover. Upon reaching the sun, Hsuriya, using two parrots as his messengers, sent a letter to Thusandi along with a precious stone. During their mission, the

irresponsible birds stopped to socialize with other parrots and temporarily forgot about the letter and its enclosure. A man and his son found the letter and removed the valuable stone, substituting bird droppings in its place. Eventually, the parrots carried out their task and delivered the letter. When Thusandi discovered the "gift" that her paramour had sent her, she angrily threw two of her eggs into the river. One egg floated upstream until a gardener and his wife retrieved it from the water and placed it in a golden casket. The egg hatched out a male infant, who was raised by the couple and named Hseng Nya. Later, he came to be called Udibwa which means "born of an egg." When Udibwa was grown, he married the daughter of a Shan ruler and fathered two sons. One son became emperor of China and the other became the father of the Palaung people. Thusandi's second egg washed ashore on the bank of the river. There a fisherman and his wife found it and put it into a golden pot. Soon it hatched out a baby boy of such noble appearance that the couple named him Min Rama, because they believed he must be of the ruler Rama Min's family. Min Rama grew up to become king of Pagan.[96]

NOTES

CHAPTER V

[1]The more commonly used term--Child-Exposure Motif--is best abandoned in favor of this designation in order to distinguish clearly between tales in which a newborn child is involved and those describing the exposure of older children. Sargon was exposed in infancy as were all other heroes whose birth stories appear below.

[2]See G. Smith, "Early History of Babylonia," *Transactions of the Society of Biblical Archaeology* 1 (1872), pp. 46-47; and H. F. Talbot, "A Fragment of Ancient Assyrian Mythology," ibid., pp. 271-80.

[3]Smith, ibid., p. 47.

[4]Talbot, "Fragment of Ancient Assyrian Mythology," p. 272.

[5]See the discussion of the history of the study of the Sargon Legend in Chapter I.

[6]C. P. Tiele appears to have introduced the title in *Handbücher der alten Geschichte* I/4 (Gotha, 1886), p. 114. Later Güterbock used the term in "Historische Tradition," p. 62 as did Jacobsen in *The Sumerian King List*, p. 145.

[7]For other examples of the application of folklore methodology to the study of ancient Near Eastern material, see O. R. Gurney, "The Tale of the Poor Man of Nippur and its Folktale Parallels," *AnSt* 22 (1972), pp. 149-58; S. Niditch and R. Doran, "The Success Story of the Wise Courtier: A Formal Approach," *JBL* 96 (1977), pp. 179-93; and Dorothy Irvin, *Mytharion*, AOAT XXXII (Neukirchen-Vluyn, 1978).

[8]Stith Thompson, *The Folktale* (New York, 1946), p. 415.

[9]See S. Thompson, *Motif-Index of Folk-Literature*, Indiana University Studies Nos. 96-97, 100-101, 105-6, 108-12 (Indiana, 1932-36), Vol. V, p. 9. Cf. M 371, p. 63, and S 141, p. 309 (Vol. V).

[10]Cf. Thompson, *The Folktale*, p. 415.

[11]See *FF Communications* No. 184 (Helsinki, 1961).

[12]The type might be called, in the style of the other titles, "The Hero Who Was Exposed at Birth."

[13]As Robert Drews has observed in "Sargon, Cyrus and Mesopotamian Folk History," *JNES* 33 (1974), p. 388, n. 8.

[14]This is assuming a date of composition for the Legend between the thirteenth and eighth centuries. It is not unlikely that the Sargon story is actually older than the composition of the Legend and may go back in oral form as far as the early second millennium, if not before. On the problem of dating the text, see Chapter III.

[15]See Chapter VI, pp. 215-16. The list of tale versions that appears below depends, in part, on the following collections: O. Rank, *The Myth of the Birth of the Hero* (New York, 1964); D. Redford, "The Literary Motif of the Exposed Child," *Numen* 14 (1967), pp. 209-28; T. Gaster, *Myth, Legend, and Custom in the Old Testament* (New York, 1969), pp. 224-30, 380-82; and G. Binder, *Die Aussetzung des Königskindes Kyros und Romulus*, Beiträge zur klassischen Philologie, X (Meisenheim am Glan, 1964), pp. 123-250. For additional bibliography see Redford, ibid., p. 211, n. 9; and cf. n. 96, below.

[16]See below (Chapter VI), *Analysis of the Type*.

[17]Cf. a version of the Slandered Queen tale such as Siegfried and Genovefa (see Grimm Brothers, *Deutsche Sagen, gesammelt durch die Brüder Grimm* [Munich and Leipzig, 1911], II no. 532, pp. 228-32), which combines calumniation of the queen with the exposure and subsequent animal nursing of her son. For a discussion of the genre, see M. Schlauch, *Chaucer's Constance and Accused Queens* (New York, 1927). As an example of the Maiden Without Hands type, see *The Pentamerone of Giambattista Basile*, ed. N. M. Penser (London and New York, 1932), III, 2 pp. 232-40.

[18]N. M. Holley's claim that the Babylonian Tammuz was cast upon the waters as an infant and "lay in a submerged boat" (see "The Floating Chest," *Journal of Hellenic Studies* 60 [1949], p. 43) is based on a misinterpretation of IV *R* pl. 30, no. 2 by S. Langdon. Cf. *CAD* Vol. Ṣ, p. 174, s.v. *ṣiḫḫirūtu*.

[19]For a recent treatment of the birth of Moses including the latest bibliography, see Brevard S. Childs, *The Book of Exodus*, The Old Testament Library (Philadelphia, 1974), pp. 4-20. Cf. Childs's earlier work, "The Birth of Moses" in *JBL* 84 (1965), pp. 109-22.

[20]The Babylonian Talmud has been translated into English under the editorship of Rabbi Dr. I. Epstein, see *The Babylonian Talmud Seder Nashim* (London, 1936), III, pp. 60-65. On the dating of the Babylonian Talmud, see *Encyclopaedia Judaica*, s.v. "Babylonian Talmud." Note that the Midrash preserves an account of the birth of Moses taken almost verbatim from the Babylonian Talmud; see *Midrash Rabbah*, trans. H. Freedman and M. Simon (London, 1939), Vol. III, pp. 26-33 I 19-25. Cf. L. Ginzberg's rendition of the birth story based on a number of Rabbinic sources including Sotah and Shemot Rabbah (L. Ginzberg, *The Legends of the Jews* [Philadelphia, 1910], II, pp. 262-69).

[21]The original source of this tale is uncertain. According to L. Ginzberg (*Legends*, Vol. XI, p. 169), the story is preserved in *Rab Pe'alim* 12 a, which cites as earlier sources the writings of Rabbi Nathan Shapiro and *Sefer Ma'asiyot* of Rabbi Nissim Gaon. Ginzberg is not able to locate the birth legend in either source. For his own account of the tale, see *Legends*, Vol. IV, p. 3. Cf. Binder, *Aussetzung des Kyros und Romulus*, p. 172 for additional bibliography. Note that this story combines elements from the tales of Moses, Oedipus, and Jonah, and the type known as "the Milk of the Mother." On this last type see E. Cosquin's study, "Le lait de la mère et le coffre flottant," *RQH* N.S. 39 (1908), pp. 370-95.

[22]This tale was originally published in Constantinople in 1712 and reprinted by A. Jellinek in 1853 (see *Beit ha-Midrash*, 3rd ed. [Jerusalem, 1967], I, pp. 25-34). For an English translation, see L. Ginzberg, *Legends*, Vol. I, pp. 186-91. Certain internal evidence indicates an Arabic original and hence a Medieval date of composition. Cf. Jellinek, ibid., pp. xv-xvi and *Encyclopaedia Judaica*, s.v. "Abraham: In Medieval Literature."

[23]This version of the Nimrod legend, which obviously reflects the influence of the Oedipus story, is found in the introduction to the Arabic romance of *'Antar* and in al-Kisā'ī's *Kitāb Ḳiṣāṣ al-Anbiyā'*. According to the *Encyclopaedia of Islam*, 1st ed., s.v. "Al-Kisā'ī," this author's identity and dates are uncertain. For an English summary of the tale, see ibid. under Namrud; and cf. I. Goldziher, *Mythology Among the Hebrews*, trans. R. Martineau (New York, 1967), pp. 188-89.

[24]See Heinrich Otten, *Eine althethitische Erzählung um die Stadt Zalpa*, Studien zu den Boğazköy-Texten, XVII (Wiesbaden, 1973), esp. pp. 6-7. This is the oldest known version of the exposed-hero tale. It is preserved on a tablet dated, on the basis of the *Ductus*, to the Old Hittite period. A copy of the text (Bo. 70/10) was published as *KBo* XXII no. 2. The reverse of the tablet duplicates KBo III 38. E. Laroche referred to the composition in his *Catalogue des textes hittites*, Etudes et Commentaires, LXXV (Paris, 1971), p. 2 no. 3 as "Fragments nommant la ville de Zalpa." Cf. Güterbock, *ZA* 44 (1938), pp. 101-11.

[25]The story of the Sun God and the Cow, preserved in Hittite on a clay tablet from Boğazköy, is Hurrian in origin. See H. Ehelolf's treatment, "Das Motiv der Kindesunterschiebung in einer hethitischen Erzählung" in *OLZ* 29 (1926), pp. 766-69. A copy of the text was published by A. Walther in *KUB* XXIV as no. 7, ii 46 - iv 59. Cf. Laroche, *CTH*, p. 63, no. 363. Laroche calls this "the Tale of the Fisherman." J. Friedrich offered a transliteration and translation in "Churritische Märchen und Sagen in hethitischen Sprache," *ZA* 49 (1950), pp. 225-33. An English translation may be found in T. Gaster's *The Oldest Stories in the World* (New York, 1952), pp. 164-67; cf. p. 170.

[26]See *The Odes of Pindar*, trans. J. Sandys, Loeb Classical Library (London and New York, 1915), pp. 57-61.

[27]Sophocles, *Oedipus The King*, Vol. I, trans. F. Storr, LCL (London and New York, 1912), see especially the Argument to *Oedipus The King*, pp. 2-3. A more concise rendition of the tale is preserved by Apollodorus who, nevertheless, follows Sophocles' version closely. See Apollodorus, *The Library*, Vol. I, trans. J. G. Frazier, LCL (London and New York, 1921), Book III, v. 7-9, pp. 343-49. For a valuable bibliography of classical references to the Oedipus tale, see ibid., p. 343, n. 3. Another version of the Oedipus story based on a water exposure has been reconstructed from the Scholia on *The Phoenician Women* (Euripides) 26; Hyginus's *Fabulae*, LXVI; and a clay vessel on which two scenes from the tale are depicted, see E. Bethe, *Thebanische Heldenlieder* (Leipzig, 1891), pp. 67-75 and esp. n. 40.

[28]Note that Sophocles wrote two plays entitled *Tyro* (now lost) that presumably included an account of the exposure of Pelias and Neleus in an ark on water. According to Aristotle, the foundling twins were eventually recognized by the ark in which they were exposed. See Aristotle, *The Poetics*, trans. W. H. Fyfe, LCL (London and New York, 1927), Book XVI 4 and n. g., p. 59; and cf. Apollodorus, *The Library*, Vol. I, pp. 82-83, nn. 1-2. A full account of the tale of Pelias and Neleus appears below as tale 27. The story of the birth of Aegisthus (see below, tale 40 and n. 61), which is preserved mainly by Hyginus, may also derive from a lost work of Sophocles concerning Thyestes, so Frazier in Apollodorus, *The Library*, Vol. II, trans. J. G. Frazier, LCL (London and New York, 1921), p. 168, n. 1.

[29]Herodotus, [*The Histories*], trans. A. D. Godley, LCL (London and New York, 1920), pp. 139-61. This part of *The Histories* was probably based on earlier works about Persia called *Persica*. On the question of Herodotus's use of the *Persica* of Dionysius of Miletus, Hellanicus of Lesbos, and Charon of Lampsacus as source material, see Robert Drews, *The Greek Accounts of Eastern History* (Cambridge, 1973), pp. 20-30. For another version of the birth of Cyrus, see tale 37.

[30]Harpagus's disobedience lead to the mutilation of his own son by Astyages, cf. *The Histories*, Book I 119, p. 155.

[31]Euripides, *Ion*, Vol. IV, trans. A. S. Way, LCL (London and New York, 1912); see especially the Argument to *Ion* on p. 3.

[32]Euripides, *Bacchanals*, Vol. III, trans. A. S. Way, LCL (London and New York, 1912). For a convenient summary of the plot, see the Argument, p. 3. Note the apparently unrelated version of the birth of Dionysus told by Pausanias, which appears below as tale 29.

[33]A number of other exposed-hero tales have been based, directly or indirectly, on lost works of Euripides: for example, Apollodorus's versions of Amphion and Zethus (see n. 45) and Atalanta (n. 48) and Hyginus's accounts of Aeolus and Boeotus (n. 63) and Hippothous (n. 64).

[34]Menander, *The Principal Fragments*, trans. F. G. Allinson, LCL (London and New York, 1921). A summary of the plot appears on pp. 3-8. Note that the name of the child, if it was mentioned in the play, is not preserved. A fifth act is partially preserved but does not contribute to the tale of the exposed infant. This play is an example of the New Comedy; cf. Gilbert Murray, "Ritual Elements in the New Comedy," *Classical Quarterly* 37 (1943), pp. 46-54.

[35]Diodorus of Sicily, *Library of History*, Vol. I, trans. C. H. Oldfather, LCL (London and New York, 1933), pp. 357-71. Diodorus drew on a number of sources for material on Semiramis including Ctesias of Cnidus (early fourth century, Cleitarchus (third century), and "certain of those who at a later time crossed into Asia with Alexander." He was also aware of the opinions of Athenaeus and "certain other historians" that Semiramis was only a courtesan (Book II 20.3). See Oldfather's discussion of the sources behind Diodorus, ibid., pp. xxvi-xxvii. For a recent treatment of the figure of Semiramis, see Wilhelm Eilers, *Semiramis*, Österreichische Akademie der Wissenschaften Philosophisch-historische Klasse Sitzungsberichte, CCLXXIV/2 (Vienna, 1971), esp. pp. 12-14.

[36]*Library of History*, Vol. II, pp. 451-53. This tale may have been taken from an encyclopedia of myth (*Kyklos*), compiled by Diodorus of Mitylene, a second-century Alexandrian mythographer used by Diodorus (see ibid., p. ix).

[37]Ibid., II, pp. 369-71. Diodorus may have taken this story from the *Praise of Heracles* by Matris of Thebes (third century); cf. the Introduction to Volume II, p. ix.

[38]Ibid., II, pp. 269-71. According to Diodorus, this account of the Mother Goddess, Cybele, was current among the natives of Phrygia.

[39]Diodorus of Sicily, *Library of History*, Vol. IX, trans. R. M. Geer, LCL (Cambridge and London, 1947), pp. 229-31. This tale may derive from a *History of Agathocles* by Duris, a Greek writer of the fourth-third centuries B.C. (see p. vii of the Introduction).

[40]Josephus, *Jewish Antiquities*, Vol. IV, trans. H. St. J. Thackeray, LCL (London and New York, 1930), pp. 255-63. The author apparently had available to him (in addition to Exodus) a mass of traditional lore, Midrash, and Aggadah on which this version was based, see the Introduction, pp. xii-xiii.

[41]Cf. Matthew I.18-II.23. On the dating of the Gospel, see *The Oxford Annotated Bible Revised Standard Version*, ed. H. G. May and B. M. Metzger (New York, 1962), p. 1239. Despite the absence of the standard exposure motif, other features present in the birth tale argue for its inclusion as a defective or incomplete version of our tale type. See Rank's treatment of the birth of Jesus in his *Birth of the Hero*, pp. 50-54; and cf. Redford, "Motif of the Exposed Child," p. 218. According to Redford, "The abandonment of the child in a deserted spot is replaced by a flight *through* the desert to Egypt"; cf. Matthew II.20-23.

[42] *Plutarch's Lives*, Vol. I, trans. Bernadette Perrin, LCL (London and New York, 1914), s.v. Romulus, pp. 97-113. In this chapter, Plutarch offered a number of theories concerning the origin of the name of Rome. In his view, this version was the most credible and had the most vouchers. He cited his sources as Diocles of Peparethus and Fabius Pictor. The former had written a "Founding of Rome" (p. 113).

[43] Ibid., pp. 95-97. Plutarch dismissed this version of the birth of Romulus and Remus as "altogether fabulous" and untrue. He attributed the tale to Promathion, an obscure Greek historian (not listed in *OCD*), who had written a history of Italy (p. 97). Cf. M. Grant's discussion of the versions of the Romulus and Remus myth in his *Roman Myths* (New York, 1971), pp. 98-116.

[44] Apollodorus, *The Library*, Vol. I, trans. J. G. Frazier, LCL (London and New York, 1921), pp. 153-64. On the problem of dating, see the Introduction, esp. p. xvi. While Apollodorus is dated to the second century B.C., according to the *OCD*[2], "the extant work of this name (*Bibliotheca*), which presents an uncritical summary of the traditional Greek Mythology, belongs to the first or second century A.D." s.v. "Apollodorus," p. 83. *The Library* is a storehouse of Greek myths and legends based on a variety of written sources and folklore material. According to Frazier, this tale of the birth of Perseus seems to derive from folk literature (cf. *The Library*, Vol. I, pp. xix-xxviii).

[45] Ibid., I, pp. 337-39. Apollodorus's version appears to be related to Euripides' lost play *Antiope* (ibid., p. 337, n. 2). Cf. Hyginus's version in *Fabulae* VIII, which is also believed to derive ultimately from Euripides.

[46] Ibid., II, pp. 45-47. Cf. n. 2 on p. 47 for a discussion of the derivation of the name Alexander.

[47] Ibid., I, pp. 81-85. Note (1) the strong resemblance of plot elements to the tale of Amphion and Zethus (see above, tale 25), and (2) that the legend of Pelias and Neleus was known to Menander, who mentions it in his play *The Arbitrants* (see above, tale 14). Apollodorus apparently followed a different tradition of the Pelias and Neleus story from that of Menander or Sophocles in the lost play *Tyro* (see n. 28). For a discussion of the various accounts of the exposure of Pelias and Neleus, see ibid., pp. 82-83, n. 2.

[48] Ibid., I, pp. 399-401. Frazier discusses the many versions of the Atalanta story and their differences, while providing a valuable bibliography of classical references in n. 2 on pp. 398-99. Among the authors cited by Apollodorus in his discussion of the Atalanta myths is Euripides; see ibid., pp. 401-2 and p. 399, n. 2.

[49] Pausanias, *Description of Greece*, Vol. II, trans. W. H. S. Jones, LCL (London and New York, 1926), p. 153. The author cites the inhabitants of Brasiae as the source of this tale, which is unknown elsewhere in Greece. Cf. Euripides' version

of the birth of Dionysus (tale 13).

[50]Ibid., III, p. 269. Pausanias describes this story as a local legend of the people of Dyme, who have a sanctuary built for Attis.

[51]Ibid., I, pp. 385-87. The author presents this version of the Asclepius tale as the tradition preserved by the Epidaurians to explain the presence of the famous sanctuary of Asclepius just outside of Epidaurus.

[52]Aelian, *On the Characteristics of Animals*, Vol. III, trans. A. F. Scholfield, LCL (Cambridge and London, 1958), pp. 39-41. Aelian used a number of early Greek sources on mythology, natural history, and paradoxa. This tale may have come from Ctesias of Cnidus, an early fourth-century Greek author of a *Persica* that included a history of the Assyrian and Median empires. After reciting the story, Aelian dismisses it as a legend (p. 41).

[53]Longus, *Daphnis and Chloe*, trans. G. Thornley and revised by J. M. Edmonds, LCL (London and New York, 1916), pp. 11-247. Longus's dates are uncertain. Thornley would place him tentatively between the second and third centuries A.D. (see p. vii); the *OCD* (s.v. "Longus," p. 513) suggests a third-century date as most probable; and *OCD*^{2} (p. 619) leaves the question open claiming that any period between the second and sixth centuries is possible.

[54]*Heliodorus An Aethiopian Romance*, trans. Thomas Underdowne and revised by F. A. Wright (London, 1923). A summary of the romance appears in the *OCD*^{2}, s.v. "Heliodorus" (4), pp. 493-94.

[55]Antoninus Liberalis, *Les mêtamorphoses*, trans. M. Papathomopoulos (Paris, 1968), pp. 50-51. On dating the text to the third century A.D., see ibid., p. ix, n. 2. According to a marginal note, the tale is said to derive from Book II of the Metamorphosis of Nicander of Colophon, a second-century B.C. writer. Papathomopoulos provides a useful commentary and bibliography on pp. 138-40. Cf. Binder, *Aussetzung des Kyros und Romulus*, p. 136.

[56]As an indication that the tale is only partially preserved, note that there is no explanation of how Miletus came in contact with Minos as an adult.

[57]*Lexicographi Graeci I 3 Svidiae Lexicon*, ed. A. Adler (Stuttgart, 1967), s.v. *lagos*, pp. 226-27. Suda (Suidas) is taken as the name of the lexicon, not the author. The text was based on classical sources and abridgments of other works. The author drew on Hesychius of Miletus for some biographical material; cf. *OCD*^{2}, s.v. "Suidas," p. 1020. For a discussion of the sources bearing on Ptolemy Soter including this birth story, see J. Hubaux and M. Leroy, *Le mythe du phênix*, Bibliothèque de la Faculté de Philosophie et Lettres de l'Université de Liège, LXXXII (Liège-Paris, 1939), pp. 203-4.

[58]This version of the birth of Cyrus is known from an epitome of the *Historiae Phillippicae* of Pompeius Trogus, prepared by Marcus Junianus Justinus in the third century A.D. Trogus's universal history, which consisted of 44 books, was based partly on Timagenes of Alexandria (first century B.C.), a contemporary of Trogus's, and Deinon's Persian Tales (fourth century B.C.). See *Histoire universelle de Justin extraite de Trogue Pompée*, trans. J. Pierrot and E. Boitard, Bibliothèque Latine-Francaise, VIII (Paris, 1827-29), I, pp. 12-21.

[59]Ibid., II, pp. 86-89.

[60]Ibid., II, pp. 334-39.

[61]*The Myths of Hyginus*, trans. and ed. Mary Grant, University of Kansas Publications Humanistic Studies, LIV (Lawrence, 1960), pp. 79-80. According to the opinion of Rose and others, the text of the *Fabulae* is an epitome rather than the original work of Hyginus, which must have been written before 207 A.D. (see the Introduction, pp. 1-3). The birth of Aegisthus is found in fragmentary form in a number of sources including Apollodorus, *The Library*, Vol. II, trans. J. G. Frazier, LCL (London and New York, 1921)*Epitome* II, 14 pp. 186-89; Dio Chrysostom, *Discourses*, Vol. V, trans. H. L. Crosby, LCL (Cambridge and London, 1951) Discourse 66.6, p. 95; the Scholiast Lactantius Placidus (on Statius, *Thebais* iv. 306); and the First and Second Vatican Mythographers, *Scriptores rerum mythicarum Latini*, ed. G. H. Bode (Cellis, 1834), Vol. I, no. 22, pp. 7-8, no. 147 pp. 125-26. For additional bibliography of classical references, see Apollodorus, *The Library*, Vol. II, p. 168, n. 1 and p. 164 n. 1. The version presented in Hyginus's *Fabulae* LXXXVII-III (cf. CCLII) is believed to be based on Sophocles' account of Thyestes, see *The Fragments of Sophocles*, ed. A. C. Pearson (Amsterdam, 1963), Vol. I, no. 246, pp. 185-87.

[62]From this incident the name Aegisthus is said to derive, for in Greek a she-goat is called "aega" (*Fabulae* LXXXVII).

[63]See Grant, *Myths of Hyginus*, pp. 143-44. In Rose's opinion, this version derives partly from Euripides (*Melanippe Desmontis*) and partly from other writers (p. 144).

[64]See ibid., p. 144, where Grant writes, "no one will doubt that this chapter is related to Euripides, since it is very like the *Arbitration* of Menander, which, as is well known, took much from him." Cf. above tale 14.

[65]*History of the Langobards by Paul the Deacon*, trans. William D. Foulke (New York, 1907), pp. 26-29. Paul drew on local legends and sagas for the tales that appear in his history. The story of Lamissio was presented as credible by the author, who referred to the histories of the ancients for precedents for multiple births.

[66]The Judas story is one of a number of Christian legends written in the Middle Ages that were based on the Oedipus tale. The earliest text known is a Latin version by Jacques de

Varaggio in the thirteenth century. For a translation and discussion, see L. Constans, *La legende d'Oedipe* (Paris, 1881), pp. 95-97, and Apollodorus, *The Library*, Vol. II, trans. J. G. Frazier, LCL (London and New York, 1921), Appendix, pp. 374-75.

[67]The story of the birth of Karna is found in the Vana Parva section of the Hindu classic, the *Mahabharata*, an enormous epic composed in Sanskrit over a period of 800 years (cf. John B. Noss, *Man's Religions* [New York, 1974], p. 192). For an English translation see P. C. Roy, *The Mahabharata of Krishna-Dwaipayana-Vyasa*, 2nd ed. (Calcutta, 1955), Vol. III, pp. 648-56, and passim.

[68]The story of Eḷakamara is found in the *Jātakas*, a collection of tales about the Buddha's former births. The text is preserved in Pali but may have derived from a Singhalese original. The traditional date of the Pali translation is the fifth century A. D. An English translation was prepared under the editorship of E. B. Cowell, *The Jātaka or Stories of the Buddha's Former Births* (Cambridge, 1895), Vol. V, no. 536, pp. 229-31. Cf. Vol. III, no. 327, p. 60.

[69]See the Nigrodha-Jātaka, ibid., Vol. IV, no. 445, pp. 22-25.

[70]This Buddhist tale is preserved in a commentary to the *Dhammapada*, which is attributed to Buddhaghosa in the fifth century. Copies of the text are written in Pali in Cambodian characters. A translation was published by E. Hardy, "The Story of the Merchant Ghosaka," *Journal of the Royal Asiatic Society of Great Britain and Ireland* (1898), pp. 741-94. A similar tale about a Bodhisattva is found in a Chinese work by Lu Tu-tsi in the third century. Cf. Binder, *Aussetzung des Kyros und Romulus*, pp. 196-97, no. 71, I-II for additional bibliography.

[71]This story belongs to a collection of tales about the Indian hero Vikramaditya. It is found in a work written in Mongolian known as the *History of Ardshi-Bordshi Chan*. Ardshi-Bordshi Chan was the Mongolian title of a fifth-century ruler of Malava, King Bhoga. A German translation was published by B. Jülg in *Mongolische Märchen, Die neun Nachtrags-Erzählung des Siddhi-Kur und die Geschichte des Ardschi-Bordschi Chan* (Innsbruck, 1868), pp. 207-13, 73-79.

[72]This Indian tale is found in a Chinese work by Fa-hien, a Buddhist who traveled to India in the fifth century A. D. A summary of the tale appeared in E. Cosquin's "Le lait de la mère et le coffre flottant," *RQH* 39 (1908), pp. 359-60. The tale served an etiological purpose, explaining the existence of a tower near the town of Vaisali. Cf. James Legge, *A Record of Buddhistic Kingdoms, being an Account by the Chinese Monk Fa-hien of his Travels in India and Ceylon in Search of the Buddhist Books of Discipline* (Oxford, 1886), XXV, pp. 73-74; and perhaps the most recent translation, which was published in the Peoples Republic of China in 1957, *A Record of the Buddhist Countries by Fa-hsien*, trans. Li Yung-hsi (Peking, 1957), XXX, pp. 55-56.

[73]The author of this Jainist text is unknown. A translation was published by C. Krause, *Prince Aghata: Die Abenteurer Ambadas*, Indische Erzähler, IV (Leipzig, 1922), and J. Schick, *Corpus Hamleticum* (Leipzig, 1932), I/2, pp. 378-80. According to Krause, the small novel (*Aghaṭakumarakatha*) was probably written before A.D. 1190.

[74]The story of Candagutta is preserved in a Pali text, the *Vaṃsatthappakasinī* or *Mahāvamsa Ṭīkā*. C. Lassen offered a summary of the legend in *Indische Altertumskunde* (Leipzig, 1874), II, pp. 205-6, n. 1. Candagutta was a great Indian king, who overran the Greek garrisons left by Alexander the Great and conquered most of India. For a discussion of the date of composition, see G. P. Malalasekera, *Vaṃsatthappakasinī: Commentary on the Mahāvamsa*, Pali Text Society (London, 1935), pp. civ-cxi.

[75]The *Hēmacandras Parisiṣtaparvan* is a Sanskrit text from the eleventh-twelfth centuries A. D. J. Hertel published a partial translation in *Ausgewählte Erzählungen aus Hēmacandras Parisiṣtaparvan*, Bibliothek morgenländischer Erzähler, I (Leipzig, 1908), pp. 68-78.

[76]The story of Trakhan was collected from the oral lore of the village of Gilgit in northern India. The people spoke a dialect of Sanskrit with many Persian words. The tale was collected and published in English by Ghulam Muhammad, "Festivals and Folklore of Gilgit," *Asiatic Society of Bengal, Memoirs* 1 (1905), pp. 93-127, especially 124-25.

[77]See R. Greeven, "Ajab Salar and Palihar," *North Indian Notes and Queries* 2 (1893), p. 164, no. 608. Note the interesting combination of the exposure tale with the David and Goliath motif. Either the presentation of the tale is incomplete or else only a fragment of the story is preserved.

[78]This account represents the literary Panjabi version of the tale of Sassi and Punnun attributed to the poet Hasham Shah. Shah's version, which is said to consist of 126 stanzas is summarized by R. C. Temple (see *The Legends of the Punjab* [Bombay, 1901], p. 24) prior to his publication of an incomplete and confused version "told by a bard from the Hushiarpur District" (see pp. 25-37). According to Temple, the tale "properly belongs to Sindh and Southern Baluchistan" (p. 24).

[79]The birth legend of Zarathustra is found here in a Pahlavi text, which is a summary of the older lost Spend Nask of the Avesta. According to the *Denkhart*, the work was completed by Aturpad in the first half of the ninth century A. D. For an English translation, see *Pahlavi Texts* Pt. 5, trans. E. W. West, The Sacred Books of the East, ed. F. M. Muller, Vol. XLVII (Oxford, 1897), pp. 35-39. Another version of the birth of Zarathustra appears below as tale 62.

[80]The *Shah Namah*, the "Book of Kings," is the national epic of Persia. It was composed by the poet Firdausi about A. D. 1000 from much older material. Firdausi's sources included a prose version of the *Shah Namah*, an ancient Pahlavi chronicle by Khudainama, and the *Bastan Namah*, a book of chronicles of

kings. For an excellent translation of the epic, see *The ShahNama of Firdausi*, 9 volumes, trans. A. G. Warner and E. Warner, Trübner Oriental Series (London, 1905-25). The story of the birth of Faridun is found in Vol. I (vv. 37-63), pp. 147-75. A convenient synopsis of the tale was published by Rank in *Birth of the Hero*, pp. 40-41.

[81]See *ShahNama* Vol. I (vv. 131-48), pp. 239-55; cf. Rank, *Birth of the Hero*, pp. 23-24.

[82]See *ShahNama*, Vols. II-IV (vv. 564-1396), pp. 232-69; cf. Rank, *Birth of the Hero*, pp. 39-40.

[83]See *ShahNama* Vol. V (vv. 1756-74), pp. 290-311; cf. Rank, *Birth of the Hero*, p. 22.

[84]Musk is used here to protect the infant from the offensive odor of the bitumen; so we infer from tale 3 (Moses) where bitumen is applied on the outside of the ark and slime within.

[85]John Wilson published a translation of the *Zaratush Namah* in his work, *The Parsi Religion* (Bombay, 1843), see especially pp. 480-88. A discussion of the text and the legend of the birth of Zoroaster appears on pp. 417-21. Cf. A. V. Williams Jackson's discussion of the birth and childhood of the prophet in *Zoroaster The Prophet of Ancient Iran* (New York, 1919), pp. 26-29.

[86]Hartmann von Aue's version of the story of Gregorius, written in Middle High German, is believed to be based on a French poem, "Vie du Pape Gregoire," or a Latin work that has not survived. For a recent treatment of the poem including a discussion of sources and of related legends, see Edwin H. Zeydel and Bayard A. Morgan, *Gregorius A Medieval Oedipus Legend By Hartmann Von Aue*, University of North Carolina Studies in the Germanic Languages and Literatures, XIV (Chapel Hill, 1955). Cf. *Gregorius The Good Sinner Hartmann von Aue*, Bilingual Edition, trans. Sheema Z. Buehne (New York, 1966).

[87]This version of the Tristan saga was collected by Jon Arnason and originally published in Icelandic in his important work *The Folktales and Fairy Tales of Iceland* (Leipzig, 1862-64), Vol. II, p. 320. Two other incomplete versions of the Tristan tale were also mentioned by Arnason (ibid., pp. 315-19, 321-24). Under the title "Die rechte Braut," the tale appeared in the Rittershaus Collection of folktales (see Adeline Rittershaus [Bjarnason], *Die neuislandischen Volksmärchen* [Halle, 1902], XXVII, pp. 113-15. For an English translation of "The True Bride," see "Wishfulfillment and Symbolism in Fairy Tales," by Franz Riklin, trans. W. A. White in *Psychoanalytic Review* 1 (1913), pp. 458-59. Cf. the so-called classic form of the Tristan romance, the epic poem of Gottfried von Strassburg based on the earlier version of Thomas, *Gottfried von Strassburg Tristan with the "Tristan" of Thomas*, trans. A. T. Hatto, The Penguin Classics (Edinburg, 1960). For a brief but valuable discussion of the development of the Tristan legend, see *The Saga of Tristram and Isönd, Translated with an introduction by P. Schach* (Lincoln, 1973), pp. xiii-xxiii. According to Schach, the Tristram saga was especially

active in Iceland "for here the story, in whole or in part, was imitated, adapted, recast, and parodied over a period of centuries" (p. xiv). Cf. P. Schach, "Tristan in Iceland," *Prairie Schooner* 36 (1962), pp. 151-64; and M. Schlauch, *Romance in Iceland* (Princeton and New York, 1934), passim. For a study of the problem of sources of the Tristan legend, see Helene Newstead, "The Origin and Growth of the Tristan Legend," *Arthurian Literature in the Middle Ages*, ed. Roger Sherman Loomis (Oxford, 1959), pp. 122-33; and Gertrude S. Loomis, *Tristan and Isolt: A Study of the Sources of the Romance*, 2nd ed. (New York, 1960).

[88]The original story of the birth of Superman that appeared in 1939 in Detective Comics is reprinted in *Superman From the Thirties to the Seventies*, with an introduction by E. Nelson Bridwell (New York, 1971), pp. 20-21. Cf. *Secret Origins of the Super Heroes*, with an introduction by Carmine Infantino (New York, 1976).

[89]This Celtic folktale was collected by J. O'Donovan from an inhabitant of Tory Island, the presumed residence of Balor Bemen. See J. O'Donovan, *Annals of the Kingdom of Ireland by the Four Masters* (Dublin, 1851), Vol. I, pp. 18-21, n. s. A more recent treatment of the tale was prepared by A. H. Krappe, *Balor With the Evil Eye* (Lancaster, 1927), pp. 1-5. An unrelated account of the struggle between Balor and Lugh is preserved in a fifteenth-century manuscript that may derive from an eigth- or ninth-century original, so Whitney Stokes, "The Second Battle of Moytura," *Revue celtique* 12 (1891), pp. 52-130, see esp. p. 101.

[90]This fairy tale appears with slight variations from India to Europe. The version given here was collected by August Dozon and published in *Collection de chansons et de contes populaires, III Contes albanais* (Paris, 1881), pp. 7-15. A Greek version of the tale was published by P. Kretschmer in *Neugriechische Märchen* (Jena, 1919), no. 58, pp. 257-67. For a Rumanian variant, cf. Binder, *Aussetzung des Kyros und Romulus*, p. 243, n. 5.

[91]A translation of this tale was published by Denis D. Cardonne under the title, "Cruauté inouie d'un père" in *Mélanges de littératures orientales*, Vol. II (Paris, 1770), pp. 69-82. Originally, the story appeared in a collection of Turkish tales by Ahman ben Hamdam Katkhuda (Suhaili), 1625-1640.

[92]The story of Ahmed Aga is found among a collection of Ottoman Turk folktales gathered by Ignaz Kunos during the years 1886-1901. The tale appears under the title "Die beiden Geschwister" in Kunos's *Turkische Volksmärchen aus Stambul* (Leiden, 1905), pp. 339-48.

[93]This tale of infant exposure is preserved in a Chinese inscription from the second century B. C. A treatment of the text was published by J. J. M. de Groot in his *Chinesische Urkunden zur Geschichte Asiens, II Die Westlande Chinas in der vorchristlichen Zeit* (Berlin and Leipzig, 1926), pp. 23-24.

[94]This Muslim legend is preserved in a Malayan document from an original Javanese text concerning the establishment of Islam on the island of Java. E. Cosquin published a translation and discussion of the legend in "Le lait de la mère et le coffre flottant," *RQH* 39 (1908), pp. 355-57.

[95]This tale, a variant of the dragon myth found throughout Indo-China, is taken from the Palaung Chronicle. The Palaungs are a hill people of Burma that speak a dialect of Mon-Khmer. J. G. Scott published a translation of the tale in *Indo-Chinese Mythology*, The Mythology of All Races, ed. L. H. Gray, reprint ed., Vol. XII (New York, 1964), pp. 276-77. Note the trace of Indian influence in the name given to the father of the hero. Hsuriya is derived from the Sanskrit name of the sun god, Surya. Cf. the story of the birth of Karna whose father is identified as Surya (see above, tale 45).

[96]The earlier collections of Rank, Redford, Gaster, and Binder (see above n. 15) mention a number of birth stories that have not been included in our list. Many of these may be dismissed rather easily as unrelated to our tale, while others bear some resemblance to the structure of the type as we define it (in Chapter VI) and are rejected with some hesitancy. We now list the most important of these tales and the reason for their exclusion. Tales belonging to other types: "the Girl With the Maimed Hands," see *The Pentamerone of Giambattista Basile*, ed. N. M. Penzer (London and New York, 1932), Vol. I, pp. 232-40; "Siegfried," see Rank, *Birth of the Hero*, pp. 56-59; "Wolfdietrich," see Friedrich von der Leyen, *Deutsches Sagenbuch* (Munich, 1912) II, pp. 224-38. Tales that do not preserve infant exposure: "Augustus," see Suetonius, *The Lives of the Caesars*, Vol. I, trans. J. C. Rolfe, LCL (London and New York, 1914), s.v. Augustus xciv, 1-6, pp. 263-69; "Pyrrhus," see *Plutarch's Lives*, Vol. IX, trans. B. Perrin, LCL (London and New York, 1920), s.v. Pyrrhus II, pp. 349-51; "Fabius," see ibid., III, s.v. Fabius I 1-2, p. 119; "Horus," see R. T. Rundle Clark, *Myth and Symbol in Ancient Egypt* (London, 1959), pp. 186-87;"Lohengrin," Rank, *Birth of the Hero*, pp. 59-64. Mention of infant exposure, but no tale: "Hiru-go," see "'Ko-Ji-Ki,' or 'Records of Ancient Matters,'" trans. B. H. Chamberlain, *Asiatic Society of Japan, Transactions* Supplement 10 (1882), pp. 19-20; "Scyld," see *Beowulf Translated into Modern English Rhyming Verse by Archibald Strong* (London, 1925), I, 45-52. Exposure of an older child: "T'u Kueh," see S. Julien, *Documents historiques sur les Tou-Kioue (Turcs)* (Paris, 1877), p. 25.

CHAPTER VI

ANALYSIS OF THE TYPE

A quick scan of the versions of the tale that we have collected reveals a variety of literary genres. Some are myths, others are legends, *Märchen*, *novellae*, or hero tales.[1] It is obvious that the form the tale type may assume is fluid. What is it, then, that gives a folktale its own identity, distinguishes it from other types, and, at the same time, provides the stability that permits it to withstand variations in form and differences of time and place? Clearly, the structure of the plot determines the characteristic pattern of the type. The more complex the basic structure, the greater the ability of the tale to maintain its identity.

Turning our attention to the plot structure of the versions of "the exposed-hero tale," let us first determine the principal traits or "components" of the type and then the possibilities of variation, that is, the "factors" or details.

There seem to be seven basic components comprising the type:

I. Explanation of abandonment
II. Infant of noble birth
III. Preparations for exposure
IV. Exposure
V. Infant protected or nursed in an unusual manner
VI. Discovery and adoption
VII. Accomplishments of hero

Each of these components is subject to variations in detail. The factors held to be most significant for the study of the type are here listed with the tales in which they occur:

I. Explanation of abandonment: All but 64
   a. Fear or shame over circumstances of birth: 1, 7, 9, 12, 14, 15, 17, 22, 25, 27, 29-31, 34-36, 38-42, 45, 55, 59, 63, 68
   b. To save the hero's life: 2, 3, 5, 8, 13, 20, 46, 52, 58, 60, 65
   c. To avert an unfavorable prophecy: 4, 6, 10, 11, 19, 24, 26, 32, 37, 44, 48-51, 56, 62, 66, 71

d. Child is unwanted: 18, 28, 33, 43, 48, 53, 54, 72

II. Infant of noble birth: All but 4, 6, 19, 28, 43, 44, 47, 58, 62, 64

a. Noble or royal parent: 1-3, 5, 7, 10-12, 14, 16-18, 20, 22, 24-26, 29, 32-40, 42, 45, 46, 49-52, 54-56, 59-61, 63, 66-72

1. Father is king: 10, 18, 26, 34, 36, 46, 49, 50, 52, 54, 56, 59, 61, 67, 70

2. Mother is queen: 7, 10, 17, 26, 34, 46, 54, 61

3. Mother is princess: 11, 12, 16, 24, 25, 32, 35, 37, 39, 42, 45, 49, 55, 60, 63, 67, 71, 72

4. Mother is priestess: 1, 22

b. Divine parent: 8, 9, 12, 13, 15-17, 21-25, 27, 29-31, 35, 41, 42, 45, 55, 57

c. Animal parent: 8, 72

III. Preparations for exposure: 1-5, 7, 10-12, 14, 19-22, 24, 29, 33, 34, 39, 42, 44-46, 48, 50, 52-57, 61-67, 69, 71

a. Box, basket, chest, receptacle, etc.: 1-4, 7, 8, 11, 12, 20-22, 24, 29, 44-46, 48, 50, 52-57, 61, 63-65, 67, 69, 71, 72

1. Receptacle made waterproof: 1-4, 19, 45, 61, 71

2. Comfortable fittings or valuables (placed in receptacle): 3, 5, 14, 33, 34, 42, 45, 46, 53, 61, 63

b. Parent's agent observes fate of abandoned infant: 2, 3, 19, 20, 46, 61

IV. Exposure: All but 58

a. In or near water: 1-4, 6-9, 20, 22-24, 29, 39, 43-46, 50, 51, 53-57, 61, 63, 64, 66-69, 71, 72

b. In wilderness, forest, mountain, or desolate area: 10, 11, 14-18, 25-28, 30, 31, 33, 35, 37, 39-42, 47-49, 57, 59, 60, 62, 68-70

c. In a cave: 5, 12, 33, 57, 62

d. Multiple exposures: 8, 37, 39, 42, 46, 48, 57, 62, 67-69

e. Mother and child exposed together: 24, 29

V. Infant protected or nursed in an unusual manner: 2-6, 8, 9, 13, 15-18, 20, 22, 23, 26, 28-33, 35-43, 46-49, 52, 57-59, 61-63, 66, 68, 70

a. By an animal

1. Goat: 30, 31, 33, 40, 46
2. Cow: 41, 48, 52, 57, 58, 62
3. Sheep: 33
4. Mare: 42, 57, 62
5. Bitch: 31, 37, 39
6. Deer: 16
7. Bird: 15, 22, 23, 32, 36, 59
8. Wolf: 22, 23, 35, 70
9. Bear: 26, 28
10. "Ferocious animal": 6, 18, 39
11. Serpent/dragon: 9, 49
12. Bees: 38
13. Whale: 4

b. By a human or humanoid

1. Nursed by a deity: 5, 8, 13, 17, 47, 63, 66
2. Nursed by a human who is the natural mother: 2, 3, 17, 20
3. Nursed by another female: 4, 29, 43, 61

VI. Discovery and adoption: All but 5, 6, 9, 13, 36, 38, 39, 49, 57, 62

a. Herder: 16, 26, 31, 37

1. Goatherd: 33, 46
2. Cowherd: 11, 15, 23, 25, 35, 41, 48
3. Shepherd: 10, 14, 18, 21, 30, 33, 40, 42, 52, 60, 69
4. Horseherd: 27
5. Swineherd: 22

b. Other commoner: 54, 58, 65-67

1. Hunter: 28, 52
2. Fisherman: 8, 24, 63, 68, 71, 72
3. Gardener: 1, 32, 51, 72
4. Launderer: 56, 61
5. Mender: 46
6. Charioteer: 45
7. Charcoalman: 14

c. Aristocracy/deity

1. Royal person: 2-4, 10, 16, 17, 20, 41, 43, 44, 50, 55, 64, 70

2. Merchant/rich person: 34, 47, 48, 53, 69
3. Cleric: 12, 34, 63
4. Deity: 7, 17, 51

VII. Accomplishments of hero: All but 7, 8, 14, 29, 30, 33, 36, 53, 56, 68
a. Noteworthy deeds: 1-6, 9-11, 13, 15-28, 31, 32, 34, 35, 37-41, 43-46, 48-52, 55, 57-67, 69-72
b. Kingship: 1, 6, 10-12, 15, 16, 19, 21, 22, 24, 25, 32, 37-39, 41-43, 45-47, 49, 51, 52, 54, 58-61, 63, 67, 70, 72

VIII. Miscellaneous factors
a. Twin heroes involved: 22, 23, 25, 27, 41, 53, 67, 69, 72
b. Dream, omen, or prophecy and its fulfillment: 4-6, 9-12, 17, 19-21, 23, 24, 26, 32, 34, 37, 38, 40, 43-45, 48, 49, 51, 56, 58, 60, 62, 65-67, 69
c. Disclosure of the hero's origin: 4, 5, 10, 11, 12, 14, 16, 19, 22, 25, 26, 28, 33, 34, 39-41, 44-46, 50, 52-54, 56, 58-61, 63, 67, 69
1. Hero is informed of the secret of his birth: 4, 11, 12, 16, 22, 25, 26, 28, 33, 34, 39-41, 41, 44-46, 50, 53, 54, 58-61, 63, 69
2. Hero informs natural parent of his identity: 5, 19, 34, 54, 67
3. Birth tokens lead to disclosure of identity: 12, 14, 40, 56, 61
4. Mother's milk miraculously flows: 4, 50, 71
d. Etymology of hero's name given: 2, 4, 6, 9, 12, 15, 17, 18, 20, 26, 27, 33, 40, 42, 43, 46, 47, 52, 65, 68, 72
e. Etiological element present: 17, 22, 29, 30, 35, 41, 50, 72
f. Miraculous events surrounding birth: 3, 5, 8, 13, 17, 20, 21, 23, 24, 30, 31, 34, 45, 49, 51, 55, 57, 62
1. Miraculous conception: 8, 17, 21, 23, 24, 30, 34, 45, 49, 55, 57
2. Miraculous birth or growth of the infant: 3, 5, 13, 20, 49, 57, 62

g. Incest: 4, 6, 7, 10, 30, 35, 40, 44, 53, 61, 63, 71
   1. Incest without consequences: 7, 30, 35, 40, 53, 61, 63, 71
   2. Incest with slaying of the father: 4, 6, 10, 44

h. Adopted child slays natural child: 41, 44

i. Mutilation of limbs: 30, 48, 52

j. Jealousy of principal wife over inferior wife: 13, 17, 49, 50, 67, 69

k. Death letter: 48, 51, 68

l. Adoptive parents childless: 8, 10, 11, 14, 15, 20, 44-47, 55, 61, 65, 69

m. Repetition of components: 8, 9, 33, 37, 39, 42, 46, 48, 57, 58, 62, 67-69, 72

List of Heroes

For convenience in the use of the following tables, a list of heroes is offered, corresponding to the order of appearance in our collection of tale versions:

A. *Akkadian*
1. Sargon

B. *Hebrew*
2. Moses
3. Moses
4. Joshua
5. Abraham

C. *Arabic*
6. Nimrod

D. *Hittite*
7. The Sons of the Queen of Kaneš
8. The Sun God and the Cow

E. *Greek*
9. Iamus
10. Oedipus
11. Cyrus
12. Ion
13. Dionysus
14. Charisius and Pamphila
15. Semiramis
16. Telephus
17. Heracles
18. Cybele
19. Agathocles
20. Moses
21. Jesus
22. Romulus and Remus
23. Romulus and Remus
24. Perseus
25. Amphion and Zethus
26. Paris/Alexander
27. Pelias and Neleus
28. Atalanta
29. Dionysus
30. Attis
31. Asclepius
32. Gilgameš
33. Daphnis and Chloe
34. Charicleia
35. Miletus
36. Ptolemy Soter

F. *Latin*
37. Cyrus
38. Hieron
39. Habis
40. Aegisthus
41. Aeolus and Boeotus
42. Hippothous
43. Lamissio

F. Latin (cont.)
44. Judas

G. Indian
45. Karna
46. Eḷakamara
47. Nigrodha
48. Ghosaka
49. Vikramaditya
50. The Thousand Sons
51. Aghaṭa
52. Candagutta
53. Kuberadatta
54. Trakhan
55. Palihar
56. Sassi

H. Persian
57. Zarathustra
58. Faridun
59. Zal
60. Kai Khusrau
61. Darab
62. Zarathustra

I. German
63. Gregorius

J. Icelandic
64. Tristan

K. English
65. Superman

L. Irish
66. Lugh

M. Albanian
67. The Jealous Sisters

N. Turkish
68. Abu'l Giwaliq
69. The Children of Ahmed Aga

O. Chinese
70. Kun-bok

P. Malayan
71. Raden Paku

Q. Palaung
72. Udibwa and Min Rama

Introduction to Tables 1-5

Before proceeding with a discussion of the individual components and factors that make up the exposed-hero tale, we offer in the following tables a tabulated summary of our componential analysis.

Table 1 indicates the presence or absence of a component in any given version. In similar fashion, Table 2 identifies the factors found in individual tales. The frequency of occurrence of both components and factors is recorded in Table 3. From these tables, we may conclude that all components are found in a majority of the tales; however, components I, II, IV, and VII occur in a significantly higher percentage of tales than components III and V. The factors, on the other hand, vary greatly in their frequency of occurrence and in their concentration in specific groups of tales.

Tables 4 and 5 supply the following supplementary information: (1) the approximate date of the first and last known occurrence of a factor and the tale in which it is recorded,[2] and (2) the earliest known occurrence of a factor in a language family, the specific language in which it is attested, and the tale involved.

Table 1

Component Analysis

	I	II	III	IV	V	VI	VII
1	+	+	+	+		+	+
2	+	+	+	+	+	+	+
3	+	+	+	+	+	+	+
4	+		+	+	+	+	+
5	+	+	+	+	+		+
6	+			+	+		+
7	+	+	+	+		+	
8	+	+		+	+	+	
9	+	+		+	+		+
10	+	+	+	+		+	+
11	+	+	+	+		+	+
12	+	+	+	+		+	+
13	+	+		+	+		+
14	+	+	+	+		+	
15	+	+		+	+	+	+
16	+	+		+	+	+	+
17	+	+		+	+	+	+
18	+	+		+	+	+	+
19	+		+	+		+	+
20	+	+	+	+	+	+	+
21	+	+	+	+		+	+
22	+	+	+	+	+	+	+
23	+	+		+	+	+	+
24	+	+	+	+		+	+
25	+	+		+		+	+
26	+	+		+	+	+	+

Table 1 - continued

	I	II	III	IV	V	VI	VII
27	+	+		+		+	+
28	+			+	+	+	+
29	+	+	+	+	+	+	
30	+	+		+	+	+	
31	+	+		+	+	+	+
32	+	+		+	+	+	+
33	+	+	+	+	+	+	
34	+	+	+	+		+	+
35	+	+		+	+	+	+
36	+	+		+	+		
37	+	+		+	+	+	+
38	+	+		+	+		+
39	+	+	+	+	+		+
40	+	+		+	+	+	+
41	+	+		+	+	+	+
42	+	+	+	+	+	+	+
43	+			+	+	+	+
44	+		+	+		+	+
45	+	+	+	+		+	+
46	+	+	+	+	+	+	+
47	+			+	+	+	+
48	+	+	+	+	+	+	+
49	+	+		+	+		+
50	+	+	+	+		+	+
51	+	+		+		+	+
52	+	+	+	+	+	+	+

Table 1 - continued

	I	II	III	IV	V	VI	VII
53	+	+	+	+		+	
54	+	+	+	+		+	+
55	+	+	+	+		+	+
56	+	+	+	+		+	
57	+	+	+	+	+		+
58	+				+	+	+
59	+	+		+	+	+	+
60	+	+		+		+	+
61	+	+	+	+	+	+	+
62	+		+	+	+		+
63	+	+	+	+	+	+	+
64			+	+		+	+
65	+	+	+	+		+	+
66	+	+	+	+	+	+	+
67	+	+	+	+		+	+
68	+	+		+	+	+	
69	+	+	+	+		+	+
70	+	+		+	+	+	+
71	+	+	+	+		+	+
72	+	+		+		+	+

Roman numbers I-VII refer to components (see p. 211)
Arabic numbers refer to individual versions (see pp. 215-16)
Plus sign (+) indicates presence of component

Table 2

Factor Analysis

	I				II							III				IV					Va			
	a	b	c	d	a	1	2	3	4	b	c	a	1	2	b	a	b	c	d	e	1	2	3	4
1	+				+				+			+	+			+								
2		+			+							+	+		+	+								
3		+			+							+	+	+	+	+								
4			+									+	+			+								
5		+			+									+				+						
6			+													+								
7	+				+		+					+				+								
8		+								+	+	+				+			+					
9	+									+						+								
10			+		+	+	+										+							
11			+		+			+				+					+							
12	+				+			+		+		+						+						
13		+								+														
14	+				+									+			+							
15	+									+							+							
16					+			+		+							+							
17	+				+		+			+							+							
18				+	+	+											+							
19			+										+		+									
20		+			+							+			+	+								
21										+		+												
22	+				+				+	+		+				+								
23										+						+								
24			+		+			+		+		+				+				+				
25	+				+			+		+							+							
26			+		+	+	+										+							
27	+									+							+							
28				+													+							
29	+				+					+		+				+				+				
30	+									+							+				+			
31	+									+							+				+			
32			+		+			+																
33				+	+									+			+	+			+		+	
34	+				+	+	+							+										
35	+				+			+		+							+							
36	+				+	+																		

Table 2 - continued

	Va									b			VI													
	5	6	7	8	9	10	11	12	13	1	2	3	a	1	2	3	4	5	b	1	2	3	4	5	6	7
1																						+				
2											+															
3											+															
4									+			+														
5										+																
6						+																				
7																										
8										+											+					
9							+																			
10																+										
11															+											
12																										
13										+																
14																+										+
15			+												+											
16		+											+													
17										+	+															
18						+										+										
19																										
20											+															
21																+										
22			+	+														+								
23			+	+											+											
24																					+					
25															+											
26					+								+	+												
27																	+									
28					+															+						
29												+														
30																+										
31	+												+													
32			+																				+			
33														+		+										
34																										
35				+											+											
36			+																							

Table 2 - continued

	c				VII		VIII																				
	1	2	3	4	a	b	a	b	c	1	2	3	4	d	e	f	1	2	g	1	2	h	i	j	k	l	m
1					+	+																					
2	+				+									+													
3	+				+											+		+									
4	+				+			+	+	+			+	+					+		+						
5					+			+	+		+					+		+									
6					+	+		+						+					+		+						
7				+															+	+							
8																+	+									+	+
9					+			+						+													+
10	+				+	+		+	+										+		+					+	
11					+	+		+	+	+																+	
12			+			+		+	+	+		+		+													
13					+											+		+						+			
14									+			+														+	
15					+	+								+												+	
16	+				+	+			+	+																	
17	+			+	+			+						+	+	+	+							+			
18					+									+													
19					+	+		+	+		+																
20	+				+			+						+		+		+								+	
21					+	+		+								+	+										
22					+	+	+		+	+					+												
23					+		+	+								+	+										
24					+	+		+								+	+										
25					+	+	+		+	+																	
26					+			+	+	+				+													
27					+		+							+													
28					+				+	+																	
29															+												
30															+	+	+		+	+			+				
31					+											+											
32					+	+		+																			
33									+	+				+													+
34		+	+		+			+	+	+	+					+	+										
35					+										+				+	+							
36																											

Table 2 - continued

	I				II							III				IV					Va			
	a	b	c	d	a	1	2	3	4	b	c	a	1	2	b	a	b	c	d	e	1	2	3	4
37			+		+			+									+		+					
38	+				+																			
39	+				+			+								+	+		+					
40	+				+												+				+			
41	+									+							+					+		
42	+				+			+		+				+			+		+					+
43				+												+								
44			+									+				+								
45	+				+			+		+		+	+	+		+								
46		+			+	+	+					+		+	+	+			+		+			
47																	+							
48			+	+								+					+		+			+		
49			+		+	+		+									+							
50			+		+	+						+				+								
51			+		+											+								
52		+			+	+						+										+		
53				+								+		+		+								
54				+	+	+	+					+				+								
55	+				+			+		+		+				+								
56			+		+	+						+				+								
57										+		+				+	+	+	+			+		+
58		+																				+		
59	+				+	+											+							
60		+			+			+									+							
61					+	+	+					+	+	+	+	+								
62			+														+	+	+			+		+
63	+				+			+				+		+		+								
64												+				+								
65		+										+												
66			+		+											+								
67					+	+		+				+				+			+					
68	+				+											+	+		+					
69					+							+				+	+		+					
70					+	+											+							
71			+		+			+				+	+			+								
72				+	+			+			+	+				+								

Table 2 - continued

	Va									b			VI													
	5	6	7	8	9	10	11	12	13	1	2	3	a	1	2	3	4	5	b	1	2	3	4	5	6	7
37	+												+													
38								+																		
39	+					+																				
40																+										
41															+											
42																+										
43												+														
44																										
45																									+	
46														+										+		
47										+																
48															+											
49							+																			
50																										
51																						+				
52																+				+						
53																										
54																			+							
55																										
56																							+			
57																										
58																										
59			+																+							
60																+										
61												+											+			
62																										
63										+											+					
64																										
65																			+							
66										+									+							
67																			+							
68																					+					
69																+										
70				+																						
71																					+					
72																					+	+				

Table 2 - continued

	c				VII		VIII																				
	1	2	3	4	a	b	a	b	c	1	2	3	4	d	e	f	1	2	g	1	2	h	i	j	k	l	m
37					+	+		+																			+
38					+	+		+																			
39					+	+			+	+																	+
40					+			+	+	+		+		+					+	+							
41	+				+	+	+		+	+					+							+					
42						+								+													+
43	+				+	+		+						+													
44	+				+			+	+	+									+		+	+				+	
45					+	+		+	+	+						+	+									+	
46					+	+			+	+				+												+	+
47		+				+								+												+	
48		+			+			+															+		+		+
49					+	+		+								+	+	+						+			
50	+				+				+	+			+		+									+			
51				+	+	+		+								+									+		
52					+	+			+					+									+				
53		+					+		+	+									+	+							
54						+			+	+	+																
55	+				+											+	+									+	
56								+	+			+															
57					+											+	+	+									+
58					+	+		+	+	+																	+
59					+	+			+	+																	
60					+	+		+	+	+																	
61					+	+			+	+		+							+	+						+	
62					+			+								+		+									+
63			+		+	+			+	+									+	+							
64	+				+																						
65					+			+						+												+	
66					+			+																			
67					+	+	+	+	+		+													+			+
68														+											+		+
69		+			+		+	+	+	+														+		+	+
70	+				+	+																					
71					+								+						+	+							
72					+	+	+							+	+												+

Horizontal row of numbers and letters refers to factors (see pp. 211-15)

Vertical column refers to individual versions (see pp. 215-16)

Plus sign (+) indicates presence of factor

Table 3

Frequency of Occurrence of Components and Factors

	Number of Tales	Percent
I	71	98.6
a	26	36.1
b	11	15.3
c	18	25.0
d	8	11.1
II	62	86.1
a	48	66.7
1	15	20.8
2	8	11.1
3	18	25.0
4	2	2.8
b	22	30.6
c	2	2.8
III	40	55.6
a	32	44.4
1	8	11.1
2	11	15.3
b	6	8.3
IV	71	98.6
a	34	47.2
b	30	41.7
c	5	6.9
d	11	15.3
e	2	2.8
V	45	62.5
1	5	6.9
2	6	8.3
3	1	1.4
4	3	4.2
5	3	4.2
6	1	1.4
7	6	8.3
8	4	5.6
9	2	2.8

Table 3 - continued

	Number of Tales	Percent
10	3	4.2
11	2	2.8
12	1	1.4
13	1	1.4
b1	7	9.7
2	4	5.6
3	4	5.6
VI	62	86.1
a	4	5.6
1	2	2.8
2	7	9.7
3	11	15.3
4	1	1.4
5	1	1.4
b	5	6.9
1	2	2.8
2	6	8.3
3	4	5.6
4	2	2.8
5	1	1.4
6	1	1.4
7	1	1.4
c1	14	19.4
2	5	6.9
3	3	4.2
4	3	4.2
VII	62	86.1
a	58	80.6
b	34	47.2
VIII		
a	9	12.5
b	33	45.8
c	32	44.4
1	25	34.7
2	5	6.9
3	5	6.9

Table 3 - continued

	Number of Tales	Percent
4	3	4.2
d	21	29.2
e	8	11.1
f	18	25.0
1	11	15.3
2	7	9.7
g	12	16.7
1	8	11.1
2	4	5.6
h	2	2.8
i	3	4.2
j	6	8.3
k	3	4.2
l	14	19.4
m	15	20.8

Table 4

Date of Appearance of Factors

	I				II							III				IV				
	a	b	c	d	a	1	2	3	4	b	c	a	1	2	b	a	b	c	d	e
B.C.																				
16th	7				7		7					7				7				
15th																				
14th																				
13th		8							1?	8	8		1?						8	
12th																				
11th																				
10th															2?					
9th																				
8th									1?				1?							
7th																				
6th																				
5th			10			10		11									10	12		
4th																				
3rd														14						
2nd																				
1st				18											2?					

Table 4 - continued

	I a	b	c	d	II a	1	2	3	4	b	c	III a	1	2	b	IV a	b	c	d	e
A.D.																				
1st																				
2nd									22											24
3rd																				29
4th																				
5th																				
6th																				
7th																				
8th																				
9th																				
10th															61			62		
11th																				
12th														63						
13th																				
14th																				
15th													71							
16th																				
17th				54?	54?		54?													
18th																				
19th	55	66		54?	54?	67	54?	72		55	72	72				55	69		69	
20th		65																		

Table 4 - continued

	Va													b			VI		
	1	2	3	4	5	6	7	8	9	10	11	12	13	1	2	3	a	1	2
B.C.																			
16th																			
15th																			
14th																			
13th														8					
12th																			
11th																			
10th															2?				
9th																			
8th																			
7th																			
6th																			
5th											9								11
4th																			
3rd																			
2nd								70											
1st						16	15			18					2?		16		

Table 4 - continued

	Va													b			VI		
	1	2	3	4	5	6	7	8	9	10	11	12	13	1	2	3	a	1	2
A.D.																			
1st									26						20				
2nd	30		33?		31				28							29		33?	
3rd					37			35				38					37		
4th		41		42															
5th	46										49							46	48
6th			33?															33?	
7th																			
8th										6?									
9th																			
10th																			
11th							59						4			4			
12th										6?									
13th		62		62															
14th																			
15th																			
16th																			
17th																			
18th																			
19th														66					
20th																			

Table 4 - continued

	VI											c				VII		VIII		
	3	4	5	b	1	2	3	4	5	6	7	1	2	3	4	a	b	a	b	c
B.C.																				
16th															7					
15th																				
14th																				
13th						8	1?									1?	1?			
12th																				
11th																				
10th												2?								
9th																				
8th							1?									1?	1?			
7th																				
6th																				
5th	10													12					9	10
4th										45?										
3rd											14									
2nd																				
1st												2?								

Table 4 - continued

	VI 3	4	5	b	1	2	3	4	5	6	7	c 1	2	3	4	VII a	b	VIII a	b	c
A.D.																				
1st		27	22		28										51?			22		
2nd																				
3rd													34							
4th										45?										
5th									46											
6th																				
7th					52?															
8th																				
9th																				
10th																				
11th				58				61							51?					
12th														63						
13th					52?															
14th																				
15th																				
16th																				
17th																				
18th																				
19th	69					72	72	56				55	69				67	69	69	69
20th				65												65				

Table 4 - continued

	VIII 1	2	3	4	d	e	f	1	2	g	1	2	h	i	j	k	l	m
B.C.																		
16th										7	7							
15th																		
14th																		
13th							8	8									8	8
12th																		
11th																		
10th					2?													
9th																		
8th																		
7th																		
6th																		
5th	11		12						13			10			13			
4th																		
3rd																		
2nd																		
1st		19			2?	17												

Table 4 - continued

	VIII																	
	1	2	3	4	d	e	f	1	2	g	1	2	h	i	j	k	l	m
A.D.																		
1st																		
2nd														30				
3rd																		
4th													41					
5th				50												48		
6th																		
7th														52?				
8th																		
9th																		
10th																		
11th																		
12th																		
13th									62			44	44	52?				
14th																		
15th				71						71	71							
16th																		
17th																68		
18th																		
19th	69	67	56			72	55	55							69		69	69
20th					65													

Table 5

Earliest Occurrence of Factor According to Language Group

	I				II							III				IV			
	a	b	c	d	a	1	2	3	4	b	c	a	1	2	b	a	b	c	d
Semitic	+	+	+		+				+			+	+	+	+	+		+	
Akkadian	1				1				1			1	1			1			
Hebrew		2												3	2			5	
Arabic			6																
Indo-European	+	+	+	+	+	+	+	+	+	+	+	+	+	+	+	+	+	+	+
Hittite	7	8			7		7			8	8	7				7			8
Greek			10	18		10		11	22				19	14	19		10	12	
Latin																			
Indian																			
Persian																			
German																			
Icelandic																			
English																			
Irish																			
Albanian																			
Miscellaneous	+		+	+	+	+		+			+	+	+			+	+		+
Turkish	68																		68
Chinese					70	70											70		
Malayan			71					71					71			71			
Palaung				72							72	72							

Table 5 - continued

	IV	Va													b		
	e	1	2	3	4	5	6	7	8	9	10	11	12	13	1	2	3
Semitic											+			+	+	+	+
Akkadian																	
Hebrew														4	5	2	4
Arabic											6						
Indo-European	+	+	+	+	+	+	+	+	+	+	+	+	+		+	+	+
Hittite															8		
Greek	24	30		33		31	16	15	22	26	18	9				17	29
Latin			41		42								38				
Indian																	
Persian																	
German																	
Icelandic																	
English																	
Irish																	
Albanian																	
Miscellaneous									+								
Turkish																	
Chinese									70								
Malayan																	
Palaung																	

Table 5 - continued

	VI														c			
	a	1	2	3	4	5	b	1	2	3	4	5	6	7	1	2	3	4
Semitic										+					+			
Akkadian										1								
Hebrew															2			
Arabic																		
Indo-European	+	+	+	+	+	+	+	+	+	+	+	+	+	+	+	+	+	+
Hittite									8									7
Greek	16	33	11	10	27	22		28		32				14	10	34	12	
Latin																		
Indian												46	45					
Persian							58				61							
German																		
Icelandic																		
English																		
Irish																		
Albanian																		
Miscellaneous				+					+	+					+	+		
Turkish				69												69		
Chinese															70			
Malayan									71									
Palaung										72								

Table 5 - continued

	VII		VIII														
	a	b	a	b	c	1	2	3	4	d	e	f	1	2	g	1	2
Semitic	+	+		+	+	+	+		+	+		+		+	+		+
Akkadian	1	1															
Hebrew					4	4	5		4	2		3		3			
Arabic				6											6		6
Indo-European	+	+	+	+	+	+	+	+	+	+	+	+	+	+	+	+	+
Hittite												8	8				
Greek	9	10	22	9	10	11	19	12		9	17			13	7	7	10
Latin																	
Indian									50								
Persian																	
German																	
Icelandic																	
English																	
Irish																	
Albanian																	
Miscellaneous	+	+	+	+	+	+			+	+	+				+	+	
Turkish			69	69	69	69				68							
Chinese	70	70															
Malayan									71						71	71	
Palaung											72						

Table 5 - continued

	VIII					
	h	i	j	k	l	m
Semitic						
Akkadian						
Hebrew						
Arabic						
Indo-European	+	+	+	+	+	+
Hittite					8	8
Greek		30	13			
Latin	41					
Indian				48		
Persian						
German						
Icelandic						
English						
Irish						
Albanian						
Miscellaneous			+	+	+	+
Turkish			69	68	69	68
Chinese						
Malayan						
Palaung						

I. Explanation of Abandonment

Only one tale (64 [Tristan]) fails to preserve any indication of an explanation of abandonment. Here an exposure does in fact occur, and the absence of this component is explained from the fact that the Tristan story represents an extremely defective and incomplete version of the type.[3] In a few tales, such as 21 and 60, one finds an explanation of abandonment albeit in an attenuated or obscured form.

Obviously, an explanation of abandonment is one of the basic traits of the type, essential for an understanding of the whole tale. Variations exist in the reasons given for the exposure of the infant hero and the most important of these are now listed:

a. Fear or Shame over Circumstances of Birth

Fear or shame plays a part in twenty-six versions of the tale. The factor occurs in all groups but is more common in Greek, Latin, and Persian stories. With the exception of the Sargon Legend, it is not found in versions written in a Semitic language. In almost all cases, the shame is based on illegitimacy resulting from relations with a deity, incestuous relations, or rape. Fear often accompanies the shame arising from the possibility of discovery by the girl's parents. Abandonment also takes place because of shame over the pedigree of a parent or the physical appearance of the child.

b. To Save the Hero's Life

Abandonment for the purpose of saving the infant's life occurs in eleven versions. It is found in all groups except the Latin. The most frequent threats prompting the exposure of the hero are genocide and fear of elimination of the hero as a future rival to a king.

Identifying the reason for abandonment in the hypothetical archetype is very difficult. Factors a and b are found in the earliest sources, while c is first attested only slightly later. On the other hand, d may be excluded from consideration because of its late appearance, its infrequency, and its absence from important linguistic and cultural groups (Semitic and Persian). Perhaps it is safest to observe that factor b seems likely to belong to the original form of the tale based on water exposure. The presence of a vessel argues for a desire to spare the life of the infant. If the mother had wished to drown her child, she could have simply thrown him into the water. Factor a (more likely than c) might be expected to have been present in the original tale that included land exposure.

II. Infant of Noble Birth

Sixty-two versions of the tale credit the abandoned hero with a royal or noble descent. This component is unquestionably an original element of the exposed-hero tale. The ten versions that do not preserve the trait occur sporadically throughout the collection and are all found in relatively late sources. The exact nature of the hero's nobility varies from tale to tale.

a. *Noble or Royal Parent*

In forty-eight versions, the infant is of noble birth by descent from a parent who is a member of royalty. The father is identified as king in fifteen versions, the mother as queen in eight, as a princess in eighteen, and as a priestess in two.[4] These relationships are most characteristic of versions preserved in Greek, Latin, and Indian sources. It should be noted that there are no examples of a king, queen, or princess as parent among tales written in a Semitic language. In tale 5, Abraham's father Terah is described as a "prince in the household of King Nimrod." This is not to be taken literally, however, but merely as an expression of Abraham's noble descent. Terah is not considered to be a son of King Nimrod in the tale. The story of the birth of Abraham is quite late, originating in the Medieval period, and no doubt was subject to the influence of tales emanating from other linguistic-cultural groups.[5]

b. *Divine Parent*

The exposed hero was sired by a deity in twenty-two stories. Sixteen of these occur in Greek sources where the feature should be considered an original element. Concerning the deity in question, five tales involve a sun god, namely, the Hurrian sun god, Apollo (three versions), and Surya.[6] Five versions involve Zeus, four Poseidon/Neptune, and one each

Heracles, Mars, Nana and Agdistis, Derceto, the Holy Spirit, the Kingly Glory of Ahura Mazda, a demon, and a magic phallus.

c. Animal Parent

Two sources separated chronologically by at least three and a half millennia designate an animal as parent of the hero. Tale 8 identifies a cow as mother, while tale 72 speaks of a dragon princess.

As we have indicated, the original form of the tale must have included the component of the noble birth of the hero. The identification of the father as a male god and the mother as a princess is the normal relationship found in the Greek subtype of the tale, and--with some variation--appears throughout the Indo-European group.

III. Preparations for Exposure

Forty versions indicate some preparation taken prior to the actual exposure. The component is found in all periods and geographic areas, yet two groups of tales, the Semitic and Indic, show a significantly higher incidence of occurrence than the others (especially Greek and Latin). This no doubt reflects the predominance of water exposure over land exposure in the Semitic and Indic tales. Despite the fact that this component is preserved in only slightly more than half of the collected versions, it is certainly an original element of the type.

a. Box, Basket, Chest, Receptacle, etc.

The infant hero is placed in a box, basket, or chest in thirty-two versions of the tale. Twenty-one are prior to exposure on water, ten before exposure on land, and one before a flight through space. In two cases, the receptacle has been transformed into a jar, and the hero is abandoned on water in one tale and on land in the other. In eight tales we find the added precaution of caulking the vessel in which the hero is placed. Naturally, this detail occurs only in cases of water exposure. Four of the eight tales originated in the Hebrew tradition[7] and one in Akkadian.

A small number of tales mention another kind of preparation, the use of comfortable materials for the hero's vessel or the insertion of valuables, money, or clothes. This detail occurs sporadically throughout the collection.

b. Parent's Agent Observes Fate of Abandoned Infant

This detail occurs in only six versions. Note the difference in the function of the parental agent. In the Hebrew and Indic versions preserving the factor (tales 2, 3, 20, 46),[8] the agent is concerned with the welfare of the child. In the lone Greek occurrence (tale 19), the father's servants stand watch to make sure that the exposed infant dies.

Of the variations of the component that we have discussed, one can be safely assumed to represent an element of the original tale. This is the presence of a vessel to contain the infant hero. The detail is found in tales involving water exposure and, more significantly, in some tales based on land exposure, where the receptacle no longer serves a purpose.

IV. Exposure

As the single most important element of the tale type, this component is found, in one form or another, in seventy-one versions. It does not seem to be preserved in tale 58, the birth story of Faridun, since the hero is placed directly into the care of the peasant who raises him. One might expect such a tale to lack an explanation of abandonment as well, but in fact one exists, indicating that we are dealing with a genuine version of the type, although in a confused and defective state. Other versions such as the stories of Dionysus (13), Jesus (21), and Kai Khusrau (60) have altered the normal form of the exposure element so that it is hardly recognizable.[9]

a. In or Near Water

The hero is abandoned in or near a river or some other body of water in thirty-four versions of the tale. Water exposure occurs in all groups of tales but is significantly more common to some than others. It is found in five of six versions written in Semitic, eight of twelve Indic sources, and eight of ten versions included in the miscellaneous group. In contrast, water exposure occurs in only six of the twenty-eight tales written in Greek.[10]

b. In Wilderness, Forest, Mountain, or Desolate Area

There are thirty examples of infant exposure that take place in the wilderness. Including factor c (exposure in a cave), which is only a variant of b, this type of exposure accounts for slightly more than half the total number of tales. Land exposure is characteristic of Greek, Latin, and Persian versions of the exposed-hero tale.

d. Multiple Exposures

Eleven tales suffer from repetition of the exposure component. They are spread throughout the collection with the exception of the Semitic group and should be interpreted as confused variants that developed in the process of transmission from a simpler original form.[11] Four of these combine water and land exposure, the two basic forms of the tale.

e. Mother and Child Exposed Together

As a twist on the exposure theme, two Greek tales have the mother and her infant exposed together.

V. Infant Protected or Nursed in an Unusual Manner

This component is present in forty-five versions of the tale. The occurrences fall into two categories: one involves an animal as nurse, the other a human or divine being. The first variation seems to be a regular feature of Greek versions and is well represented among Latin, Indian, and Persian tales. In contrast to the Indo-European examples, the Semitic group shows a preference for the other form of the trait. Note, however, that the Sargon Legend lacks the component entirely. Of the seven components that we have identified, this one is most likely not to belong to the hypothetical archetype, assuming that the original tale was based on water exposure. Clearly, there is no room for an episode of animal nursing if the hero is abandoned on water. Whether the other variation (human or divine nursing) was present is uncertain. Providing the hero with a divine nurse would add to his stature, but the trait does not appear to be essential. The Sargon Legend, in this respect, may be closest to the original form of the water-exposure tale.

Assuming that one form of the tale included animal nursing, then the identification of the original animal would be of interest. This is no easy task, however, for the possibilities are all infrequently attested and about equally distributed throughout the Indo-European family. With but little confidence, one might suggest the wolf on the basis of its presence in a Chinese tale (70) from the second century B.C., as well as its other occurrences. Since the hero is most frequently discovered by a herder (shepherd), one might expect an animal that is a member of the herd or a natural predator of the herd. Having the hero nursed by a dangerous animal would also emphasize his special powers.

VI. Discovery and Adoption

The act of discovery and adoption is an integral component of the exposed-hero tale and is preserved in sixty-two of the seventy-two versions. There are two basic variations on the theme depending upon the social class of the person finding the infant. In forty-eight versions, the individual is a commoner; a noble or other prominent person plays a role in twenty-two tales, and a deity appears in three tales.

The hypothetical archetype most likely involved a commoner. Not only does this variation occur more frequently, but it makes the tale more interesting by stressing the "rags to riches" career of the hero. About half of the tales that deal with a peasant identify him as a herder of one sort or another. The type that appears most often is the shepherd, who was probably found in the original form of the land-exposure subtype.

Among the tales involving a commoner other than a herder, a variety of professions is encountered. Most of the stories in this group belong to the water-exposure type. The profession most frequently attested is that of fisherman, and here, I believe, we find the original occupation of the commoner in this tale form. The other workers represented in this group--gardener, hunter, launderer, etc.--are variants whose occupations relate less directly to the sea.

VII. Accomplishments of Hero

Sixty-two versions of the type refer to specific accomplishments of the hero or allude, in a general way, to the source of his fame. This component, which represents an original element of the archetype, is expressed in two forms: the accomplishment of noteworthy deeds of various nature and the elevation of the hero to the throne.

The presence of the second form (acquisition of kingship) in the archetype is possible but not certain. Although the detail is found in only thirty-four versions, it occurs throughout the collection without regard to linguistic, cultural, geographical, or historical boundaries.

VIII. Miscellaneous Details

Scattered among the versions of the exposed-hero tale are individual factors that do not appear explainable as variations of the main components. Only a few occur in a significant number of tales and are worthy of consideration as original elements of the tale. Many others seem to be loan factors that have entered into versions of our tale from other tale types.

a. Twin Heroes Involved

The modification of the exposed-hero tale to accommodate twin heroes is obviously a late development that appears in stories of Greek and Roman heroes. Clearly, the Greek tales 25 and 27 are closely related, sharing an added detail not generally present in other versions of the tale, namely, revenge on an evil stepmother who had persecuted the twins' mother. Somewhat removed (but still related) is tale 41, which is written in Latin. The versions of Romulus and Remus (22-23), however, apparently follow a different line of descent.

b. Dream, Omen, or Prophecy and Its Fulfillment

Thirty-three versions present some prophecy, dream, or omen which is eventually fulfilled. The factor occurs frequently in Greek, Latin, Indian, and Persian stories. Its presence in three late tales written in a Semitic language is evidence of Greek influence, since all three preserve elements of the Oedipus plot.

c. Disclosure of the Hero's Origin

The true identity of the abandoned hero is dramatically revealed in the denouement of thirty-two versions. There are four variations in the way this is accomplished:

1. Hero is informed of the secret of his birth.

2. Hero informs natural parent of his identity
3. Birth tokens lead to disclosure of identity
4. Mother's milk miraculously flows (indicating the true relationship between hero and mother)

This factor is frequently attested among Indo-European versions of the tale (32 times). Variation 1 represents the original form of the detail occurring five times more often than the nearest alternatives (2 and 3).

d. Etymology of Hero's Name Given

An explanation of the origin of the hero's name occurs in twenty-one versions of the tale. Even though the factor appears in less than one-third of the total number of tales, it is found in some of the oldest stories in each linguistic-cultural group (with the exception of Persian) and may represent an original element of the type.

e. Etiological Element Present

There are eight exposure stories that include an etiological element in their narrative. All but one are found in tales belonging to the Indo-European family in which the detail appears to have originated. The remaining tale (72) from Burma shows traces of Indian influence.

f. Miraculous Events Surrounding Birth

In eighteen versions, miraculous events of one kind or another accompany the birth of the hero. This detail, which is attested in all important linguistic-cultural groups, occurs in some of the oldest sources of the tale. Two forms are discernible: miraculous conception and miraculous birth or growth of the hero. The first variation (miraculous conception) is more common and probably represents the original form of the factor. In the eleven cases of miraculous conception, two heroes are conceived in a flash of light, two are conceived by the spirit of a deity, two by eating a special substance, and three are conceived under other unusual circumstances. In addition, there are two cases of virgin birth and one pregnancy induced by a magic phallus.[12]

g. Incest

An incest motif is present in twelve stories. It may be accompanied by patricide, in which case it represents an adaptation of the Oedipus tale, or it may occur without such consequences. Incest is not an original element of the exposed-hero tale.

h. Adopted Child Slays Natural Child

This unusual detail is preserved in two versions written in Latin. Its presence in the exposed-hero tale is extraneous, and its source unclear.

i. Mutilation of Limbs

Mutilation takes place in three versions of the tale and is associated with a fourth (11 [Cyrus]). All cases involve tales from the Indo-European group. Two of these bear some resemblance to each other, the stories of Candagutta and Cyrus. In the Indian tale, mutilation follows as a result of Candagutta's participation in a game of "play-king." Herodotus's account of the birth of Cyrus also includes an episode where the hero plays "king" as a youth; however, the mutilation of the son of Harpagus does not follow as a consequence of this activity but occurs for another reason in a later section of the narrative.[13]

j. Jealousy of Principal Wife over Inferior Wife

This detail, which is also extraneous to the exposed-hero tale, is present in six stories. One form of the factor, preserved in tale 49, is quite reminiscent of the relationship between Sarah and Hagar after the birth of Ishmael (see Genesis 16).

k. Death Letter

Three tales include this factor, which may represent a loan element from another type.

l. Adoptive Parents Childless

Fourteen tales specifically state that the foster parents of the abandoned hero are childless or imply the same by indicating that they recently lost an infant at birth. With two exceptions, the detail is confined to tales originating in the Indo-European cultural tradition. It is preserved in Josephus's account of the birth of Moses but not in the versions written in Hebrew (2, 3). The detail is also present in a late story written in Turkish. It is quite likely that the factor represents an original element of some subtypes of the tale.

m. Repetition of Component

Fifteen tales reveal a significant defect in the structure of the plot by the repetition of one or more of their components. Such deterioration is thought to occur in the process of oral transmission.[14] Note that the Semitic group is curiously free of this defect. For versions involving multiple exposures, see IV d.

Relationships Among Components and Factors

It should be apparent that certain components and factors are interrelated and interdependent. The main connections may be stated as follows:

1. The explanation of abandonment (I) and the exposure (IV) are related. If a tale version possesses the first component, one may be fairly certain that the other component follows. This holds true in all cases except 58 and 64. In the story of Faridun (58), the structure of the tale is defective, and there is no exposure. The component has apparently dropped out as the hero is passed directly to the commoner who acts as foster parent. The tale concerning Tristan (64) also suffers from a disjointed and incomplete narrative structure. All information surrounding this hero's origins prior to his discovery and adoption is missing.
2. Components III (preparations for abandonment) and IV (exposure) are related, with the latter trait dependent upon the former in the sense that whenever a tale includes preparations for abandonment, an actual exposure takes place.
3. Caulking the vessel (III a 1) is dependent upon the presence of a box, basket, or chest (III a) and upon an exposure on water (IV a).
4. The discovery or adoption by a fisherman (VI b 2) appears only after an abandonment on or near water (IV a).
5. Repetition of components (VIII m) and multiple exposures (IV d) are related. The occurrence of the latter qualifies as an example of factor VIII m.

The Genealogy of the Tale Type

We have observed significant variation within the versions of the exposed-hero tale, not only among those originating in different linguistic or cultural traditions, but also within the same language group. Nevertheless, the correspondence of components and the sequential structure of the tale point unquestionably in the direction of a common origin. All versions appear, ultimately, to derive from a common ancestor. The reconstruction of the *Ur*-form or archetype, the determination of the geographical point of origin, and the direction of the dissemination of the tale are the main goals in the study of the folktale following the collection of versions and their componential analysis.[15]

In attempting to apply this method to the study of the tale of the exposed hero, we encounter certain complications arising from the great antiquity of the tale and many of its versions that are not present in studies of other tales. These involve the long period during which versions appear (over 3500 years), the widespread diffusion of tales, and the fact that all exemplars represent literary versions or published accounts of oral versions.[16]

After examining the components and factors that make up the tale, it is easy to recognize the outline of a basic story recurring throughout the collection. This basic story is generally expressed in one of two ways.

In the simplest form (Type A), the exposure of the infant hero takes place on water. We may summarize this form as follows: A mother is forced to abandon her son. Wishing to protect his life, she prepares a receptacle to contain him. The vessel is placed on a body of water and floats along until someone finds it, rescues the infant, and adopts him. The child grows up to become a great hero. Type A is found in Mesopotamia, Israel, and India, among other places.

A second form of the tale (Type B) involves exposure on land. An infant is exposed to die in a desolate area but is kept alive by an animal who nurses him. Eventually, a local inhabitant discovers the babe, takes him, and raises him. The infant grows up to become a famous hero. This form is well attested in Greece, Italy, India, and Persia.

Subtypes of the Tale

In a large collection of versions, groups of tales will emerge that seem to share similar details as well as a geographic, linguistic, or cultural center. These groups are known as subtypes. It is often advisable to begin the analysis of complex tales by identifying the various subtypes and postulating their hypothetical original form. From these subtype archetypes, one attempts to reconstruct the ultimate archetype that theoretically produced all forms of the tale.[17]

We now turn to a discussion of subtypes and subtype archetypes of the exposed-hero tale, recognizing that these represent abstractions which may never have existed. Nevertheless, they are useful tools in the comparative study of a folktale.[18]

A Semitic Subtype

Six versions of the type are written in Semitic languages (1-6), and one version (20), although written in Greek, remains essentially a Hebrew tale. One might expect to reconstruct the hypothetical Semitic archetype on the basis of these six or seven tales. It seems necessary, however, to eliminate most of the versions from consideration, for the stories of Joshua, Abraham, and Nimrod are very late in comparison to the others and bear the unmistakable influence of Greek and Christian sources. We are now left with tales 1, 2, 3, and 20. The first two go back to the early first millennium B.C., while the latter pair are found in sources dating from the first century A.D. to the fifth century A.D. But three of the four tales (2, 3, 20) are versions of the same story, the birth of Moses. To use all four versions equally with the Sargon narrative in the reconstruction of the Semitic subtype would give unfair weight to the Moses tale. Hence, whatever generalizations that may be made about a Semitic archetype should be based on tales 1 and 2.[19]

Listing the components of the type in relation to these two versions, we find:

I. Explanation of abandonment (1,2)
II. Noble birth (1,2)
III. Preparations for exposure (1,2)
IV. Exposure (1,2)

V. Nursed in an unusual manner (2)
VI. Discovery and adoption (1, 2)
VII. Accomplishments of hero (1, 2)

The Akkadian and Hebrew tales preserve the same principal traits with one exception. Component V is found in the Moses story but not in the Sargon Legend. For reasons that will be discussed later,[20] this component can probably be eliminated from consideration as an original trait of the subtype archetype.

Turning to the question of the factors present in the subtype, we note an apparent conflict in the explanation of abandonment given in tales 1 and 2. Moses is exposed to save his life, but Sargon is apparently abandoned out of fear and shame; he was born illegitimately to a priestess who was most likely prohibited by her office from bearing children. Nevertheless, a connection exists, for there is an additional element involved in Sargon's abandonment. His mother also wanted to save his life as evidenced by the elaborate precautions taken in caulking the reed basket that served as his vessel. This correspondence does not settle the question of the original motive for exposure in the hypothetical archetype but merely points to a rationale suggested by the structure of the tale.

On the issue of noble birth, both tales attribute this trait to the hero in a rather indirect manner. Neither is identified as the offspring of a king or god as is the case in other subtypes of the tale. Their nobility is implicit in the status accorded their parents--Moses' parents as Levites and Sargon's mother as high priestess.

Both accounts agree on the care taken prior to exposure and on the highly significant detail that the infant was abandoned on water. The versions do not agree, however, on the status of the person discovering and adopting the child. Here it seems likely that once again the Sargon story more closely reflects the original form of the tale by placing a peasant or commoner in the role.[21]

Perhaps the safest conclusions to be drawn concerning a hypothetical Semitic archetype on which the Sargon and Moses tales would be based are (1) that the tale involved an exposure on water in a vessel specially prepared to protect the life of the hero, (2) component V was probably missing from this archetype, and (3) the hero was discovered and adopted by a peasant.

Such an archetype would resemble quite closely the simplest form of the exposed-hero tale that we have called Type A (water exposure).

A Greek Subtype

There are twenty-four versions of the tale that will be considered in the identification of a Greek subtype. Four other tales (11, 20, 22, 23), also preserved in Greek, will not be used because they clearly originate in different linguistic-cultural traditions.

An examination of versions indicates the following components and factors as constituents of a Greek subtype:

I. Explanation of abandonment--fear and shame
II. Noble birth--parents are male god and princess
IV. Exposure--land
V. Nursed in an unusual manner--by an animal
VI. Discovery and adoption--herder
VII. Accomplishments of hero--noteworthy deeds

The Greek versions of the exposed-hero tale generally include all the principal components in their narrative structure except III (preparations for exposure). The hero is exposed because of fear or shame resulting from the circumstances of his birth. He is the illegitimate, though noble, product of a union between a male deity and a princess. The infant is abandoned in a wilderness, nursed by an animal, and rescued by a herder. As an adult, he accomplishes great deeds that may or may not result in his elevation to the throne. Such is the form of the Greek subtype, which probably also represents the hypothetical subtype archetype and follows closely the pattern of Type B (land exposure).

A Latin Subtype

A subtype based on versions of the tale preserved in Latin sources would consist of these elements:[22]

I. Explanation of abandonment--fear or shame
II. Noble birth--parents are male god and princess
IV. Exposure--land and water

V. Nursed in an unusual manner--by an animal
VI. Discovery and adoption--herder
VII. Accomplishments of hero--noteworthy deeds and kingship

The Latin form of the exposed-hero tale resembles quite closely the Greek subtype as one might expect from the historical and cultural connections between the two civilizations. There is, however, one slight difference between the subtypes, namely, a higher incidence of tales with factor IV a (exposure in or near water) in the Latin group. This occurs despite the fact that the rest of the components and factors posited for the subtype follow the pattern that we have identified as Type B (land exposure).

The misleading statistical importance of IV a may be explained by the small number of tales included in the group, the occurrence of water exposure in a multiple exposure tale (in which land exposure is primary), and the fact that there are two versions of the same tale (Romulus and Remus) that preserve the factor.

Instead of postulating a separate archetype for the Latin group, it might be better to say that these tales probably derive from the subtype archetype reconstructed for the Greek versions.

An Indian Subtype

Tales originating in the Indian tradition cover a span of over two millennia. Most are preserved in sources dating from the fifth century A.D. As a group, these versions would suggest a pattern based on the following traits:

I. Explanation of abandonment--to avert a prophecy
II. Noble birth--father is king
III. Preparations for exposure--receptacle
IV. Exposure--water
VI. Discovery and adoption--peasant
VII. Accomplishments of hero--noteworthy deeds and kingship

It should be noted that the componential structure of the Indian subtype is essentially that of the Type A tale (water exposure). The details, however, are those associated with some versions of Type B (land exposure). This might suggest a history of the Indian subtype in which an archetype of Type A suffered contamination from Type B versions, resulting in the assimilation of some of its secondary detail. The geographical position of the land, surrounded by ocean and dominated by rivers, may have assured the popularity of the water-exposure form.

Perhaps further indication of this process is revealed in the story of the birth of Karna (45). This version is slightly older than the earliest of the other tales and, more importantly, its structure and components are in a better state of preservation. It consists of the same components found in the hypothetical Indian subtype but differs in the details, preserving factors I a and II a 3 and b, precisely those details present in the Greek subtype and archetype. The infant Karna is exposed from shame over the circumstances of his birth. He was born out of wedlock, the result of a liaison between the sun god and a princess. The rest of the tale follows the pattern of the water-exposure tale including the detail of caulking the vessel of the infant hero. The story of Karna may indicate one stage of the conflict in India between the Type A form of the exposed-hero tale and versions belonging to the Greek subtype.

In sum, the general characteristics thought to be present in the Indian subtype archetype would include: (1) a tale based on water exposure, (2) the hero placed in a box or other vessel, (3) discovery by a commoner, and (4) the hero's rise to kingship.

A Persian Subtype

The last group to be considered is the Persian. It is comprised of six tales preserved in late sources and two versions of the birth of Cyrus, one written in Greek, the other in Latin. As a group, these tales are more defective than any of the other linguistic-cultural units. One tale has not even retained the principal trait of exposure. Others preserve basic components in greatly distorted form. Four tales suffer from repetition of components and three from multiple exposure.

The Persian subtype, so far as it can be determined, may be described as follows:

I. Explanation of abandonment--to avert a prophecy (?)
II. Noble birth--unclear
III. Preparations for exposure--receptacle

IV. Exposure--land
V. Nursed in an unusual manner--by an animal
VI. Discovery and adoption--peasant
VII. Accomplishments of hero--noteworthy deeds and kingship

All that can be said about an archetype for the Persian group is that it would most likely follow the pattern of Type B. The presence of component III and factor III a is an indication of the confused state of versions belonging to this subtype.

The Ur-Form or Ultimate Archetype

As we turn our attention to the consideration of the hypothetical archetype that produced all forms of the exposed-hero tale, it seems possible, on the basis of our componential analysis and subtype-archetype models, to identify with confidence most of the principal traits. But the prospects of determining individual details present in the archetype are less bright.[23] There is an enormous amount of variation in the collection, and many details are attested in only a small number of tales. Even the oldest versions (1, 2, 7, 8, 9-13) manifest a great variety of minor details, suggesting that they themselves are far removed in time from the ultimate archetype.

Our study of the Semitic and Indic subtypes reveals a tale structure based on components I, II, III, IV, VI, and VII. In contrast, the subtypes postulated for the Greek, Latin, and Persian groups are composed of components I, II, IV, V, VI, and VII.

These two patterns have been designated Type A (water exposure) and Type B (land exposure) respectively. In our opinion, Type A represents the original form of the tale and Type B a significant, but secondary, development.

An explanation of abandonment (I) is an essential component of the tale. Without this trait, the tale would be bereft of much of its meaning. The reason for the exposure is, however, less certain. Possibly, factor I a is original. Fear or shame over the hero's birth is present as a motive in the three oldest versions: the tale of the Sons of the Queen of Kaneš, the Hurrian tale of the Sun God and the Cow,[24] and the

Sargon Birth Legend. In addition, it represents the original explanation for abandonment in the Greek and Latin subtypes. It is also found in the story of Karna (45), which is the best preserved version, structurally and componentially, in the Indian group. At the same time, the archetype must also have included a desire on the part of the mother to spare the life of her child. Otherwise, there is no reason for the presence of the basket or vessel that protects the hero from drowning.

In the archetype, the hero was certainly of noble birth (II). His mother was probably a princess and his father a god. This relationship is preserved in the Greek and Latin subtypes. It is possible that the pattern is reflected in the Sargon Legend as well, although in a somewhat altered form. The role of high priestess may be considered a variant form of princess, for in Mesopotamia the priestess was frequently a daughter of the king or another member of the royal house.[25] It should also be noted that the duties of high priestess might have required her participation in the sacred marriage, where her partner (the king?) would assume the role of a male god. So, conceivably, the Sargon story may represent an adaptation of the original form of the tale in which the hero's parent(s)[26] have been cast in roles reflecting Mesopotamian customs and practices.

The hypothetical archetype included **component III (preparations for abandonment)** in the form of a vessel used to contain the infant and keep him afloat. The factor is also present in some Type B versions, where it serves no purpose in the plot. In many of these land-exposure tales, the original basket or vessel has been transformed into a box, chest, cradle, etc.

Assuming that the original form of the tale had the infant hero abandoned on water (in a river), then the presence of **component V (nursed in unusual manner)** in the archetype is definitely in question. We can safely rule out an episode of animal nursing which logically should take place in a forest or wilderness setting. Nursing by a human or humanoid (deity) is still possible, though we think unlikely.

The *Ur*-form surely included discovery and adoption (VI) by a commoner, possibly a fisherman or gardener.

The accomplishment of some notable achievement (VII and VII a) obviously belongs to the archetype for the simple reason that these tales concern heroes, human and divine, and great deeds are the stuff of which heroes are made. The inclusion of factor VII b (kingship) in the archetype is problematic. It is apparently an original element in some subtypes[27] but may not have been present if the archetype dealt with the birth of a god.

That the archetype of the exposed-hero tale may have existed as an ancient myth about the birth of a god is worthy of consideration. N. M. Holley suggests as much in his study of "floating chest" stories in Greek literature.[28]

The place of origin of the exposed-hero tale can only be broadly defined as most probably the Near East--Mesopotamia or Western Asia. It seems doubtful that the tale originated with the Hittites or Hurrians in view of the confused state of versions 7 and 8.[29] One might look for a region where rivers played a major role in the lives of the people. If the point of origin is essentially correct, then the direction of dissemination may have been eastward to India, Southeast Asia, and China, and westward to Greece and Italy, possibly through Syria-Palestine.

A date of origin of the tale cannot be determined. The oldest known versions, tales 7 and 8, are preserved in sources dating from the mid-second millennium.

Both versions would appear to be far removed from the hypothetical archetype. The Hurrian tale (8) combines elements of land exposure with water exposure, suggesting that both forms of the tale circulated independently long before the middle of the second millennium. If the Sargon Legend account were based on an ancient folktale, which we think likely, then the Sargon birth story might go back to the end of the third millennium.

The Sargon Legend and the Tale of the Birth of Sargon

In the study of the exposed-hero tale, we have drawn on the Sargon Legend text for an account of the birth and exposure of the great Akkadian king. While the Sargon Legend cannot be considered folk literature, the section that we have designated as the prologue (see Chapter III) seems to be based, at least in part, on folk traditions.

That the Sargon Legend does not preserve a complete narrative account of an exposure tale is clear. Rather, we find the basic outline of a folktale worked into the framework of a semipoetic literary text. The story is related in only eight lines that reflect, just barely, the essential components of the type. Absent are all the minor details that give fullness to a narrative tale. One consequence of this assumed abridgment is a difficulty (on our part) in understanding certain aspects of the story that were probably obvious in its original form.[30]

All this seems to suggest that the author of the Sargon Legend drew on or adapted an older more elaborate account of the abandonment of Sargon for use in his composition. One might argue that the exposed-hero tale was adapted to Sargon at the time of the composition of the Legend, but this we think less likely. Such folktales and legends have been known to arise during or soon after the life of a great hero.[31] The Sumerian King List is aware of a tradition linking Sargon to a member of the date-growing profession about the beginning of the second millennium B.C.[32] An interest in Sargon's origins is also demonstrated in another early source, the so-called Sargon-Lugalzagesi Legend.[33]

That an actual folktale circulated prior to the composition of the Legend seems probable. Whether this tale existed in oral or written form at the time of the composition of our text cannot be determined.

The Exodus Account of the Birth of Moses

For a long time scholars had accepted the premise that the birth legends of Sargon and Moses were unusually similar in form and content. In recent years, studies by M. Cogan, M. Greenberg, and others have challenged this assumption by stressing the different motivations for the abandonment, by asserting a closer parallel between the Moses story and an Egyptian myth concerning Horus, and by raising the question of whether the Exodus tradition actually preserves a genuine element of exposure. These arguments have now been effectively answered by C. Cohen.[34]

Nevertheless, there are differences between the Hebrew and Akkadian stories not only in detail but on the componential level as well. These differences, which represent changes in the basic pattern of the exposed-hero tale, are found in the biblical narrative. The Hebrew innovations are:[35]

1. The concept of genocide as the motivating factor underlying the need to abandon the hero. Moses is exposed to save his life from a threat to all Hebrew male infants.
2. The hero is hidden for three months (until it is no longer possible to conceal him).
3. The role of the sister who watches over the hero from a distance as the representative of the mother.
4. The use of Pharaoh's daughter to rescue and adopt the infant hero.
5. The hiring of the natural mother to nurse her own child.

Having identified the variations of the tale that are unique to the Moses story, we come to the question of their interpretation. Two factors act to temper the severity of the abandonment.[36] The reference to a three-month period during which Moses was hidden is intended to show that his parents did all they could to protect him before being compelled to expose him on the river. Likewise, the mission of Moses' sister in watching over the infant hero demonstrates the mother's continuing concern for his safety.[37]

As Childs has most recently argued,[38] the genocide motif directed at the Hebrew male infants in Exodus I is dependent upon the birth story of Moses in Exodus II, 1-10. The primary tradition is the exposure story with the threat to the hero expanded to include the entire people. This danger then serves as the introduction to the story of the birth of Moses.

Elements of irony and perhaps scorn are aimed at the Egyptians. Using the Pharaoh's own daughter as the means by which the evil plan is thwarted and the future hero saved illustrates this point. Another instance is seen in the hiring of the infant's natural mother to serve as wet nurse.

Let us consider the *Sitz im Leben* of the Moses birth legend. According to the widely held view, the Moses birth narrative belongs to the youngest strata of Exodus tradition.[39] Possibly, at some late stage a Hebrew storyteller wished to assign to the figure of Moses an unusual birth history appropriate to his position in the Exodus tradition. To serve this purpose he turned to an ancient and popular literary device, the tale of the hero exposed at birth. As in other cases of Hebrew borrowing of ancient Near Eastern motifs, the material was adapted to reflect the spirit of Hebrew civilization. Specifically, the details of the tale were changed to soften the harshness of the exposure and bring it in line with Israel's moral sensibilities.[40]

Having accepted the premise that the Hebrew author of the Moses birth legend introduced innovations into the tale of the exposed hero, one might consider the form of the hypothetical version that served as the *Vorlage* for his adaptation. Much has been made about the use of Egyptian local color in the history,[41] but when we look within the Egyptian milieu for a prototype, no such version is known. The myth involving Isis and Horus which Greenberg has put forward as the closest parallel to the biblical tale cannot be accepted as such. As Cohen and Redford have shown, the Egyptian story is very late (the Ptolemaic period) and is not truly a version of the exposed-hero tale.[42] For one thing, the hero Horus is not abandoned in the marshes to save his life; rather, his birth takes place while his mother is in hiding there. Other major components of the tale are also lacking.

It would appear more likely that the *Vorlage* of the Moses story be sought in the direction of Mesopotamia or Western Asia. As Childs has noted, the episode in the Moses birth legend describing the hiring of a wet nurse (in this case the hero's own mother) to suckle the foundling and raise him until he is weaned seems to be based on an ancient legal tradition reflected in the Sumerian-Akkadian lexical series *ana ittīšu*.[43] In Mesopotamia, a technical term (*tarbītum*) was used to designate the duties incumbent upon the hired wet nurse in fulfilling this function.[44]

Were we to strip away all the obvious innovations present in the Exodus birth story, we should be left with a basic tale structure that might approximate the *Vorlage*.

I. Explanation of abandonment minus genocide and three-month concealment = exposure because of shame or to save the hero's life[45]

II. Hero of noble birth

III. Preparations for exposure minus role of sister = preparation of reed basket

IV. Exposure (water)

V. Nursed in an unusual manner minus hiring of wet nurse = absence of component (?)

VI. Discovery and adoption minus role of princess = discovery by commoner (?)

VII. Accomplishments of hero

After eliminating the Hebrew contributions, one finds a tale structure based on components I, II, III, IV, VI, and VII, the same pattern present in the Sargon Legend and the hypothetical archetype. The author of the Moses story may have known of and have been influenced by the Sargon tale, as he was apparently influenced by other Mesopotamian traditions, such as foundling adoption (*ana ittīšu*) and the *tarbītum*-relationship. Cuneiform documents such as an Akkadian fragment of Gilgameš found at Meggido, clay liver models from Hazor, and El Amarna correspondence, testify to the presence of cuneiform literature in Syria-Palestine during the second millennium. Of course, the Moses birth story might just as easily have derived from an unknown version of the exposed-hero tale.

The Social Basis of the Exposed-Hero Tale

Underlying all versions of the exposed-hero tale is the fact that in the ancient world, as in the modern, unwanted children were at times cruelly abandoned by their parents.[46] Children were exposed for a variety of reasons in antiquity including economic necessity,[47] birth defects, or religious taboo. In some cases, surely the explanations set forth in occurrences of the folktale served as the critical motivating factor: the social stigma attached to illegitimacy, the desire to save the life of a high-born child threatened by other claimants to the throne, or the hope of sparing a child from a fate dictated by an evil omen. It seems logical to assume that most exposures must have involved members of the lower classes for economic and social reasons. That this phenomenon was not particularly rare is attested by the existence of legal sources reflecting its practice.[48]

As Ebeling has pointed out, there were degrees of severity in the disposition of unwanted children.[49] Those who sought the death of a child would expose him on a mountain or in a desolate region where discovery would be less likely and death from exposure or wild animals virtually inevitable. A less harsh action for those who wished to preserve an opportunity for survival to the infant or who wished to ease the burden of their conscience would be abandonment in a street, a ditch, or in a vessel on water.[50]

Clearly, the existence of the exposed-hero tale is an expression of this social practice, despite the attempts by some to explain the origin of the tale or myth as an expression of psychological conflicts and subconscious processes.[51] In any event, one should at least consider the possibility that in the case of Sargon or any of the other historic heroes, the popular narrative of the unusual birth may have been based on some historical fact. Sargon, clearly a usurper, might have been born illegitimately and abandoned in some manner. It is, unfortunately, impossible either to dismiss or to prove this contention on the basis of the cuneiform evidence available, although on balance it seems rather improbable. Certainly the details of the Sargon exposure, as related in the Legend, hardly inspire confidence in their historicity. At this point in the development of Assyriology, the origins and early career of Sargon of Akkad, the greatest king in Mesopotamian tradition, remain shrouded in obscurity.

NOTES

CHAPTER VI

[1]For a discussion of the different forms of the folktale, see Thompson, *The Folktale*, pp. 7-10.

[2]In many cases a number of tales are roughly contemporary and would seem to qualify as the latest occurrence of a factor. For convenience, one tale has been selected at random to serve our purpose.

[3]In fact, the Tristan account seems to be a conflation of two different types: the exposed-hero tale and the tale of the Substituted Bride.

[4]Aside from the Sargon Legend, one other tale identifies the hero's mother as a priestess. This is tale 22, a version of the birth story of Romulus and Remus. Here the mother is described as a vestal priestess. These priestesses were supposed to represent the daughters of the royal house but often were not even patricians. During their tenure in office, they were expected to remain virgins (see *OCD*[2], p. 1116). In our study of the *ēntu* (see Chapter II, p. 38 and n. 74), we noted that the position of high priestess in Mesopotamia was customarily filled by members of the royal house.

[5]See Chapter V, n. 22. Note that in the biblical account of the birth of Moses the hero's nobility stems from the designation of his parents as Levites, which anachronistically came to imply a certain noble status.

[6]In the Palaung tale (72) of Udibwa and Min Rama, the father is identified as the son of Surya, the solar deity of India.

[7]Three of the Hebrew versions involve Moses, the fourth concerns Joshua. The Akkadian tale is, of course, the Sargon Legend.

[8]The function of the factor in the remaining Persian tale (61) is unclear, although the great care taken in the preparation of the infant's vessel would seem to indicate a sympathetic motive.

[9]Dionysus was exposed to the elements, in a sense, before he was born when his mother's body was burned away from him. Concerning Jesus, the flight through the desert to Egypt (see Chapter V, n. 41) or the forty-day period of temptation spent in the wilderness (see Luke IV. 1-2) might be interpreted as forms of the exposure component. Similarly, the mother of Kai Khusrau fled with her infant son into the wilderness to escape from the armies of Afrasiyab.

[10]And one of these derives from the Hebrew tradition, tale 20, Josephus's account of the birth of Moses.

[11]A list of the most common processes at work in the oral transmission of the folktale that result in multiform versions is given in Thompson's, *The Folktale*, p. 436, see esp. no. 5, "Repetition of an incident which occurs but once in the original tale."

[12]According to M. Grant (see *Roman Myths* [New York, 1971], p. 101), myths of this type (tale 23) "illustrate the widespread Italian veneration of sexual vigor, though there are also Celtic parallels, in a number of different settings."

[13]See Chapter V, n. 30.

[14]Cf. n. 11.

[15]In our treatment of the tale of the hero who was exposed at birth, we follow the historic-geographic method developed by Kaarle Krohn for the study of the folktale. For a systematic presentation of this method of investigation, see *Folklore Methodology By Kaarle Krohn*, trans. Roger L. Welsch (Austin and London, 1971). The work, which is based on Krohn's lectures, was originally published in German in 1926 as *Die folkloristische Arbeitsmethode* (Oslo, 1926). Cf. Stith Thompson's summary of the technique in his *The Folktale* (New York, 1946), pp. 428-48. One example of the application of the method may be seen in Thompson's study of a North American Indian tale "The Star Husband" in *The Study of Folklore*, ed. Alan Dundes (Englewood Cliffs, 1965), pp. 414-74.

[16]In the past, most studies employing the historic-geographic technique have focused on European or American Indian tales, whose collections are composed of oral versions as well as written versions preserved in relatively modern sources. The long history of our tale type and its virtual worldwide distribution have resulted in the introduction of an enormous amount of variation that makes the reconstruction of the original form very difficult.

[17]Cf. Dundes, *Study of Folklore*, p. 415; and Thompson, *The Folktale*, p. 434.

[18]Although the two oldest tale versions are preserved in Hittite, we are not justified in attempting to reconstruct a Hittite subtype archetype, since one of the tales (8) clearly emanates from the Hurrian tradition. See Chapter V, n. 25.

[19]It is admittedly dangerous to attempt to reconstruct an archetype based on only two versions.

[20]The specific form of this component represents an innovation on the part of the Hebrew storyteller. See below, *The Exodus Account of the Birth of Moses*.

[21]See above, *Analysis of Components and Factors*, VI.

[22]Plutarch's versions of the birth of the Roman heroes Romulus and Remus (22, 23), although preserved in Greek, are included in the consideration of the Latin subtype.

[23]Especially the factors included in the miscellaneous group (VIII).

[24]At least in the sense that the cow wanted to kill her "monstrous" offspring. Another motive is present in this confused variant, namely, factor I b (to save the hero's life). The sun god has the infant exposed on a ledge to protect him from his mother and assure his discovery by the fisherman.

[25]For example, Sargon appointed Enḫeduanna, his daughter, as EN-priestess. Cf. J. Renger, "Untersuchungen zum Priestertum in der altbabylonischen Zeit," *ZA* 58 (1967), p. 126 20 and n. 97; and cf. above n. 4.

[26]Note that the "unknown" father mentioned in the Legend plays an essentially insignificant role in the story.

[27]Namely, Latin, Indian, and Persian.

[28]See N. M. Holley, "The Floating Chest," *Journal of Hellenic Studies* 69 (1949), esp. pp. 40, 45-46.

[29]Both tales are defective and suffer from repetitive components or factors. In tale 7, the mother gives birth to thirty sons and later thirty daughters, although only the sons are exposed. Tale 8 preserves elements from Type A and B forms of the tale.

[30]For example, the events surrounding Sargon's conception, his mother's feelings concerning his abandonment, his paternal lineage, and perhaps even the role of Aqqi, his foster father.

[31]A version of the exposed-hero tale concerning Cyrus is known to have existed in Persia less than a century after his death. See Chapter V, tale 11, for Herodotus's account of the birth of Cyrus. The legend of Kun-bok (tale 70) is preserved in a Chinese document that is probably only slightly later than the age of the hero.

[32]Might this be a reflection of a tale about Sargon's birth and exposure?

[33]See Scheil, "Nouveaux renseignements sur Šarrukin," *RA* 13 (1916), pp. 175-79. Cf. Chapter IV *III* , 6.

[34]See C. Cohen, "Hebrew *tbh*: Proposed Etymologies," *JANES* 4 (1972), pp. 46-51; and cf. M. Cogan, "A Technical Term for Exposure," *JNES* 27 (1968), pp. 133-35; and M. Greenberg, *Understanding Exodus* (New York, 1969), pp. 36-44, 198-99.

[35]For a discussion of "those features of the story which belong to the specifically Hebrew tradition," see Brevard S. Childs, "The Birth of Moses," *JBL* 84 (1965), pp. 115-18.

[36]Also note that the Hebrew author purposely avoided use of the verb השליך, the *terminus technicus* in Hebrew for the concept of abandoning. Instead, Moses' mother is said to have "placed" (ותשם) her infant son on the river. See Cogan,

"A Technical Term for Exposure," p. 134.

[37]Regarding the role of the sister, cf. Childs, "Birth of Moses," p. 115, "the sister tempers the harshness of the exposure by keeping watch at a distance."

[38]In support of Gressmann's conclusion; see ibid., p. 118, where Childs states "we agree with Gressmann that the threat to the child in the birth story was secondarily expanded to the people in general in ch. 1." Cf. H. Gressmann, *Mose und seine Zeit* (Göttingen, 1913), pp. 1-16.

[39]See Childs, *Exodus*, p. 8 for a discussion of the analysis of Gressmann. Childs notes that "a majority of critical commentators have accepted Gressmann's analysis (Böhl, Beer, Auerbach, Rylaarsdam, Noth, Fohrer, and Clamer with reservations)." Cf. Childs, "Birth of Moses," p. 118 where the author specifically states that "our study has confirmed the position that the birth story belongs to the latest stage of the collection of the Exodus traditions."

[40]Cf. Childs, "Birth of Moses," p. 118.

[41]See Gressmann, *Mose und seine Zeit*, p. 7; and Childs, "Birth of Moses," pp. 110-11.

[42]See Cohen, "Hebrew *tbh*," p. 50; and Redford, "Motif of the Exposed Child," pp. 220-21. Cf. J. J. Finkelstein, "*šilip rêmim* and Related Matters," *Kramer Anniversary Volume*, AOATS XXV (Neukirchen-Vluyn, 1976), pp. 187-94.

[43]See B. Landsberger, *MSL* I, pp. 43-47, esp. col. iii, 21-50.

[44]See Childs, "Birth of Moses," p. 112 and nn. 15-17.

[45]For an argument against the presence of factor I c (to avert a prophecy of a coming child) in the original story, see Childs, "Birth of Moses," p. 110.

[46]Even today reports appear in the media concerning cases of infants found in trash cans or on the steps of hospitals or orphanages.

[47]So the apparent motivation for the abandonment of the children of El in the Ugaritic myth of the Gracious Gods; see T. H. Gaster, *Thespis* (New York, 1961), pp. 432-33.

[48]Cf. chap. II, commentary to the text col. i 10.2 and n. 120.

[49]E. Ebeling, "Aussetzung," *RLA* I (1932), p. 322.

[50]See B. Landsberger, *MSL* I, *ana ittīšu*, p. 44, III col. iii 29-36.

[51]Cf. O. Rank, *The Myth of the Birth of the Hero* (New York, 1964), pp. 65-96; and Joseph Campbell, *The Hero with a Thousand Faces* (Princeton, 1973).

CHAPTER VII

CONCLUSIONS

This work represents a comprehensive study of the Akkadian composition known as "the Sargon Legend" or "the Sargon Birth Legend." We have offered a new edition of the text making use of a previously unedited fragment of the second column (K 7249). In addition, our treatment has constituted a philological study of the Legend, a study of its literary and textual problems, and an analysis of one of its motifs.

Summary of Results

1. Date of Composition

Only the extreme limits of the possible date of composition can be determined with confidence. The Sargon Legend had to be composed after 2039 and before 627 B.C. The *terminus post quem* is established by the occurrence in the text of the royal epithet *šarru dannu* which is known to have originated in the eighth regnal year of Amar-Sin (2039). The *terminus ante quem* is determined by the presence of copies of the text in the library of Assurbanipal and in inventory lists of the library's collection. Nevertheless, a date of origin between the thirteenth and eighth centuries seems likely on the basis of internal evidence such as the use of idiomatic expressions that are first attested in the royal inscriptions of Middle and Neo-Assyrian kings.

2. *Sitz im Leben*

The motivation for the composition of the Sargon Legend cannot be ascertained. Possible explanations have been considered, but without a definite date of composition they remain conjectural.

3. Sources

The Sargon Legend seems to have drawn on a variety of sources including folk tradition, a source containing information on the origin of the hero, and some historiographic material whether in the form of inscription, chronicle, or historical omens. In addition, one may posit a separate source of uncertain nature for column ii.

4. Historical Value

With the exception of the tradition of the birth and exposure of Sargon, there is much in the Legend that is based on ancient tradition and corroborated by other Sargon texts.

5. The Legend as *Narû*-Literature

Column i of the Legend, although partially destroyed, appears to manifest all of the essential components of the genre known as *narû*-literature or "pseudo-autobiography." But in view of the estimated length of the text (three to four columns), one may question whether the composition is a genuine pseudo-autobiography or rather a composite work whose opening section is written in the form of a miniature *narû*.

6. Columns i and ii

On the problem of the relationship between the first and second columns, we can offer no solution. The text of column ii is too mutilated and the contents too obscure to permit its interpretation.

7. The Exposed-Hero Tale

Our study of the infant-exposure motif has lead to the identification of a tale type which we have designated as the tale of the Hero Who Was Exposed at Birth. Employing the historic-geographic technique used in the study of folktales, we have isolated the essential components and factors of the type, identified the various subtypes of the tale, and reconstructed the hypothetical archetype from which all versions, including the birth histories of Sargon and Moses, are theoretically derived.

Other Areas for Investigation

Beyond the study of the Sargon version of the exposed-hero tale, there remains much to be done before exhausting the Legend text as a source of Sargon tradition. A comprehensive investigation of all of its literary motifs is certainly beyond our present task, and we shall be content to point out some areas where further study might prove of value.

The Career of the Idealized Ruler

In Mesopotamian tradition, Sargon of Akkad stands out as prototypical ruler. The image is reflected best of all in the Sargon Legend where the hero challenges those future monarchs who wish to be considered great to accomplish the glorious deeds that had established his own reputation.

The peoples of Mesopotamia were not alone in boasting a figure of such status. Other nations in antiquity had their heroes. Among the Israelites, David was revered as the epitome of kingship, while Moses was remembered as the preeminent religious leader. The Persians look back on Cyrus with justification as the greatest king and emperor in their tradition. When the sources which tell of these "idealized rulers" are examined, certain common features emerge as if to suggest that the traditions surrounding these figures were molded according to a pattern. Some of the most striking connections are:

	Sargon	Moses	David	Cyrus
1. Mysterious origin	exposure tale	exposure tale		exposure tale
2. Humble beginnings	gardener	son of slaves	shepherd	shepherd
3. Divine favor	Ištar's lover	spokesman of YHWH	anointed by Samuel	future ordained by prophecy
4. Court official	cupbearer	prince	musician	cupbearer
5. Associated with new capital	Agade		Jerusalem	
6. Created dynasty	Akkadian		Davidic	Achaemenid

7.	Conqueror	empire		large kingdom	empire
8.	Prototype	kingship	religious leader	kingship	kingship
9.	Incurs divine wrath	sacrilege at Baby- lon	waters of Meribah	Bathsheva affair	

Do these correspondences represent coincidence, events likely to occur in the career of any ancient hero, or are there patterns of characteristics that tradition selectively preserves or attaches to the figure of a hero? Are these traits borrowed from one hero's tradition to another? A study devoted to these figures and any other relevant ones might shed some light on the problem.

Other topics, which have been mentioned only briefly in the course of this work, are also worthy of additional study. These include: the hero as lover of a female deity, the hero as adventurer and explorer of unknown regions, and the relationship of the birth story vessels of Sargon and Moses to the flood story arks in Mesopotamian and Hebrew tradition.

APPENDIX

THE NAME SARGON

This list of orthographies of the name Sargon is based largely on the collection published by Hirsch (see H. Hirsch, "Die Inschriften der Könige von Agade," *AfO* 20 [1963], p. 1 and n. 3). It has been brought up to date and expanded to include spellings of the names of Sargon I and II.

Orthographies

1. *šar-ru*-GI
   a. original inscription from Susa, *MDP* X, pp. 4-8. (Akkadian)
   b. fragment of a calcite vase, *UET* VIII, pl. 2, no. 10 2. (Akkadian)
   c. votive inscription of Ašlultum or Tašlultum (see chap. IV, Sargon family inscriptions 1), wife of Sargon, *YOS* I, p. 7, no. 7. (Sumerian)
   d. inscriptions of Enḫeduanna, daughter of Sargon, *UET* I, p. 5, no. 23 5; p. 71, no. 271 2. (Sumerian)
   e. the Maništušu Obelisk from Susa, *MDP* II, p. 29, Face C col. xiii 25. (Akkadian)
   f. Old Babylonian copies of Old Akkadian inscriptions from Nippur, *AfO* 20 (1963), p. 36 b 1 vs. col. iv 27 and passim. (Akkadian)
   g. Old Babylonian omen text, *YOS* X, pl. 43, no. 31 col. iii 5 and passim. (Akkadian)
   h. inscription from Nippur, *PBS* XII/1, pl. 11 no. 8 3. (Akkadian)
   i. copy of an inscription from Lagaš (*šar-ru*-GI-x?) *RTC* pl. 45, no. 83b:10 Face 6. (Sumerian)
   j. epic text (^{d}*šar-ru*-GI), *TCL* XVI, pl. 126, no. 64 4. (Sumerian)

k. the "Curse of Agade" (^{d}*šar-ru*-GI), *ZA* 57 (1965), p. 50 4. (Sumerian)

l. Old Babylonian onomastic list (unpublished), Oriental Institute (the Crozer Theological Seminary Collection) A 24193 r. i 41'.

m. the Cruciform Monument of Maništušu, *CT* XXXII, pl. 1, col. ii 2. (Akkadian)

2. *šar-um*-GI

a. Old Babylonian copies of Sargon inscriptions from Nippur, *AfO* 20 (1963), p. 36 b 1 vs. col. iii 27 and passim. (Sumerian)

b. economic text containing a Sargon date name, *TMH* V, Tf. V no. 151, r. 10; and *ECTJ*, p. 76 and pl. 21. (Sumerian)

3. *šar-um*-GI-*nê*

a. economic text containing a Sargon date name, *TMH* V, Tf. XXXVIII, no. 181, r. 9; and *ECTJ*, p. 90 and pl. 6. (Sumerian)

b. economic text containing a Sargon date name, *TMH* V, Tf. XXII, no. 85, r. iv 1; and *ECTJ*, p. 53 and pl. 3. (Sumerian)

4. *šar-ru-um-ki-in*

a. epic text from Uruk, *TCL* XVI, pl. 142, no. 73 a 10, 12. (Sumerian)

b. Old Babylonian economic text from Ur, *JCS* 28 (1976), p. 242, no. 11 (r.) ii 7. (Sumerian)

c. Old Babylonian copy of a Sargon letter (unpublished practice tablet), CBS 15217 obv. 3' and 13'; see chap. IV *VI* 2. (Akkadian)

5. *šar-rum-ki-in*

a. Old Babylonian omen text from the Likhachev collection, *AfO* 5 (1928-29), p. 215 8. (Akkadian)

b. Old Babylonian Sargon epic, *RA* 45 (1951), p. 174 57. (Akkadian)

6. *ša-ru-ki-in*

a. Old Babylonian Sargon *narû*?, *BRM* IV, no. 4 1. (Akkadian)

	b.	unedited Sargon epic, *Sumer* 13 (1957), p. 99, pl. 16 I 9'; and *TIM* IX, no. 48 pl. 36 I 9'. (Akkadian)
7. *šar-ru-ki-in*	a.	early Old Babylonian liver model from Mari, *RA* 35 (1938), p. 53 = pl. 1, no. 1. (Akkadian)
	b.	Old Babylonian omens, *YOS* X, pl. 42, no. 31 col. i 4 and passim. (Akkadian)
	c.	Old Babylonian omen from Larsa, *RA* 27 (1930), p. 149, no. 14 16. (Akkadian)
	d.	Old Babylonian omen, *RA* 26 (1929), p. 9, no. 4. (Akkadian)
	e.	Old Babylonian Sargon epic, *RA* 45 (1951), p. 176 120. (Akkadian)
	f.	stele of Šamši-Adad I from Nineveh, *EAK* I, p. 9 I 11. (Akkadian)
	g.	Old Babylonian practice tablet preserving a copy of a Sargon letter, *UET* VII, no. 73 i 10 (Akkadian)
	h.	the Sumerian King List, *AS* XI, p. 110 31 and passim. (Sumerian)
	i.	hymn from Kiš, *PRAK* II, p. 37 c 55. (Sumerian)
	j.	Old Babylonian epic text from Uruk, *TCL* XVI, pl. 142, no. 73 22 and passim. (Sumerian)
	k.	Neo-Babylonian omen on a model of the face of Ḫuwawa from Sippar, *AAA* 11 (1924), p. 113 1. (Akkadian)
8. *ᵈšar-ru-ginⁱⁿ*	a.	Ur III economic text from Drehem, *PDT* no. 605 6. (Sumerian)
9. *šar-gi-ni*	a.	onomastic list from Nippur, *ZA* 12 (1897), p. 355, col. ii 5. (reference to Sargon is questionable)
10. *šar-gi-in*	a.	onomastic list from Nippur, *ZA* 12 (1897), p. 355, col. ii 6. (reference to Sargon is questionable)

11. LUGAL-*ki-in*
    - a. Old Babylonian Naram-Sin legend, *RA* 16 (1919), p. 161 18. (Akkadian)

12. MAN-*ki-in*
    - a. tablet XXII of ḪAR-ra=*ḫubullu*, *MSL* XI, p. 26 6 4'. (Akkadian)

13. LUGAL-*ki-en*
    - a. omen text from Assur, *KAR* no. 152, r. 20. (Akkadian)

14. [1]LUGAL-*ú-kin*
    - a. chronicle-like text concerning Nabonidus, *AfO* 22 (1968-69), p. 5 25, 29. (Akkadian)

15. LUGAL.GI
    - a. implicit in a commentary on the series *Enūma Anu-Enlil* from Kujunjik (LUGAL. GIN:GI), *AfO* 14 (1941-44), pl. 7, col. i 3. (Akkadian)
    - b. for a possible occurrence in the Weidner Chronicle, see Weidner's emendations of Güterbock's treatment (ZA 42 [1934], p. 52 Ex. A) in *AfO* 13 (1939-40), p. 51 13. (Akkadian)

16. LUGAL.GI.NA
    - a. Old Babylonian Naram-Sin legend, *RA* 70 (1976), p. 117 L II 32'. (Akkadian)
    - b. Middle Babylonian omen text, *AfO* 16 (1952), p. 74. (Akkadian)
    - c. Neo-Assyrian omen text, *CT* XX, pl. 2, r. 9. (Akkadian)
    - d. Neo-Assyrian omen text, *CT* XXVII, pl. 23 19. (Akkadian)
    - e. the Dynasty Chronicle from Kujunjik, *CCEBK* II, p. 52, r. II 4; p. 56, r. II 14. (Akkadian)
    - f. the Historical Omens of Sargon, *CCEBK* II, p. 27, no. II 5. (Akkadian)
    - g. the Sargon Legend, *CT* XIII, pl. 42 1. (Akkadian)
    - h. inventory list of the Kujunjik collection, *Rm*. 618 (*Bezold Catalogue*, *Supp*. p. 1627), 4, 21. (Akkadian)
    - i. inventory list of the Kujunjik collection, *AOAT* XXV, pp. 313-18, 6'. (Akkadian)

j. fragment of *šar tamhări* from Kujunjik, *AfO* 20 (1963), p. 161 4. (Akkadian)

k. omen from the series *šumma izbu*, *TCS* IV, p. 76 Tablet V, no. 33 and passim. (Akkadian)

l. geographical treatise from Assur, *KAV* no. 92 4. (Akkadian)

m. fragment of *šar tamhări* from Assur, *KAV* no. 138 4. (Akkadian)

n. astrological text, *ACh Ištar* II 41-42. (Akkadian)

o. the Weidner Chronicle from Assur, Ex. A *ZA* 42 (1934), p. 52 14. (Akkadian)

p. Neo-Babylonian version of Sargon Omens, *CCEBK* II, p. 42, no. 40 8. (Akkadian)

q. omen text from Uruk, *TCL* VI, pl. 3, no. 1 r. 1. (Akkadian)

r. Neo-Babylonian inscription of Nabonidus, *VAB* IV, p. 226 II 57, 64. (Akkadian)

s. Neo-Assyrian copy of a Naram-Sin text (^{l}LUGAL.GI.NA), *CT* XIII, pl. 44 obv. 2. (Akkadian)

t. Neo-Assyrian collection of Sumerian proverbs, *BWL* p. 251, pl. 60 col. i 10. (Sumerian and Akkadian)

u. economic texts of Nabonidus, *RA* 63 (1969), p. 80 b line 4; p. 81 a line 9'. (Akkadian)

v. Late Babylonian economic text of Cyrus (^{l}LUGAL.GI.NA), *Cyr.* no. 40 16. (Akkadian)

w. Late Babylonian economic text of Cambyses, *Camb.* no. 150 4. (Akkadian)

17. MAN.GI.NA — a. astrological omen, see chap. IV n. 40. (Akkadian)

18. LUGAL.GIN — a. the Sargon--Naram-Sin Chronicle, *CCEBK* II, p. 2 1 and passim. (Akkadian)

b. the World Map from Sippar, *CT* XXII, pl. 48 10. (Akkadian)

c. the Weidner Chronicle (Ex. B), *Babyloniaca 9*(1926), p. 24, r. 7 (see pl. 2 7). (Akkadian)

d. Neo-Babylonian practice tablet from Dilbat containing part of the Sargon Legend, *CT* XIII, pl. 43 b 1. (Akkadian)

e. royal inscriptions of Nabonidus, *CT* XXXIV, pl. 23 16, 18; pl. 30 29. (Akkadian)

f. commentary on the series *Enūma Anu-Enlil* from Kujunjik (LUGAL.GIN:GI); cf. 15 a. (Akkadian)

g. economic texts of Nabonidus, *RA* 63 (1969), p. 80 a 6; p. 81 b 6'; and cf. p. 79, no. 5. (Akkadian)

h. Late Babylonian economic text of Cyrus, *Cyr*. no. 256 9. (Akkadian)

An otherwise unknown orthography x-x-*ki?-na* may be preserved in a fragment of a Late Babylonian text published by A. K. Grayson in his *BHLT*, p. 107 3, as proposed by Grayson. Cf. Sargon II, no. 12 below.

Orthographies from Border Areas

19. LUGAL.GI.EN

a. the Amarna copy of *šar tamḫāri*, *VS* XII, no. 193 20 and passim. (Akkadian)

20. LUGAL-*gi-na-aš*

a. copy of *šar tamḫāri* from Boğazköy, *KBo* III, p. 42, no. 9 6, 7, 9. (Hittite)

b. fragment of *šar tamḫāri* from Boğazköy, *MDOG* 101 (1969), p. 19 6, 10 and passim. (Hittite)

c. the Annals of Hattušili I (LUGAL-*gi-na-ša-an*) from Boğazköy, *KBo* X, p. 7, no. 2 col. iii 32. (Hittite)

		d.	fragment of *šar tamḫāri* from Boğazköy (LUGAL-*gi*-x), *KBo* XII, p. 1, no. 1 8. (Hittite)
21.	LUGAL-*gi-ni*	a.	fragment of *šar tamḫāri* from Boğazköy, *KBo* III, p. 42, no. 10 3, 8. (Hittite)
22.	LUGAL-*gi-en-ne*	a.	fragment of a text containing ritual and mythological material, *KUB* XXVII, p. 27, no. 38 col. iii 19. (Hurrian)
23.	LUGAL-*gi-e-we*$_e$	a.	fragment of a text containing ritual and mythological material, *KUB* XXVII, p. 28, no. 38, col. iv 23. (Hurrian)
24.	LUGAL-*gi-we*$_e$-*na*	a.	fragment of a text containing a list of kings, *KUB* XXXI, p. 1, no. 3 6, 10. (Hurrian)
25.	LUGAL-*ki-ni-šu*	a.	the Annals of Hattušili I, *KBo* X, p. 3, no. 1 r. 20. (Akkadian)
26.	*šar-ru-uk-ki*	a.	Ras Shamra recension A of ḪAR-*ra* XX-XXII, *MSL* XI, p. 49 col. iv 34 and cf. p. 133 45. (Akkadian)

Orthographies of Sargon as a Component of Personal Names in Old Akkadian and Ur III Texts

1.	*šar-ru*-GIM	a.	*CT* VII, pl. 25 no. 13164 12.
2.	*šar-ru*-GI-*ì-lí*	a.	the Maništušu Obelisk, *MDP* II p. 14 Face A col. xii 8.
3.	*ur-šar-ru*-GIM	a.	*Or* 4 (1924), p. 59 iB 66 50.
		b.	*PDT* no. 126 r. 1.
		c.	*Or* 47 (1930), p. 58; cf. Tf. XII 41 5.
4.	*ur-šar-ru-u*⌜*m*⌝-[GIM]	a.	*TRD* 27 16
5.	*ur*-^{d}*šar-ru*-GIM	a.	*BIN* III, 477 12.
6.	*ur*-^{d}*šar-ru-gin*	a.	*RA* 9 (1912), p. 56 SA 241.

Orthographies of the Name of Sargon I: Examples

1.	^{1}LUGAL-*ki-in*	a.	*JNES* 13 (1954), p. 212 i 33.
2.	^{1}LUGAL-*ki-en*	a.	*KAH* I, no. 63 6.
3.	^{d}LUGAL.X (GIN or GI?)	a.	*HUCA* 27 (1956), pp. 78-79 n. 332.

Orthographies of the Name of Sargon II: Examples

1.	^{l}LUGAL.GI.NA	a.	Lyon, *Sarg.* Cyl. Inschrift p. 1 l.
2.	^{d}LUGAL.GI.NA	a.	*ABL* 422 obv. 2, 3.
3.	^{ld}LUGAL.GI.NA	a.	*ABL* 1355 obv. 2.
4.	LUGAL.GIN	a.	*ABL* 524 obv. 1.
5.	^{ld}LUGAL.GIN	a.	*ABL* 1467 r. 1-3.
6.	MAN.GIN	a.	*ABL* 107 r. 3.
7.	^{l}MAN.GIN	a.	*ABL* 122 obv. 4.
8.	^{l}MAN.GI.NA	a.	*ABL* 1214 obv. 4.
9.	LUGAL-*ú-kin*	a.	*ABL* 542 obv. 2.
10.	^{l}LUGAL-*ú-kîn*	a.	*ABL* 951 obv. 10.
11.	^{l}LUGAL-*ú-ki-in*	a.	*IAMN* 9 (1933), p. 16.
12.	^{l}*sa-ru-ke-na*	a.	*LA* 2, p. 204.

Noncuneiform Occurrences of the Name Sargon

1.	סרגון (Hebrew)	a.	Isaiah XX.1. (Sargon II)
2.	סרגן (Aramaic)	a.	*AJSL* 49 (1932), p. 54 fig. 1. (Sargon II)
3.	שרכן (Aramaic)	a.	*TSSI* II, p. 104 15 and pl. 5 and *KAI* no. 233 15. (Sargon II)
4.	שרכן (Aramaic)	a.	*EPAR* no. 28. (reference to Sargon II is questionable)

Table 6

Orthographies Arranged Chronologically

	šar-ru-GI	*šar-um-GI*	*šar-um-GI-né*	*šar-ru-um-ki-in*
3rd Mill.				
Old Akkad.	1a,1b,1e			
Sumerian	1c,1d	2b	3a,3b	
Akkad. Copies	1f			4c
Sum. Copies		2a		
2nd Mill.				
Akkadian	1g,1h,1l,1m			
Sumerian	1i-k			4a,4b
Hittite				
Hurrian				
1st Mill.				
Akkadian				
Sumerian				

Table 6 - continued

	šar-rum-ki-in	*ša-ru-ki-in*	*šar-ru-ki-in*	^{d}*šar-ru-gin*^{in}	*šar-gi-ni*
3rd Mill.					
Old Akkad.					9a?
Sumerian				8a	9a?
Akkad. Copies			7g		
Sum. Copies					
2nd Mill.					
Akkadian	5a,5b	6a,6b	7a-f		
Sumerian			7h-j		
Hittite					
Hurrian					
1st Mill.					
Akkadian			7k		
Sumerian					

Table 6 - continued

	šar-gi-in	LUGAL-*ki-in*	MAN-*ki-in*	LUGAL-*ki-en*
3rd Mill.				
Old Akkad.	10a?			
Sumerian	10a?			
Akkad. Copies				
Sum. Copies				
2nd Mill.				
Akkadian		11a		
Sumerian				
Hittite				
Hurrian				
1st Mill.				
Akkadian			12a	13a
Sumerian				

Table 6 - continued

	^{1}LUGAL-*ú-kin*	LUGAL.GI	LUGAL.GI.NA	MAN.GI.NA	LUGAL.GIN
3rd Mill.					
Old Akkad.					
Sumerian					
Akkad. Copies					
Sum. Copies					
2nd Mill.					
Akkadian			16a,16b		
Sumerian					
Hittite					
Hurrian					
1st Mill.					
Akkadian	14a	15a,15b	16c-w	17a	18a-h
Sumerian			16t		

Table 6 - continued

	LUGAL.GI.EN	LUGAL-*gi-na-aš*	LUGAL-*gi-ni*
3rd Mill.			
Old Akkad.			
Sumerian			
Akkad. Copies			
Sum. Copies			
2nd Mill.			
Akkadian	19a		
Sumerian			
Hittite		20a-d	21a
Hurrian			
1st Mill.			
Akkadian			
Sumerian			

Table 6 - continued

	LUGAL-*gi-en-ne*	LUGAL-*gi-e-we$_e$*	LUGAL-*gi-we$_e$-na*
3rd Mill.			
Old Akkad.			
Sumerian			
Akkad. Copies			
Sum. Copies			
2nd Mill.			
Akkadian			
Sumerian			
Hittite			
Hurrian	22a	23a	24a
1st Mill.			
Akkadian			
Sumerian			

Table 6 - continued

	LUGAL-*ki-ni-šu*	*šar-ru-uk-ki*
3rd Mill.		
Old Akkad.		
Sumerian		
Akkad. Copies		
Sum. Copies		
2nd Mill.		
Akkadian	25a	26a
Sumerian		
Hittite		
Hurrian		
1st Mill.		
Akkadian		
Sumerian		

SELECTED BIBLIOGRAPHY

PRIMARY SOURCES FOR THE SARGON LEGEND

King, L. W. *Cuneiform Texts from Babylonian Tablets in the British Museum*. Vol. XIII. London: Harrison and Sons, 1901. Pl. 42 and 43.

Lambert, W. G. *Cuneiform Texts from Babylonian Tablets in the British Museum*. Vol. XLVI. London: Trustees of the British Museum, 1965. Pl. 45 no. 46.

Smith, George. *The Cuneiform Inscriptions of Western Asia, Vol. III: A Selection from the Miscellaneous Inscriptions of Assyria, prepared . . . by . . . Sir H. C. Rawlinson . . . , assisted by George Smith.* London: British Museum, 1870. Pl. 4 no. 7.

Strassmaier, Johann N. *Alphabetisches Verzeichniss der assyrischen und akkadischen Wörter der 'Cuneiform Inscriptions of Western Asia' Vol. II, sowie anderer meist unveröffentlichter Inschriften, mit zahlreichen Ergänzungen und Verbesserungen, und einem Wörterverzeichniss zu den in den Verhandlungen des VI. Orientalisten-Congresses zu Leiden veröffentlichten babylonischen Inschriften.* AB IV. Leipzig: J. C. Hinrichs, 1886. P. 1094.

STUDIES OF THE SARGON LEGEND

Cosquin, E. "Le lait de la mère et le coffre flottant." *Revue des questions historiques*. N. S. 39 (1908), pp. 370-74.

Delitzsch, Friedrich. *Wo lag das Paradies*. Leipzig: J. C. Hinrichs, 1881. Pp. 208-9.

Ebeling, Erich. *Altorientalische Texte und Bilder zum alten Testament*. Ed. H. Gressmann. 2nd ed. Berlin and Leipzig: Walter de Gruyter, 1926. Pp. 234-35.

Grayson, A. K. *Ancient Near Eastern Texts Relating to the Old Testament*. Ed. J. B. Pritchard. 3rd ed. Princeton: Princeton University Press, 1969. P. 119.

Güterbock, H. G. "Die historische Tradition und ihre literarische Gestaltung bei Babyloniern und Hethitern bis 1200." *Zeitschrift für Assyriologie* 42 (1934), pp. 62-65.

Gutschmid, Alfred. *Neue Beiträge zur Geschichte des alten Orients*. Leipzig: Teubner, 1876. Pp. 108-10.

Jensen, Peter. "Aussetzungsgeschichte." In *Reallexikon der Assyriologie*, I. Berlin and Leipzig: Walter de Gruyter, 1932. P. 322.

Jeremias, Albert. *Das alte Testament im Licht des alten Orients*. Leipzig: J. C. Hinrichs, 1904. Pp. 254-56.

King, L. W. *Chronicles Concerning Early Babylonian Kings*. Vol. II. London: Luzac and Company, 1907. Pp. 87-96.

Labat, René. *Les religions du Proche-Orient asiatique*. Paris: Fayard-Denoël, 1970. P. 308.

Lenormant, Francois. *Histoire ancienne de l'Orient*. Vol. IV. 9e ed. Paris: A. Lévy Libraire-Éditeur, 1881-83. Pp. 76-77.

Ménant, Joachim. *Babylone et la Chaldée*. Paris: Maisonneuve et Cie, 1875. Pp. 98-100.

Oppert, Jules. "Deux textes très anciens de la Chaldée." *Académie des Inscriptions et Belles Lettres, comptes rendus, quatrième série* 11 (1883), pp. 80-81

Pinches, Theophilus G. "Assyriological Gleanings." *Proceedings of the Society of Biblical Archaeology* 18 (1896), p. 257

Sayce, Archibald H. *Lectures on the Origin and Growth of Religion as Illustrated by the Religion of the Ancient Babylonians*. Hibbert Lectures. London: Williams and Norgate, 1887. Pp. 26-29.

Smith, George. "Early History of Babylonia," *Transactions of the Society of Biblical Archaeology* 1 (1872), pp. 46-47.

_______. "SAR-GI-NA." *Records of the Past*. Vol. V. London: S. Bagster and Sons, 1875. Pp. 56-57.

_______. *Assyrian Discoveries*. New York: Scribner, Armstrong and Company, 1875. Pp. 224-25.

_______. *The Chaldean Account of Genesis*. New York: C. Scribner, 1875. Pp. 299-300.

Speiser, E. A. *Ancient Near Eastern Texts Relating to the Old Testament*. Ed. J. B. Pritchard. Princeton: Princeton University Press, 1950. P. 119.

Talbot, H. F. "A Fragment of Ancient Assyrian Mythology." *Transactions of the Society of Biblical Archaeology* 1 (1872), pp. 271-80.

_______. "The Legend of the Infancy of Sargina the First, King of Agane." *Records of the Past*. Vol. V. London: S. Bagster and Sons, 1875. Pp. 1-4.

Tiele, Cornelis. *Handbücher der alten Geschichte*. I Serie. Vierte Abteilung: Babylonisch-assyrische Geschichte. Gotha: Perthes, 1886. Pp. 112-15.

Ungnad, Arthur. *Altorientalische Texte und Bilder zum alten Testament*. Ed. H. Gressmann. Tübingen: J. C. B. Mohr, 1909. P. 79.

Weber, Otto. *Die Literatur der Babylonier und Assyrier*. Leipzig: J. C. Hinrichs, 1907. Pp. 206-7.

Winckler, Hugo. "Legende Sargons von Agane." *Keilinschriftliche Bibliothek*. Vol. III. Ed. E. Schrader. Berlin: H. Reuther, 1892. Pp. 100-3.

Zimmern, Heinrich. *Zum Streit um die "Christusmythe."* Berlin: Reuther and Reichard, 1910. P. 26.

STUDIES (INCLUDING COLLECTIONS OF OCCURRENCES) OF THE INFANT-EXPOSURE MOTIF

Binder, Gerhard. *Die Aussetzung des Königskindes Kyros und Romulus*. Beiträge zur klassischen Philologie, X. Meisenheim am Glan: Verlag A. Hain, 1964.

Cosquin, E. "Le lait de la mère et le coffre flottant." *Revue des questions historiques*. N. S. 39 (1908), pp. 353-425.

Gaster, Theodore H. *Myth, Legend, and Custom in the Old Testament*. Vol. I. New York: Harper and Row, 1969, Harper Torch Books, 1975. Pp. 224-30, 380-82.

Grant, Michael. *Roman Myths*. New York: C. Scribner's Sons, 1971. Pp. 98-103.

Holley, N. M. "The Floating Chest." *Journal of Hellenic Studies* 66 (1949), pp. 39-47.

Rank, Otto. *The Myth of the Birth of the Hero*. Ed. Philip Freund. New York: Alfred A. Knopf, 1959, Vintage Books, 1964.

Redford, Donald B. "The Literary Motif of the Exposed Child." *Numen* 14 (1967), pp. 209-28.

Rose, H. J. *A Handbook of Greek Mythology*. New York: Dutton and Company, 1959. Pp. 288-90, no. 14.

Thompson, Stith. *Motif-Index of Folk-Literature: A Classification of Narrative Elements in Folktales, Ballads, Myths, Fables, Medieval Romances, Exempla, Fabliaux, Jest-Books, and Local Legends*. 6 Vols. Indiana University Studies Nos. 96-97, 100-101, 105-6, 108-12. Bloomington: Indiana University Press, 1932-36. Vol. V, L 111.2.1, M 371, and S 141.

Text A - K 3401

Text B - K 4470

Top: Text C – BM 47449
Bottom: Text D – K 7249